Whatever happened to equal opportunities in schools?

Gender equality initiatives in education

Edited by
Kate Myers

Open University Press
Buckingham · Philadelphia

Open University Press
Celtic Court
22 Ballmoor
Buckingham
MK18 1XW

e-mail: enquiries@openup.co.uk
world wide web: http://www.openup.co.uk

and
325 Chestnut Street
Philadelphia, PA 19106, USA

First Published 2000

A catalogue record of this book is available from the British Library

ISBN   0 335 20304 3 (hb)   0 335 20303 5 (pb)

Library of Congress Cataloging-in-Publication Data
Whatever happened to equal opportunities in schools? / Kate Myers, editor.
      p.   cm.
   Includes bibliographical references (p.) and index.
   ISBN 0–335–20304–3 (hb). – ISBN 0–335–20303–5 (pb)
   1. Educational equalization – Great Britain.   2. Sex discrimination in education – Great Britain.   3. Sex differences in education – Great Britain.   4. Educational change – Great Britain.   I. Myers, Kate.
LC213.3.G7W53   1999
379.2'6–dc21   99–23609
                                                                              CIP

Typeset by Graphicraft Limited, Hong Kong
Printed in Great Britain by St Edmundsbury Press Ltd, Bury St Edmunds, Suffolk

This book is dedicated to the memories of
Lynda Carr (1946–1996), Myra McCulloch
(1949–1997), and Ros Moger (1949–1999)

Three special women who all walked the talk

£16·99
29/05/02

Contents

Notes on contributors

Sue Adler is a librarian who has worked in London since 1974. She was the Inner London Education Authority's (ILEA) Equal Opportunities (Gender) librarian and, in the ILEA's final year, an equal opportunities inspector (part-time). She is co-author, with Jenny Laney and Mary Packer, of *Managing Women: Feminism and Power in Educational Management* (Open University Press 1993) and is the author of a children's book on Nelson Mandela (1993). She has compiled many lists of children's resources, including *Ms Muffet Fights Back* and *Equality Street* for Penguin Books. She has contributed chapters to *Genderwatch! After the Education Reform Act*, *Reading the Difference* (edited by K. Myers 1992) and *Equality Matters* (edited by H. Claire, J. Maybin and J. Swann 1993).

Ruth Blunt is principal officer for gender equality at the National Union of Teachers' (NUT) headquarters. Her policy areas also include disability equality and lesbian and gay equality. Before becoming an employee of the NUT, Ruth was a science teacher in the London Borough of Hillingdon, at Swakeleys School, a girls' comprehensive with a mixed sixth form. A committed trade unionist, she was NUT school representative for a number of years and the first equal opportunities officer for Hillingdon NUT. Between 1986 and 1990, Ruth Blunt was a councillor in the London Borough of Ealing, serving on the women's committee and the education committee.

Marina Foster is a project leader working in schools giving academic and pastoral support to African Caribbean pupils, first with Berkshire County Council and now with Reading District Council. Marina is a black teacher, who came to the UK from South Africa in the apartheid era. She studied for the Froebel Diploma at Roehampton College as a United Nations Fellow and stayed on to study at several British universities. She worked as an in-service and resources development tutor at the Centre for Urban Educational Studies in the ILEA from 1973 until 1983. She was appointed as a senior lecturer and member of Berkshire's Team for Racial Equality in Education, which was based at Bulmershe College of Education from 1984 to 1992. During this period, the team organized and ran Department of Education and Science (DES) funded courses and exhibitions for schools, headteachers and lecturers on equal opportunities, race and gender, and contributed to the implementation of Berkshire's race equality policy. An unpublished work resulting from these courses is 'Policies for equality: The Seven Schools Project', which charts the progress of seven secondary schools through the processes of development policies on race and gender. She was on the editorial committee of the ILEA journal *Multi-Ethnic Education Review* and an editorial member of the journal *Dragon's Teeth* for seven years.

Diana Leonard is Professor of the Sociology of Education and Gender at the Institute of Education, University of London. She has published extensively on the sociology of gender and the family and has recently completed two Economic and Social Research Council (ESRC) funded research projects on Gender and Special Educational Needs (SEN) in Mainstream Junior Schooling and on the Family Work of Young People, their Educational Achievement and Post 16 Careers. Since October 1997 she and colleagues at the institute and the University of Birmingham have been working on a new project on Gender and Learning, and at the institute and Goldsmiths College on Violence Resilient Schools. Her other interests include the experiences of women (home and international) doctoral students.

Anne Madden is Head of the Education and Training Unit at the EOC. She started her professional career as a research assistant at the University of Adelaide, South Australia and joined the EOC in 1979. She has worked on casework, formal investigations, policy and development work within the Education and Training Unit and has produced a wide range of articles and publications for the EOC on issues across all sectors of education and training. She represents the EOC on a number of advisory and consultative groups, including the Women into Science and Engineering (WISE) National Coordinating Committee and the Qualifications and Curriculum Authority (QCA) Gender Advisory Group. She is responsible for briefing commissioners and attending ministerial meetings and select committees on education matters. She is vice-chair of the governing body of Brooklands Primary School, Trafford.

Frances Magee is Director of Education for the London Borough of Haringey. Previously she was the chief adviser in Lewisham and before 1990 held several posts in the inspectorate of the ILEA, including being its inspector for equal opportunities. Before going into local authority officer posts, she taught in schools in London and Cambridgeshire, starting her teaching career in 1965. She has taught in primary, secondary and community education as well as being a teacher in the youth service. The majority of her work has been in inner-city, multi-ethnic communities. She has been involved in classroom action research since the 1970s; her major themes have been on language and learning, equal opportunities, world studies and the arts. While still working in school, she collaborated with several major research and curriculum development projects and publications in these areas. She has also worked in the informal sector with other women, for other women. In her present post she still seeks to find time for researching, for promoting learning and understanding and to support others to secure ways of teaching which build on what we have learned so far about equality of opportunity.

Val Millman taught in primary and secondary schools prior to working on a number of projects, including the Schools Council's Sex Differentiation Project, the Lower Attaining Pupils Project and the Technical and Vocational Educational Initiative (TVEI). She is now an education adviser with Coventry City Council, where one of her curriculum responsibilities is equality of opportunity, and she is leading a secondary school Raising Achievement of Girls and Boys project. She is also leading Coventry Local Education Authority's (LEA) research and development work on the impact of 'pupil transience' on attainment and achievement. Within the fast developing field of careers education and guidance, she is working with Coventry primary and secondary schools to develop Preparation for Adult Life programmes. These aim to equip children and young people for their rapidly changing personal world, in which social, economic and labour market structures are becoming increasingly uncertain and insecure. Val is currently undertaking further research in this area at the University of Warwick. Since her work at the Schools Council in the early 1980s, she has continued to write extensively on the development of educational practices which promote gender equality, especially through the work-related curriculum. Her articles, which have been included in a range of publications, have most recently focused on work-related curriculum initiatives in primary schools.

Frances Morrell Since 1994 Frances Morrell has been the Director of Studies for the European Commission programme European Citizenship 1999. She is also the joint chief executive of Arts Inform and a member of the graduate school, London School of Economics. Previously she has been chair NCVCQ subject advisory Performing Arts and Entertainment Industries Committee and the director of the Speaker's Citizenship Programme 1989–94. Between 1981 and 1987 she was the deputy, then leader of the ILEA. Before that she was policy adviser to the Secretary of State for Industry, then to the Secretary of State for Energy, and policy adviser to the Fabian Society.

Kate Myers is Professor of Professional Development in Education at the University of Keele. Previously she was an associate director of the International School Effectiveness and Improvement Centre, Institute of Education, University of London, and a freelance education consultant. Before going into higher education (HE), she was the project manager of the Schools Make A Difference (SMAD) project in the London Borough of Hammersmith and Fulham. She has previously been a pastoral head in an ILEA comprehensive school, ILEA coordinator of the Schools Council's Sex Differentiation

Project, an advisory teacher, director of the Schools Curriculum Development Council/Equal Opportunities Commission (SCDC/EOC) Equal Opportunities Project, and a senior inspector in the London Borough of Ealing.

Paddy Orr has been an independent education consultant and registered inspector working in secondary and primary schools since 1993. Before that for 18 years he was a member of Her Majesty's Inspectorate of Schools (HMI), based first in the West Midlands and then in East Anglia. Among other roles for several years he had national responsibility for equal opportunities (gender) and was a member of national working groups on equal opportunities. Before joining HMI he taught in England, Scotland and abroad in comprehensive, secondary modern and international schools.

Barbara Smail is the Director of Regional Affairs for the British Association for the Advancement of Science and plays an active role in promoting the public understanding of science through the association's programmes for both young people and adults. Trained as a chemist, she worked in business before moving into education and became head of chemistry in a comprehensive school in south Manchester. In 1979, she became the research fellow/schools liaison officer for the EOC's Girls Into Science and Technology (GIST) Project. In the early 1980s, she acted as evaluator for the first Women and Physics courses set up by the universities of Manchester, Glasgow and Sussex and chaired the Association for Science Education's Policy Working Party on Gender and Science Education. She has been on the staff of the British Association since 1984 and has worked in a number of roles. She has been particularly concerned to provide access to science, engineering and technology for under-represented groups and to find ways of opening the doors of communication between the scientific community and the general public.

Hazel Taylor is an education management consultant. Her work portfolio ranges across higher education, LEAs and individual schools, and includes a part-time post as consultant headteacher to a school in special measures. She specializes in working with new heads, including mentoring and consultancy via Headlamp, and with schools in difficulty. She teaches the school-based MA in managing school improvement for the University of North London, and is also a senior consultant for the Centre for Educational Leadership and School Improvement at Christ Church University College, Canterbury. She is a National Professional Qualification for Headteachers (NPQH) assessor. She was head of an inner-city mixed comprehensive school for six years, until 1997, and before that was a senior secondary adviser in the London Borough of Enfield. Her work as equal opportunities adviser for the London Borough of Brent spanned the mid-1980s, following years of teaching English in the ILEA. She is a non-executive director of a National Health Service (NHS) Community Care Trust, where she is chair of the clinical governance committee.

Preface

We have written this book to try and set the record straight and to see what, if anything, can be learnt from work that took place in schools in the 1970s and 1980s addressing gender equality issues. We have focused on gender equality knowing that this is only one dimension of equality. Race, class, disability and sexuality are all components that are inextricably inter-linked. Although focusing on gender, the contributors have endeavoured to disaggregate other areas of inequality by, for example, exploring issues pertaining to black girls and working-class white boys.

Acknowledgements

Acknowledgements are due to the pupils in Maitland House, Haverstock School during the 1970s and early 1980s who first alerted me to many of the issues discussed in *Whatever Happened to Equal Opportunities in Schools?*

Without the contributors there would be no book. For most of them writing their chapters was on top of full-time demanding jobs involving a huge amount of extra work. For those that did so, thanks for responding so patiently and indulgently to the pressure from me to keep to deadlines. Thanks also to all the people who have been instrumental in getting this book produced, in particular Sue Adler, Bernadette Callan, Maureen Cox and Shona Mullen.

Kate Myers

Abbreviations

ATs	advisory teachers
CDT	craft design and technology
CREG	Centre for Research on Gender
CUES	Centre for Urban Educational Studies
CVCP	Committee of Vice Chancellors and Principals
CRE	Commission for Racial Equality
CSE	Certificate of Secondary Education
DASI	Developing Anti-Sexist Innovations project
DES	Department of Education and Science
DfE	Department for Education
DfEE	Department for Education and Employment
DTI	Department for Trade and Industry
EAZ	Education Action Zone
EOC	Equal Opportunities Commission
ERA	Education Reform Act (1988)
ESRC	Economic and Social Research Council
FEDA	Further Education Development Agency
FEFC	Further Education Funding Council
FI	Formal Investigation
GLC	Greater London Council
GNVQ	General National Vocational Qualification
GCE	General Certificate of Education
GCSE	General Certificate of Secondary Education
GIST	Girls Into Science and Technology project
GRIST	Grant related in-service training
HE	higher education
HEFCE	Higher Education Funding Council for England
HMI	Her Majesty's Inspectorate of Schools

ILEA	Inner London Education Authority
INSET	in-service education and training
ISIP	International School Improvement Project
LEA	local education authority
LEAC	Local Education Authorities Consortium for Equal Opportunities
LMS	local management of schools
NCB	National Children's Bureau
NFER	National Foundation for Educational Research
NPQH	National Professional Qualification for Headteachers
NUT	National Union of Teachers
Ofsted	Office for Standards in Education
QCA	Qualifications and Curriculum Authority
SATs	Standardized Attainment Tasks
SCAA	Schools Curriculum and Assessment Authority
SCDC	Schools Curriculum Development Council
SDA	Sex Discrimination Act
SEN	special educational needs
SMAD	Schools Make A Difference project
TIMMSS	Third International Mathematics and Science Study
TTA	Teacher Training Agency
TVEI	Technical and Vocational Educational Initiative
WedG	Women and Education Group
WISE	Women Into Science and Engineering
WERC	Women's Education Resource Centre

Chapter one

How did we get here?

Kate Myers

Then

In 1975–6, when the Sex Discrimination Act (SDA) was implemented, 23.1 per cent of girls compared with 22.6 per cent of boys obtained five or more higher grades at Ordinary level (O level) or grade 1 Certificate of Secondary Education (CSE), the equivalent of today's five A–C grades in the General Certificate of Secondary Education (GCSE) (DES, May 1988). Although comparisons over time are notoriously difficult, it does seem that then, as now, girls were doing better than boys at 16 plus. So what was the problem and why were so many women and a few men galvanized to try and do something about girls' achievement? What is or was all the fuss about? (And as I shall show later, there certainly was a fuss when teachers and schools tried to address the issues.)

Then as now, although girls were apparently doing better at school up to the age of 16, this was not replicated in the workplace or further education (FE). At the end of the 1970s, 61 per cent of women were employed in only ten occupations, many of them low paid and low status (*New Society*, 5 July 1979). Most women in waged work were clerks, cashiers, shop assistants, secretaries, maids, cleaners and nurses. As far as further education was concerned 'it is only on catering, nursing and secretarial courses that girls outnumber boys' (*New Society*, 5 July 1979). Not surprisingly women earned a lot less than men. In April 1977, the average gross weekly earnings for a male non-manual worker was £86.02. Non-manual women workers earned £52.06 (*Social Trends*, 1978).

Although girls were generally doing better than boys up to school leaving age, it seemed that some skills and qualifications were more important than others in preparing young people for the workplace. Expectations of what was appropriate work for men and women were fairly traditional (even more than now) and from birth to grave, images reinforced expectations. It was difficult to find a greeting card or clothes for a new-born baby that did not have specific explicit and implicit messages regarding the new-born's sex and impossible to find one for a black friend. Although (as far as I know) no one went as far as pink or blue coffins, overt differentiated and discriminating expectations followed men and women throughout their lives. It is not appropriate here to rehearse whatever physiological and biological differences there may be between males and females. The important points as far as schooling is concerned are as follows:

- 'Differences between male and female performance on tests of verbal and spatial ability have been recorded but the results do not fit into a simple pattern of sex differences' (Arnot *et al.* 1998: 56). Indeed the differences *within* each sex are greater than the average difference between them, so for example there is a far greater difference between the tallest and smallest men than between the average height of a man and a woman. The range on any scale including height and weight is so great that it is unreliable and inequitable to determine a curriculum on expectations of the average. Too many girls and too many boys will not conform to the stereotype.
- Many expectations are culture specific so finding more female doctors in the former Soviet Union compared with the USA no doubt had more to do with status and salary than biology.
- Many expectations are role specific so for example embroidery is gener-ally considered a female skill whereas the sewing needed for suits (tailors) and bodies (surgeons) is male.
- Expectations change over time – not so long ago, indeed in Margaret Thatcher's time as a young Member of Parliament (MP), the idea of a woman Prime Minister was inconceivable.

Bearing all this in mind the schooling experience and our curriculum should open doors for our young people, not close them.

The school curriculum

The advent of the SDA encouraged some educationalists to look behind the statistics and start to examine the differentiated school curriculum – differentiated through structure and content. Most primary and secondary schools were offering girls and boys distinctly different curriculum experi-ences. Describing their findings about curricular differences for boys and girls from a study that took place in 1973, HMI reported 'All in all, the different treatment of boys and girls in primary schools is a subtle process, in step with the social attitudes of the time, and more likely to be modified by changes in those than by any other means. The subtlety of the process does not diminish its power: attitudes learnt early often persist' (DES 1975: 3). (See Paddy Orr's Chapter 2.)

It was not so subtle in secondary schools where overt differences in the craft curriculum for example, with girls entering secondary school taking courses in needlework, domestic science and home economics, and boys taking courses in woodwork, technical drawing and metalwork were common place. The curriculum of this period reflected the different expectations that society had of girls and boys and women and men. Expectations, aspirations and reality were all distinctly gender related, as demonstrated by the world outside school which was manifested by gender-segregated work patterns and leisure activities. But in some respects, the world was slowly starting to change.

> It is important . . . that the secondary education of girls should no longer educate them primarily for a domestic role. With the increase in modern labour-saving aids to household management, and the new attitudes beginning to develop in almost all countries towards the practical sharing of partnership in marriage and in the parenthood of the children, there will be an increasing place in the secondary curriculum during the adolescent years . . . for concentrating the education of both boys and girls on the personal relationships in marriage and the home rather than on cookery, knitting and laundry, as well as in the world of work.
>
> (Byrne 1978: 7)

Unfortunately, in spite of all these new labour-saving devices 13-year-old girls and boys were more influenced by the old rather than the new order when it came to 'option choice'. This was pre-National Curriculum when the cohort we now describe as Year 9 were allowed to choose their subject for the 16 plus examination courses of the time – the General Certificate of Education (GCE) O level and the CSE. This 'choice' was taken when vulnerable adolescents were most likely to be influenced by peer group pressure and what society expected of male and female roles. The consequence was 'in mixed schools there is marked differentiation between the subjects studied by pupils' (Pratt *et al.* 1984: 27).

Even when both sexes were following the same curriculum, they were exposed to what many would now consider stereotyped views of race and gender. This happened in school through curriculum content, textbooks and expectations. There were overt and more subtle examples of expectations of male and female behaviour; even when women role models were chosen they were often viewed through somewhat jaundiced lenses. Take, for example, a textbook of the period describing Queen Elizabeth I: 'She was mean about money, but she had known poverty; she was cautious and crafty, but she knew danger only too well. She was vain; her jewels, her wardrobe, her wigs and her make-up became almost a legend, but then she was a woman' (Larkin 1975: 17). (There is no mention of the way men of the time adorned themselves with wigs, make-up and jewels.)

Although girls were doing marginally better overall at 16 plus, they were doing very badly in some subject areas and these subject areas (particularly physical sciences and mathematics) seemed to be very significant for the world of work and adult life.

Projects

In the late 1970s and early 1980s a range of initiatives were launched to address some of these issues. Many were supported by the Equal Opportunities Commission and some by a small number of LEAs. Several of them are described in this book.

> The period from the mid-1970s until the mid-1980s . . . might be viewed as one where the extent of equal opportunities development, although underpinned by legislation, depended on the commitment of individual politicians, teachers and local authorities. Equal opportunities policy development, hence, might originate from local political allegiance, individual teachers or headteachers, an 'awareness raising' incident or involvement in one of several funded curriculum development projects (Whyte *et al.* 1984; Millman and Weiner 1985). Initiatives were often short-term, small-scale, temporary and local.
>
> (Arnot *et al.* 1996: 12)

Few if any of these projects were seen as 'mainstream' and many attracted derision from the media. I later used the term 'equiphobia' to describe the reaction such initiatives received.

Equiphobia

Equiphobia is an irrational hatred and fear of anything to do with equal opportunities (Myers 1990: 295). My own first encounter with the media was soon after I had been given a responsibility for equal opportunities at Haverstock School in north London. Such posts were new at the time and I was interviewed by Richard Garner for the *Times Educational Supplement* (*TES*) which on 3 July 1981 ran a sympathetic piece about the job and the issues under the headline 'School creates new post to tackle sexism' (Garner 1981). The item was picked up by Peter Simple for his regular column in the *Daily Telegraph*, which ran an item on 23 July under the headline 'Totalitarian days'. Introducing a policy that meant all new books purchased should where possible be non-sexist, as I described to the interviewer ('we do have a policy of trying to buy non-sexist fiction': Garner 1981), was likened to the Nazis and the Cultural Revolution. Simple went on to say:

they [the pupils] should reflect that the cult of 'equal opportunities' is, in one respect, potentially more drastic than National Socialism or Communism. It does not stop at eliminating books written by people of a hated race, class, religion or ideology. Since men and women will have different and varying functions for as longs [*sic*] as they reproduce their kind, every book about human beings can be banned as 'sexist'.

(Simple 1981)

My reply to the newspaper was not published.

Headlines and articles in this vein became regular features in the tabloids as soon as any new initiative that tried to raise the achievement or aspirations of girls or black pupils was discovered by the hacks. 'Sexist snoopers plan is attacked' (Will Stewart, *Daily Express*, 20 January 1987), 'Loonies ban sexist Robin Redbreast!' (John Kay, *Sun*, 19 March 1987: see Chapter 7 about Ealing for more discussion about this particular headline) and 'Outcry at £48,000 race spies in school' (Melanie Whitehouse, *Daily Express*, 22 September 1989). Homophobia was rife too: 'I won't give my son to the Loonies' (Bruce Kemble, *Evening Standard*, 4 September 1989). It was a difficult climate in which to operate sensibly and rationally. For some reason, now the concern is about boys' underachievement, similar initiatives do not seem to attract the same kind of response. Indeed government ministers and even chief inspectors find it a proper subject to address.

Now

There is no doubt that things have changed. Attitudes about what is possible for men and women, boys and girls to do and aspire to are more open. Girls are doing even better and in a wider range of subjects in schools. But women at work are still faced with the 'glass ceiling' and in spite of the 'new man', working women with children (and other carer responsibilities) are still faced with at least two jobs – the 'double shift'. Young women (and men) still receive mixed messages about the role of women. Yes, 'girls' can be powerful but at the same time 'page 3' type portrayals ensure that they are still downgraded and demeaned. They are not allowed to forget their real role in life or get too uppity, and they are still primarily the carers – responsible for childcare and for elderly relatives – regardless of their other obligations.

The recent concerns expressed in the mainstream as well as the education media about the underachievement of boys has put equal opportunities back on the agenda. But as before, we need to take a closer look at the figures before being able to suggest effective strategies for dealing with the situation.

First, which boys are underachieving? Some boys are actually doing very well and we need to be very clear which subgroup of boys we are concerned about.

Second, what is happening to girls in and post-school? Overall at 16 plus, they are doing better than boys but they are still not doing so well in some subject areas. Regardless of their actual ability, girls tend to have less confidence in their academic achievement and self-report their ability lower than boys. A 1998 survey of 9000 Year 9 students revealed some interesting differences with regard to their attitudes to lessons, teachers, discipline and behaviour and life after school. Although the girls scored higher on the National Foundation for Educational Research (NFER) non-verbal reasoning test and more of them were aiming to go to university (68 per cent compared with 62 per cent of boys), their self-report of their work was lower than the boys. 'Interestingly, in view of their job aspirations [and attainment] more boys (55%) think their work is "very good" or "above average" than the girls (44%) and 50% of the boys compared with 48% of the girls believe that their teachers would endorse this view' (Myers *et al.* 1998: 9). If girls are likely to underestimate their ability and boys likely to overestimate it, some existing structures such as the tiered entry system in GCSE mathematics (where a choice is made about level of entry) may not be helpful in eliminating bias (Elwood 1995; Murphy and Elwood 1998). (The same issues may apply whenever girls – and indeed perhaps women – are in a situation of describing their abilities, such as in records of achievement and appraisal.)

Health issues and feelings of self-worth are often connected, and the increase in smoking and alcohol consumption among young women (Cabinet Office 1999) is an area of growing concern. Girls are also 'more likely than boys to worry about their weight and to go on a diet. Half of all girls in Year 11 (aged 15/16) were not happy with their weight and one in four were on a diet' (Cabinet Office 1999: 1). In addition: 'Britain has the highest teenage conception rate and the highest teenage motherhood rate in Western Europe' (Cabinet Office 1999: 1).

Third, what happens to girls when they get in the workplace?

> Equal pay is a prime concern for the Equal Opportunities Commission (EOC). Throughout their working lives women generally earn less than men; this is as true for women managers as for women in other jobs. Women who work full-time currently earn 80 per cent of men's hourly pay on average.
>
> (EOC 1996: 1)

This was written twenty-one years after the SDA. Two years later, Will Hutton writing in the *Observer* stated: 'Ominously, the gap between men's and women's pay has widened for the first time in 10 years . . . women's earnings . . . are now slipping despite the support of Sex Discrimination and Equal Pay Acts' (*Observer*, 1998: 3).

In spite of their considerable achievements at 16 plus, 'for some [girls], opportunities do not match earlier aspirations and achievement. Society's attitudes and/or the expectations of teenage girls themselves may inhibit them from achieving their full potential' (Cabinet Office 1999: 2). Girls may be doing even better in their education at 16 plus but there is a long way to go in the workplace.

Fourth, what about life outside school and the workplace? How can young men and women participate in equal relationships in the context of the 'laddish' culture we are now enjoying? The workplace as we know it is changing in such a dramatic way with heavy industrial and manual jobs diminishing at a rapid rate and the current and potential impact of information technology (IT) on both work and lifestyles. The global economy and the increasingly talked about '24 hour society' means that our world is changing fast. We need to be educating our young people to take active and fulfilling roles, regardless of their sex or ethnicity in this brave new world.

Contributors in this book have attempted to look back at some of the initiatives that took place in the 1980s which tried to address attitudes to and expectations of girls and young women. How successful were these initiatives? What if anything can we learn from these projects to help us look behind the figures and current concern about boys?

The book

Part I concentrates on national initiatives. Paddy Orr (Chapter 2), formerly an HMI with national responsibility for equal opportunities, traces various government actions from 1975 and in Chapter 3, Anne Madden, head of Education and Training at the EOC, reflects on the EOC's role and contribution since the SDA. In Chapter 4, Ruth Blunt, principal officer for gender equality at the National Union of Teachers, describes the NUT's contribution to equality issues.

Local level is the focus of Part II. The approaches of three different LEAs are described and analysed from the perspectives of elected members, officers and advisers. In Chapter 5, Frances Morrell, who was chair of the ILEA Education Committee, discusses the ILEA's range of initiatives. In Chapter 6, Hazel Taylor, who was the inspector for gender equality in Brent, describes what happened in the first authority in the UK that created this type of post. My own chapter about gender equality work in Ealing was first published in 1991 as part of an Open University (OU) course about Curriculum and Learning (reproduced here with kind permission of the OU). It is brought up to date with reflections from some of the key players at the time, including Hilary Benn (then chair of the Education Committee), Alan Richardson (then senior secondary inspector) and Penny Clayton, a primary headteacher.

Some significant projects are discussed in Part III. In Chapter 8, Val Millman, who was the development officer for the Schools Council's Sex Differentiation Project, describes the project's aims and outcomes. In

Chapter 9, Barbara Smail, who was one of the project officers for the Girls Into Science and Technology (GIST) Project, reflects on her personal experience of the project and discusses the current situation regarding young women and science.

In Chapter 10, Frances Magee chronicles the project that took place at the now closed Hackney Downs School, focusing on anti-sexist work with boys. Diana Leonard (Chapter 11) describes an example of the contribution of higher education through her connections with the Women and Education Group (WedG) and the Local Education Authorities' Consortium (LEAC) for Equal Opportunities initiative based at the Institute of Education, University of London.

In Part IV, Marina Foster discusses in Chapter 12 many of the concerns about the lack of integration between race and gender and how in reality gender equality often meant equality for white women and girls only. In Chapter 13, Sue Adler looks at books, readers and reading during this period and describes how the ILEA tried to tackle the issues around bias and stereotyping. In Part V, I attempt to bring together salient points from the contributions, reflect on lessons learned during this period and suggest how we could use these lessons to inform the current debate about equality in education.

References

Arnot, M., David, M. and Weiner, G. (1996) *Educational Reforms and Gender Equality in Schools*, Research Discussion Series no. 17. Manchester: Equal Opportunities Commission.

Arnot, M., Gray, J., James, M., Ruddock, J. with Duveen, G. (1998) *Recent Research on Gender and Educational Performance*, Office for Standards in Education (Ofsted) Reviews of Research. London: The Stationery Office.

Byrne, E. (1978) *Equality of Education and Training for Girls (10–18 years)*. London: Commission of the European Communities.

Cabinet Office (1999) *Fact Sheet*. London: Cabinet Office.

DES (1975) *Curricular Differences for Boys and Girls*. London: HMSO.

DES (1988) *Statistical Bulletin*, May. London: DES.

Elwood, J. (1995) Undermining gender stereotypes: examination and coursework performance in the UK at 16, *Assessment in Education*, 2(3): 283–303.

EOC (1996) *Briefings on Women and Men in Britain: Pay*. London: EOC.

Garner, R. (1981) School creates new post to tackle sexism, *Times Educational Supplement*, 3 July: 6.

Larkin, P.J. ([1959] 1975) *Britain's Heritage*, book II. London: Hulton Educational.

Millman, V. and Weiner, G. (1985) *Sex Differentiation in Schools: Is There Really a Problem?* York: Longman.

Murphy, P.F. and Elwood, J. (1998) Gendered experiences, choices and achievement: exploring the links, *International Journal of Inclusive Education*, 2(2): 95–118.

Myers, K. (1990) Book review of 'Equal Opportunities in the New Era', *Education*, 5 October: 295.

Myers, K., MacBeath, J. and Robertson, I. (1998) Changing your life through Study Support: How will we know if it makes a difference? Paper presented to the American Educational Research Association (AERA) Conference, San Diego, CA, April.

Pratt, J., Bloomfield, J. and Seale, C. (1984) *Option Choice: A Question of Equal Opportunity*. Windsor: NFER-Nelson.

Simple, P. (1981) Totalitarian days, *Daily Telegraph*, 23 July.

Social Trends (1978) London: HMSO.

Whyte, J., Deem, R., Kent, L. and Cruickshank, M. (eds) (1984) *Girl Friendly Schooling*. London: Methuen.

Part I

Country-wide initiatives

Chapter two

Prudence and progress: national policy for equal opportunities (gender) in schools since 1975

Paddy Orr

THE CONTEXT

The years since 1975 have seen complex developments in social and economic policy which have had a major impact on education. The search for social justice which informed much political thinking in the post-war years has been overtaken by more pragmatic concerns for efficiency and competitiveness. In education this has led to a stronger emphasis on achievement, cost-effectiveness and preparation for working life.

Government approaches to equality of opportunity in education need to be interpreted in the context of these broader developments. Government has sought to reduce differences in the curricular experiences of boys and girls and ensure that both sexes are equally well prepared for a wide range of career and employment possibilities. Because these objectives are more obviously the concern of secondary than primary schools, the secondary phase has received more attention than the primary. Any intentions that the governments of the time may have had to intervene more ambitiously to promote equality of opportunity have been constrained by a number of factors.

- First, there are limitations to what can be attempted nationally in a locally administered education system.
- Second, at a time of rapid change and innovation in education, equal opportunities has been seen as only one of a number of issues arguing for priority in the allocation of resources. Intervention has been considered only if it could be shown to serve broader objectives such as raising standards or preparing pupils more effectively for working life.

- Third, there have been difficulties because the term 'equality of opportunity' can be interpreted in different and conflicting ways: to some it implies no more than offering opportunities; to others it implies, much more radically, the need to ensure that those opportunities are accepted. Such differences in viewpoint have made Conservative governments, in particular, reluctant to involve themselves in matters seen as controversial by many of their supporters.

Partly for these reasons, the promotion of equal opportunities for girls and boys has never, in itself, been a major focus of national educational policy. Nevertheless, the need for gender equality has been implied in much that governments have initiated since the mid-1970s, in reforming the curriculum on the one hand and in seeking to raise standards in schools on the other. In fact, equality of opportunity is now generally accepted as a necessary guiding principle in educational provision. Few would question that it is as important for girls to do well at school as it is for boys; that both sexes should have equal experience of those aspects of the curriculum thought to be essential; and that girls and boys should be helped to make genuine choices from the same range of educational and employment opportunities.

Such points of view reflect a considerable shift in public attitudes since 1975. In that year HMI published the results of a survey of curricular differences for boys and girls in schools, carried out in response to a government request (DES 1975a). The authors were anxious to establish whether the curriculum enabled girls to compete on equal terms with boys, and whether curricular differences militated unfairly against girls' personal development and career prospects. They sought to trace the origins of the striking differences that existed between the subject choices of boys and girls in secondary schools, where they found a 'prevailing picture of traditional assumptions being worked out through the curricular patterns . . . , and of support for and acceptance of these patterns by the majority of teachers, parents and pupils' (DES 1975a: 24).

Curricular differences 1975

In reporting on the primary schools in the survey, HMI highlighted a lack of mechanical and spatial experience in the early years, which put girls in particular at a disadvantage. HMI also identified a failure to pay sufficient attention in the preparation of early reading materials to boys' 'more robust interests'. In the junior years, boys and girls were separated for games, although not usually for other aspects of physical education. Junior boys and girls were normally taught craft separately, and boys were more likely than girls to engage in a wider variety of crafts, involving the use of a range of tools and materials leading to three-dimensional modelling and construction and the use of measurement. Above all, it was felt that the majority of teachers had different expectations of the aptitudes and interests of boys and girls, and that in this respect teachers' attitudes were typical of the time. The authors felt that these differences in expectation were more likely to be modified by changes in public attitudes than by any other means. Almost all secondary schools were found to separate boys and girls for some subjects below the age of 16, mainly by giving separate provision within a subject, as in physical education, or by providing different courses for boys and girls, as in home economics and needlework for girls and woodwork and metalwork for boys. Curricular separation was accentuated in the provision for 14 to 16-year-olds, and in GCE Advanced level (A level) and vocational courses taken by students over the age of 16. In particular, girls' and boys' experience of science was very different after the age of 14. Despite these weaknesses, the survey found that a number of schools in the early 1970s were already seeking ways to reduce sex differentiation in the curriculum. For example, in some middle schools opportunities for mixed classes in the crafts were on the increase, and there appeared to be some movement away from practices likely to restrict boys and girls to activities traditionally assumed to be appropriate to their sex.

The passing of the Race Relations Act in 1976 had little immediate impact on schools. It was not seen by schools as having implications for curricular provision or organization, and the interrelationship between gender and ethnicity in patterns of pupil performance had at this point received little attention.

POLICY INITIATIVES SINCE 1975

Since 1975, government policy to promote equal opportunities (gender) in schools has concentrated on three areas: first, initiatives designed to help girls and boys respond fully to the changing demands of the labour market; second, the reform of the curriculum; and third, the need to raise standards of achievement.

Preparation for working life

Already in the mid-1970s, in government policy statements which mentioned gender issues, there were usually oblique references to labour market needs – in particular the under-representation of girls in science and technology and the employment to which these subjects might lead. For instance, in 1977 HMI published a working paper on *The 11 to 16 Curriculum* (DES 1977a) which included comments on a government Green Paper, *Education in Schools*, published in the same year (DES 1977b). The authors wrote:

The Green Paper . . . points out that care must be taken to see that girls do not, by their choice of subject, limit their career opportunities, and that schools do not, by their assumptions, decisions or choice of teaching materials limit the educational opportunities offered to girls. It may become necessary in some way to encourage girls to broaden their aspirations and to feel confident of success in science and technology, although the Green Paper gives no guidance on what form that encouragement might take. Schools, however, do not provide science education solely for employment. Science must also be seen as an integral part of a general education for all pupils.

(DES 1977a: 10)

This extract illustrates the tension between liberal thinking about education, and the more instrumental perspective that schooling prepares young people for the demands of working life. Several other themes emerged in the mid-1970s which had implications for the way in which equality of opportunity was interpreted by the governments of the time. The Great Debate initiated by the then Prime Minister James Callaghan in 1976 emphasized the central need to raise standards in schools, if Britain was to survive in an increasingly competitive world. Schools would have to be much more efficient. The days of the post-war boom had passed. In addition, a much larger measure of agreement about the nature and purpose of the curriculum in primary and secondary schools would be needed if these improvements were to be realized. James Hamilton, Permanent Secretary at the DES, said in June 1976 at the annual conference of the Association of Education Committees: 'I believe that the so-called secret garden of the curriculum cannot be allowed to remain secret after all, and that the key to the door must be found and turned.'

Curricular reform

As far as gender equality was concerned, however, the early stages of curricular reform were not auspicious. The results of a survey carried out by Pratt *et al.* (1984) on behalf of the Equal Opportunities Commission showed that the patterns of subject choice in secondary schools had changed little despite the passing of the Sex Discrimination Act in 1975. Schools had responded to the SDA by removing organizational restrictions on boys and girls taking up subjects or courses. In most schools, this was the limit of the response made. Concern to promote equality of opportunity by means other than organizational adjustments to the curriculum were largely subordinated to broader national educational priorities.

During the 1980s, government sought to achieve a nationally agreed framework for the 5 to 16 curriculum, with nationally agreed objectives for its various components, and breadth, balance and relevance for all pupils in the way the curriculum was organized. In 1981, a DES publication, *The School Curriculum*, outlined government intentions. The document included several references to equality of opportunity: 'The equal treatment of men and women embodied in our law needs to be supported in the curriculum' and 'It is essential to ensure that equal opportunities are genuinely available to both boys and girls' (DES 1981: para. 20). The document also stressed, once again, the need for girls and boys to avoid restricting their choices of employment or career by making inappropriate subject choices. It emphasized the importance of a secure grounding in science and technology during the primary years and the desirability of a balanced science curriculum for all up to the age of 16.

The Conservative government's White Paper, *Better Schools* (DES 1985a), summarized government policy, and set out intentions for improvement of the curriculum, assessment and examinations, and the management of schools. The principal aims for all sectors of education were, first, to raise standards at all levels of ability in order to prepare young people more effectively for adult life, and second, since education was an investment in the nation's future, to secure the best possible return from the resources which were found for it. As part of the strategy for improvement, the White Paper pointed out that a 'broad agreement about the objectives and content of the school curriculum . . . could help to remove preconceptions based on a pupil's sex or ethnic origin' (DES 1985a: 9).

Education Reform Act 1988

Widespread debate and consultation about the nature and purpose of the curriculum followed and the eventual result was the introduction of the National Curriculum through the Education Reform Act 1988. This enabled government to assume greater control over what pupils should learn and how they should spend their time in schools. The National Curriculum and other aspects of the Education Reform Act were intended to secure a general improvement in educational standards by making schooling more relevant to the needs of particular groups of pupils, including boys and girls.

The National Curriculum restricted pupils' choice of subjects, and so helped to reduce gender differentiation. A review of recent research on educational performance (Arnot *et al.* 1998) published by Ofsted shows that there has been a narrowing of the gender gap in patterns of entry to GCSE.

Modifications to the National Curriculum since its introduction have led to some increase in flexibility in curricular planning, and, currently, additional choice is specifically being encouraged through the introduction of

Part One General National Vocational Qualifications (GNVQs) for 14 and 15-year-olds. This has considerable implications because of the gender associations of the vocational courses available – for example health and social care and manufacturing and engineering. Nevertheless, the extent to which pre-16 vocational choices for Part One GNVQs encourage gender differentiation varies considerably from school to school. Much depends on the way a school organizes the course and the amount of time allocated to it (Ofsted 1997).

If the National Curriculum has led to a reduction in sex differentiation in the curriculum up to the age of 16, there is little evidence of a similar reduction in subject or course choices after this age, particularly in the subjects traditionally dominated by boys. One of the aims of National Curriculum balanced science at GCSE – to reduce gender imbalances in science in A level and other post-16 courses – has not been achieved. The problem of girls' under-representation in physics at A level remains acute, although girls do as well as boys in balanced science up to the age of 16. The most striking change at A level has been the rise in student numbers in most subjects other than the physical sciences and mathematics (Department for Education and Employment (DfEE) 1994). The increase has been more rapid for girls than boys. The participation rate for all students has more than doubled since 1975, and more girls than boys now take A levels (DES 1975b; DfEE 1998a).

Employment opportunities

The limited success since the late 1970s of government initiatives to encourage girls to take up scientific and technological opportunities beyond 16, whatever its other causes, may owe something to changing perceptions of desirable employment in adult life, and to shifts in the patterns of employment opportunities. Many young men and women studying mathematics or science-based courses do not, in fact, end up in employment which draws on qualifications gained in these subjects. Despite this, as the authors of a report on science and mathematics in schools pointed out in 1994, there is no evidence of a 'substantial failure to supply sufficient qualified graduates for employment in engineering or science-related fields' (Ofsted 1994: 1).

Opportunities in the service sector – commerce, banking, communications, marketing, media, law, accountancy – provide counter-attractions for higher attaining girls which do not necessarily require specialist subject preparation at A level or even, in most cases, in higher education. Such opportunities may deflect attention from potentially attractive but 'non-traditional' areas in science, technology and computing. For example, opportunities in computing have increased, but the great majority of highly paid posts in computing go to young men.

If one takes account of all types of work, young women are as well placed as young men to take advantage of the great majority of developing employment opportunities, which are increasingly concentrated in the service sector. Many involve part-time and largely unskilled work. However, the collapse of traditional opportunities in unskilled work has mainly been in areas favoured by men. Young people with poor literacy or numeracy skills may find it difficult to get a job, and here also young men are more likely to be at a disadvantage than young women.

Standards of achievement

The need to raise the standards achieved by girls and boys has increasingly been a central element of national policy. To support this objective, much has been done to introduce systems for the collection of data, and to establish the extent and influence of gender bias in teaching approaches, syllabus content and assessment procedures. Government agencies such as the Assessment of Performance Unit (APU) have contributed extensively to increased understanding. In recent years, HMI and Ofsted inspection reports have often included comments on differences between boys' and girls' achievements, attitudes and behaviour. HMI has at different times supported initiatives and published the results of surveys or investigations into, for example, girls' experience and achievement in science (DES 1980) and mathematics (DES 1989), and boys' experience and achievement in modern languages (DES 1985b) and English (Ofsted 1993). Ofsted, in conjunction with the EOC, has published an analysis of performance differences between boys and girls at school, with accompanying suggestions for improvement (Ofsted/EOC 1996). Ofsted has also sponsored the publication of an extensive review of recent research into gender and educational performance (Arnot *et al.* 1998). Currently, the government is promoting initiatives to raise boys' achievement in literacy. It is also introducing arrangements for target-setting in all schools. However, in the circular on the topic (DfEE 1998), there is no suggestion that schools should set separate targets for boys and girls, or that they should take account of particular issues such as the low attainment of 'working-class' boys, or the narrow aspirations of many sixth form girls, or girls from certain minority ethnic groups. The omission is presumably to avoid imposing extra bureaucratic burdens on schools. This may be a false economy. Well-organized information about the performance of different groups of pupils is essential, if targets for improvement are to be soundly based.

It is impossible to tell how much effect government policy initiatives, as opposed to the extensive work of other partners in the education service, have had on gender patterns of attainment. Nor can one quantify the influence in this context of changing attitudes and expectations within and beyond schools. Nevertheless, girls now leave school with better qualifications than used to be the case. They have caught boys up among those gaining three or more A level passes, the important category for university entrance. Their overall performance at A level matches that of boys, although boys tend to get more of the highest and lowest grades. In GCSE, girls outperform boys at every level. Because of inconsistencies in the statistical evidence, it is difficult to make precise comparisons with earlier years, but it appears that the gap between boys' and girls' performance at GCSE is greater than it was in 1986, just before GCSE was introduced. In English, girls do better than boys throughout the years of compulsory schooling. Their performance in mathematics and science is broadly similar to boys' (Ofsted/EOC 1996).

Ethnicity and social class

Gender, of course, is not the only factor affecting attainment. Ethnicity and social class are also crucial, as are the interrelationships between these different elements. Unfortunately, most available data do not take more than one variable into account, often because of the small sample sizes. Data from a large sample who took GCSE in 1985 indicate that, whatever their gender or ethnic origin, pupils from higher social class backgrounds do better on average in the GCSE examinations they take. These data also show that the relative achievements of boys and girls vary with ethnic background. The pattern in this 1985 sample of girls outperforming boys in GCSE was uniformly true only for white pupils: it was not true for Asian pupils, whatever their social class background (Gillborn and Gipps 1996: 17). Since 1990 schools have been required to make annual returns to their LEAs of ethnically based statistics on pupils (DES 1989a). However, schools and LEAs do not always make the best use of these data to monitor standards or plan provision. For example, an Ofsted inspection report on Manchester LEA, published in 1998, points out that although the LEA sent schools analyses by gender of GCSE results, it did not provide analyses by ethnicity, 'a major omission in a multi-cultural city' (Ofsted 1998: 38).

Single-sex schools

The extent to which single-sex schooling may affect achievement has long been a subject of debate, in the UK and elsewhere. If socio-economic variables and pupils' prior attainment are taken into account, there is still no conclusive evidence that girls or boys in single-sex schools attain more or less highly than in mixed schools. Recent statistical analyses by Ofsted show that, overall, girls' schools do better than mixed and boys' schools in terms of ethos, efficiency and quality of education. However, the better standards may do no more than reflect the well-established differences in the attitudes and performance nationally of girls and boys. In other words, gender is the determinant, rather than type of school. The evidence of Ofsted inspections suggests that relatively few single-sex schools, apart from girls' schools in more advantaged areas, seek as a matter of policy to exploit the opportunities provided by their single-sex status to broaden girls' or boys' educational and employment aspirations. Inevitably, this limits the effect the schools might have.

The numbers of single-sex schools have reduced markedly since the mid-1970s, mainly as a result of local reorganization of educational provision. There were 1300 maintained single-sex schools in 1975; in 1985 there were 400; in 1995 there were 227, with slightly more girls' than boys' schools (Ofsted/EOC 1996). The reduction has had a clear impact on the number of women headteachers in secondary schools. In 1975, one-quarter were women. In 1985, the proportion was one-sixth. However, since 1985, the proportion has risen to reach one-quarter again. Women make up just over a half of all teachers in maintained secondary schools (DfEE 1997b).

Specific reforms

Educational reforms and other initiatives introduced while the Conservative government was in power in the 1980s and 1990s raised awareness of equal opportunities issues, but often as much by default as deliberate intention. The Technical and Vocational Education Initiative had a widespread impact in making schools more aware of stereotyping, yet the main aims of the scheme did not include a reference to equal opportunities. The requirement to avoid stereotyping and the need to ensure that, as far as possible, boys and girls were educated together were subsets of one of the aims. Nevertheless, the quality of every scheme's provision for equal opportunities became an important criterion for the allocation of funding. The Education Reform Act 1988 introduced the National Curriculum, with implications for reducing sex differentiation. It established a testing system which provided detailed information about the performance of boys and girls in Standard Assessment Tasks (SATs) at the ages of 7, 11 and 14. The stipulation introduced in 1990 that schools should each year make returns of ethnically based statistics provided an opportunity for schools and LEAs to monitor attainment by ethnicity and gender. The Education Act 1992 created an inspection system which evaluates provision for equal opportunities. The publication for parents of National Curriculum assessments and GCSE examination results has raised national awareness of gender issues in attainment.

Role of HMI

HMI also contributed to the developing awareness of equal opportunities issues, but did not generally take a lead in doing so. The role of HMI was to evaluate the effects of educational policy, not to initiate it. Because inspectors were deployed nationally, HMI could gather evidence on which government might base policy decisions, but there was no guarantee that the evidence would be used, and it was always possible for political imperatives to take precedence in government decision making. Furthermore, HMI were recruited from all areas and levels of education, and represented all shades of opinion. Their corporate judgements were reached through shared and detailed analysis of evidence. The procedures encouraged objectivity, but also caution. 'Controversial' areas such as the anti-sexist (or anti-racist) initiatives favoured by a few LEAs in the 1980s were unlikely to be a major focus of inspection and reporting, although locally based HMI were expected to keep a watching brief on what went on. From the late 1970s onwards, there were central HMI committees for ethnicity and disadvantage, but not for gender. Gender issues were dealt with mainly through specialist subject committees, or through liaison with organizations such as the EOC. During the 1980s, the science and mathematics committees made important contributions to the debate about girls' performance in these subjects. However, not until the later 1980s were official arrangements established within HMI for coordinated attention to all aspects of equal opportunities. A central committee was formed, with a remit to advise on inspection procedures and monitor the working practices of HMI. The work of this group led eventually to the approach to equal opportunities adopted by Ofsted in the national inspection system introduced in 1993, after HMI had been reorganized.

Ofsted inspections

Ofsted inspection procedures for all types of schools include a requirement to inspect equal opportunities. In relation to gender, three main areas have to be investigated: first, any significant variations in the relative achievements of boys and girls; second, any inequalities in access to the curriculum; and third, the extent to which leadership and management promote access to the full range of opportunities for achievement that the school provides. The *Handbook* for inspection and associated documents provide detailed guidance on how inspectors should tackle these tasks (Ofsted 1995).

The main difficulty is that inspection teams have neither the time nor, in many cases, the expertise to deal with such complex areas thoroughly. Even an evaluation of test or examination results to identify and explain 'significant variations' between boys' and girls' attainment is likely to be a major undertaking if it is to go beyond the superficial and immediate. The reading of a selection of Ofsted inspection reports shows that in the great majority of cases gender issues receive short shrift in inspections. Partly in consequence, presumably, the annual reports of inspection findings have little to say on the topic.

Government policy since 1997

The arrival of a Labour government in May 1997 has not yet led to major changes of direction in educational policy as far as equal opportunities is concerned, except in one respect. Labour policy is directed firmly towards social disadvantage and, in that context, towards the needs of boys and girls who, as a result of inadequate achievement, do not realize their full potential to contribute to society. Policy is more clearly concerned with particular social groups of pupils than was the case under the previous Conservative government, which tended to assume that because 'a rising tide lifts all the boats', there was no *a priori* need to target specific groups in order to raise standards.

'Underachievement' by boys is now the main gender issue, for a variety of reasons. Increased emphasis on and national interest in testing procedures and 'league tables' have revealed obvious gaps between girls' and boys' achievements, at GCSE in particular. The decline in opportunities for employment in manual work have accentuated the need for boys to be better qualified. The current government focus on literacy has been supported by several studies of boys' relatively low achievement in English, including one produced by the Qualifications and Curriculum Authority (QCA 1998) and another by the Basic Skills Agency (BSA 1997). The teaching approaches recommended in the Framework of the National Literacy Strategy bear some resemblance to the approaches found to be successful in these studies. However, the literacy strategy concentrates on reading and writing rather than spoken English, which is not dealt with in any detail, although differences in the performance of boys and girls are often revealed in talk. The teaching of reading through group work, which is an integral part of the framework approach, relies on groups formed on the basis of reading ability, and this may work to boys' disadvantage. It is too early to tell whether the national literacy strategy will have a marked effect on boys' performance in reading and writing. Results of early tests in pilot schools show improvement in boys' performance, but even more improvement in girls' performance.

Other initiatives are being introduced nationally to counter the low achievement of many boys. Local education authorities are required to record in their education development plans strategies for improvement, if the differences between boys' and girls' achievements in their area are greater than would be expected nationally in similar areas. As part of the national literacy strategy for Key Stage 3, three LEAs are to pilot schemes for raising boys' achievement. Three education action zones (EAZs) are proposing to develop specific strategies to raise boys' achievement. Boys' perceptions of reading will receive attention as part of the programme for the National Year for Reading. Under new arrangements for teacher training, trainee teachers will be expected to develop an awareness of gender issues such as boys' achievement and girls' choices post-16 (DfEE 1997a). However, these different initiatives are not part of a coordinated national strategy to promote equal opportunities. Recent government publications on priorities for educational policy, including the central White Paper *Excellence in Schools* (DfEE 1997c), contain almost no references to gender equality, or to ethnicity. Nevertheless, many of the developments currently proposed by the government, such as the requirement that schools should set specific targets for improvement, have obvious implications for equality of opportunity (DfEE 1998b).

CONCLUSION

Since 1975, national policy for gender equality in schools has, in the main, been dominated by three concerns: the need to raise standards, increase cost-effectiveness and respond to the demands of a changing and often unpredictable labour market. Progress has been made in promoting equal opportunities, although it has not been continuous or even, in some respects, anticipated. Changes in social attitudes and expectations, within and outside school, have undoubtedly played a major part in promoting this uneven progress. Much remains to be done. Government policy has tended to concentrate on 'single issues': the current priority is boys' achievement. Although this area is obviously important, national developments in education in the next few years – such as the review of the National Curriculum, growing involvement with information and communication technology, new approaches to the teaching of literacy and numeracy, the extension of work-related learning, new approaches to personal and social education – will have implications for a school's understanding of equality of opportunity.

The experience of recent years suggests that a number of priorities need to be followed up if challenges of this sort are to be dealt with successfully.

Schools will be better placed if they
- know more about good practice in promoting gender equality
- continue to seek to reduce differences between boys and girls in subject and course choices
- are better informed about what they can be expected to do to counter the 'anti-achievement' culture that affects many boys

- use opportunities provided by the literacy and numeracy strategies to develop their understanding of the teaching approaches that are most successful with girls and boys
- know more about how science and mathematics can be made more attractive to girls, seek to involve more girls in scientific and technological courses post-16 and ensure that good quality advice is given for post-16 choices
- know how to collect, organize and use data about the achievements and progress of different groups of pupils, so as to set appropriate targets for improvement.

National policy makers are likely to help most if they

- take careful account of gender issues in reshaping the National Curriculum
- provide more guidance about good practice in promoting equal opportunities and ensure that Ofsted inspections and other monitoring procedures are used effectively to gather evidence in this regard
- provide guidance for schools about how to set targets on the basis of efficiently gathered data on the attainment and progress of different groups of pupils
- take account, when considering inequalities, of the interrelationships between gender, ethnicity and social class
- ensure that, in policy statements and other publications, appropriate attention is paid to gender equality and other equal opportunities issues.

References

Arnot, M., Gray, J., James, M., Ruddock, J. with Duveen, G. (1998) *Recent Research on Gender and Educational Performance*, Ofsted Reviews of Research. London: The Stationery Office.

BSA (1997) *Improving Boys' Literacy: A Survey of Effective Practice in Secondary Schools*. London: Basic Skills Agency.

DES (1975a) *Curricular Differences for Boys and Girls: Education Survey 21*. London: HMSO.

DES (1975b) *Statistics of Education Volume 2, 1975 England and Wales*. London: HMSO.

DES (1977a) *The 11 to 16 Curriculum*, HMI working paper. London: HMSO.

DES (1977b) *Education in Schools*, Cmnd 6869. London: HMSO.

DES (1980) *Girls and Science*, HMI Matters for Discussion 13. London: HMSO.

DES (1981) *The School Curriculum*. London: HMSO.

DES (1985a) *Better Schools*. London: HMSO.

DES (1985b) *Boys and Modern Languages*, HMI 55/85. London: HMSO.

DES (1989a) *Ethnically-based Statistics on School Pupils*, Circular 16/89. London: DES.

DES (1989b) *Girls Learning Mathematics*, Education Observed 14. London: HMSO.

DfEE (1994) *Science and Mathematics: A Consultation Paper on the Supply and Demand of Newly Qualified Young People*. London: HMSO.

DfEE (1997a) *Requirements for Courses of Initial Teacher Training*, Circular 10/97. London: DfEE.

DfEE (1997b) *Statistics of Education [Teachers], Table 24, England and Wales*. London: DfEE.

DfEE (1997c) *Excellence in Schools*, White Paper. London: The Stationery Office.

DfEE (1998a) *DfEE/OFSTED PICSI Annex for Secondary Schools Autumn 1998*. London: Ofsted.

DfEE (1998b) *Target-Setting in Schools*, Circular 11/98. London: DfEE.

Gillborn, G. and Gipps, C. (1996) *Recent Research on the Achievements of Ethnic Minority Pupils*. London: HMSO.

Ofsted (1993) *Boys and English*. London: Ofsted.

Ofsted (1994) *Science and Mathematics in Schools: A Review*. London: HMSO.

Ofsted (1995) *The OFSTED Handbook: Guidance on the Inspection of Schools*. London: HMSO.

Ofsted (1997) *Part One GNVQ Pilot: The First Two Years 1995/97*. London: The Stationery Office.

Ofsted (1998) *Inspection of Manchester Local Education Authority, June 1998. Office of Her Majesty's Chief Inspector of Schools, in conjunction with the Audit Commission*. London: Ofsted.

Ofsted/EOC (1996) *The Gender Divide: Performance Differences between Boys and Girls at School*. London: HMSO.

Pratt, J., Bloomfield, J. and Seale C. (1984) *Option Choice: A Question of Equal Opportunity*. Windsor: NFER-Nelson.

QCA (1998) *Can Do Better: Raising Boys' Achievement in English*. London: QCA.

Chapter three

Challenging inequalities in the classroom: the role and contribution of the Equal Opportunities Commission

Anne Madden

Introduction

In this chapter I describe the education provisions contained in the Sex Discrimination Act 1975, the role and structure of the EOC, the extent of the EOC's engagement with gender equality work in education over its lifetime and the various approaches adopted to promote change. I attempt to set this within the changing historical, political and social contexts and indicate the impact of broader education reforms both on the EOC's education work and on progress towards gender equality in schools. Where possible, I evaluate the extent to which particular EOC approaches and strategies have made a positive difference and flag up some lessons for policy makers, practitioners, key education organizations and the EOC when considering strategic approaches to developing gender equality in the future.

The Sex Discrimination Act and the establishment of the EOC

In December 1975, the Sex Discrimination Act became law. This major legislation outlawed discrimination on the grounds of sex in employment, education and in the provision of goods, facilities and services, and gave individuals, for the first time, direct access to the law to claim their rights. The SDA also established the Equal Opportunities Commission. The EOC's duties are defined in Section 53 of the SDA:

- to work towards the elimination of discrimination
- to promote equality of opportunity between women and men generally
- to keep under review the working of this Act and the Equal Pay Act 1970; and when they are so required by the Secretary of State or otherwise think it necessary, draw up proposals for amending them.

The passing of the SDA was a landmark on the path towards securing equality for women and reflected the social, cultural and economic changes which had been taking place over many years. In addition to the call for equality for women on the grounds of social justice and as an inalienable right in itself, the laws of the time were recognized as no longer reflecting fairly or adequately the changed roles and behaviour of men and women. Technological advances had reduced the number of jobs requiring physical strength, and had increased those requiring manual dexterity and the capacity to manage and take responsibility. Technical innovation had limited the need for hands-on and intensive housework. At the same time, the numbers of women working as a matter of necessity to supplement low family incomes had increased significantly. The EOC's first *Annual Report* observed:

> traditional distinctions between what is men's work and what is women's work have been steadily abolished in fact, although many of our industrial and social practices continue to be based upon these assumptions. For the first time, women have actually enjoyed the freedom to contemplate a career in work on equal terms with men and to enter more fully into the social, cultural and intellectual life of the nation . . . As women have begun to reach out into the wider areas of social and industrial life, they have encountered a variety of obstacles to equality of opportunity: some direct, deliberate and overt; some unintended and indirect, and many based simply on unexamined assumptions and stereotypes about the proper role and place of women.
>
> (EOC *Annual Report* 1976: 1)

Role of the EOC

The role set down for the EOC reflected the recognized need for a body to take strategic action to change discriminatory practices and attitudes towards women (and men), which previously had been regarded as the norm. Responsibility was to be given to a body of up to fifteen commissioners, including a chair and deputy chair, and the EOC *Annual Report*, 1976, records that it was envisaged that the commission would develop a network of five to eight regional offices by 1978, employing some 220 of the envisaged total of 440 staff.

At the end of the first year of operation, there were 166 staff at the headquarters in Manchester. Offices have been opened in Wales and Scotland, and a Press Office in London, but grant-in-aid to the EOC during its existence has been insufficient to support the development of a regional network and staff numbers have not exceeded 200. Successive governments have been reluctant to fund the EOC to become the large organization envisaged for the task defined in the SDA. This has accentuated the need to prioritize some areas of work over others, and has created difficulties in developing regional and local knowledge to support policy and promotional work at grassroots levels.

It is interesting to note that the SDA and EOC began life in a time of severe economic crisis and public spending cuts. This climate served to undermine the case for equality and created discontent among employers at the additional burdens imposed by complying with sex discrimination legislation. Individuals, too, were reluctant to speak up for their equality rights for fear of losing jobs (EOC *Annual Reports* 1976, 1979). This evidence of the call for equality falling down the political and social agenda from the outset, and being regarded as a luxury rather than a critical economic and social imperative, has been a part of the history of the work of the EOC. Even now, there is concern among some employers about adopting equality measures which would impose additional burdens on business.

Gaining the support of ministers, government departments and key organizations across industry, education and service delivery for action on equality has always been regarded by the EOC as critical to achieving success and gaining the momentum to move equality forward. With only limited support from government, the task facing the EOC in changing practices and attitudes across all sectors of society has been daunting. Within education those academics and practitioners in schools, LEAs and further and higher education who have championed equality, have made a significant difference, but have been badly served by policy makers who have failed to provide the framework or financial support to ensure that good equality practice was maintained and became the norm rather than the exception.

The current call from the EOC for government to mainstream equality echoes the call to the then Secretary of State for the Home Department, Rt Hon. Merlyn Rees in 1977:

We wish to stress again our conviction that the Commission does not have an exclusive responsibility in the field of sex discrimination – all of us, from the Government and powerful organizations on both sides of industry to small, local voluntary groups and individuals, are equally implicated in the task.

The Commission believes that of all these parties, Government and its Departments have a special responsibility in providing a lead, particularly by demonstrating that dealing with questions of sex discrimination and the promotion of equal opportunities form a central part of Departmental policies and practices. It is not sufficient for private organizations to show that they have done no more than to comply with the letter of the law. It is even less acceptable, in the Commission's view, for Government Departments to limit their scope for positive initiatives and policies in the same way, and the Commission feels bound to register a sense of disappointment at the apparently low priority given to this issue by Departments of Government responsible for introducing the Sex Discrimination Act in the first place.

(EOC 1977)

With no clear policy direction on equality from government to the UK, the EOC has had to use the law, through support of individual cases, in many circumstances to define discrimination and bring about changes in practices. The commitment of the current government to mainstreaming equality is therefore very welcome and will lead, it is hoped, to the development of structures and systems which move equality forward.

The EOC and education

The SDA makes it unlawful for educational establishments (schools, colleges, universities and LEAs) to discriminate on the grounds of sex:

• in the terms of admission to an establishment
• by refusing or deliberately omitting to accept an application for admission
• in affording a pupil access to any benefits, facilities or services, or by excluding a pupil from the establishment or by subjecting the pupil to any other detriment.

These clauses are important because they established for the first time the right of girls and boys to access to the same school and the same types of school in an area, access to the same curriculum including work experience opportunities and careers education, and to all extracurricular activities, and the right not to be treated less favourably than the opposite sex in any aspect of school or college life.

It should be remembered that up until this time, the education that girls and boys had received, particularly in coeducational secondary schools, prepared them generally for different roles in society. Girls would usually be timetabled for needlework and cookery (later home economics) and boys for woodwork and metalwork (later craft, design and technology or CDT), reflecting their different 'caring' and 'breadwinner' roles. In addition, the majority of girls would 'opt' out of sciences and technology at 14, or at the earliest opportunity, while boys were encouraged to pursue these subjects and maths to examination at 16. Only in independent and grammar schools were girls actively and systematically encouraged at that time to enter GCE maths and science.

In the early days of the SDA, issues of women's role in society were very much part of the education debate. Should women be educated to the same extent as men and take up paid employment, particularly when the UK was facing high unemployment? Should women with children work or be encouraged to improve their education and re-enter the labour market or should the male breadwinner role continue to dominate education and employment opportunities? While equality legislation guaranteed, in principle, rights to the full range of educational opportunities for women and men and these rights were supported by many vocal academics, the reality for many young girls was a life which continued to reflect the traditional and limited role of their mothers.

Clearly, in seeking to ensure that schools met their legal requirements under the SDA, the EOC was faced with the need not only to bring about a change in curriculum practices, but also to challenge, in policy makers, teachers, pupils and parents, traditional assumptions about men's and women's roles in society which, in 1975, continued to shape education expectation, curriculum, choices and outcomes.

Links with the Commission for Racial Equality

The arrival of sex equality legislation and the EOC was matched by the passing of the Race Relations Act and the establishment of the Commission for Racial Equality (CRE) with parallel duties to promote racial equality.

The EOC and CRE developed close links from the outset, recognizing that issues of race and sex discrimination were often interlinked and would be fully addressed only by joint approaches. It was not until the 1980s, when the Education Section engaged in extensive curriculum development work in schools, however, that there was full recognition at the EOC of the importance of developing anti-racism strategies alongside anti-sexist work in schools to counter racist and negative teacher expectations of black girls.

What the EOC did: the early years 1976–9

The first task facing the newly established EOC was to define the major equality challenges to be tackled, and to determine the best structure and resource allocation to successfully address these issues. Departments broadly reflecting the areas outlined in the SDA – employment, education and goods, facilities and services – were established which worked to committees of commissioners reflecting these areas. The Education Section worked on casework and enforcement issues, policy and promotional work across all sectors of education and on teacher/lecturer employment and publicly funded training schemes. It is important to recognize, therefore, that while school-based education is the focus of this analysis, other work on further and higher education, youth and adult training schemes, adult education including positive action and women returners, and promotion and appointment of teachers and lecturers was being undertaken within the Education Section of the EOC.

In devising its approach to education issues, the EOC recognized that developing equality in education would require changes in national policy direction, changes in schools' systems, practices and culture and changes in individual behaviour and attitude. It therefore sought to operate on all these fronts, from its early existence.

Meeting with education ministers and responding to government consultations to build gender equality into policy development started as early as 1977. The first consultation response was to the *Education in Schools* Green Paper (DES 1977). The EOC recommended that:

- as part of the curriculum review, LEAs should be requested to report on steps taken to implement the SDA
- the proposed improvement in initial and in-service teacher training should include the development of courses of equal opportunities between the sexes
- the content as well as the quality of careers education should be improved to reflect equality of opportunity.

(EOC *Annual Report* 1977: 24)

In the same year, a commission delegation to the Secretary of State for Education and Science urged that more vigorous involvement of the DES, particularly the HMI, was needed 'since the Education Service as a whole did not consider sex discrimination as a serious problem' (EOC *Annual Report* 1977: 24).

The focus of much of the early work of the Education Section was on interpreting what the SDA meant for education practices, to inform those with responsibilities under the Act, that is LEAs, teachers, governors, what was required of them and to resolve issues of sex discrimination. It was hoped in this way to remove structural and discriminatory barriers to equality.

Formal investigations and complaints

The EOC's first Formal Investigation (FI) into alleged discriminatory allocation of girls to secondary education in Tameside LEA, was begun in 1976. While the FI concluded that there was no sex discrimination, the report set out for the first time a precise legal interpretation of the education clauses of the SDA.

It is significant that the first engagement with the law on education issues should relate to access to secondary schools. Section 23 of the SDA, regarding the duty of LEAs not to discriminate in carrying out their functions under the Education Acts, relates to access to and provision of schools and to curricular provision within and across an LEA. It has been an area of legislation which has not been recognized or applied by all LEAs and it has provoked a number of enforcement activities, in relation to access to and curriculum in single-sex schools during the life of the SDA and the EOC. In 1978, for example, the EOC advised a LEA that providing places for boys at a local fee-paying single-sex grammar school while withdrawing similar provision for girls contravened the SDA. The provision for girls was reinstated. In 1979, Avon LEA amended its selection procedures for grammar schools when it was advised that a sex quota allocation system contravened the SDA.

Several other education practices were identified during 1976 as being potentially unlawful. Of these, perhaps the issue which attracted the most complaints was the provision of different curricular options for girls and boys at age 13–14. Complaints fell into two categories:

• timetables provided for boys to do one subject while girls did another
• timetables allocated pupils to options on the ground of sex but the headteachers allowed individuals to transfer to the 'opposite sex' option on special request.

The EOC maintained that such practices had the effect of placing pupils at a disadvantage on the grounds of their sex. The problem arose mainly in those subjects where the school's resources, either in facilities or teaching staff, were limited and had to be rationed. Complaints received primarily concerned physical education (PE) and sport, and the practical subjects such as woodwork, metalwork, home economics and needlework. Attempts were made to resolve difficulties by informal negotiation initially as the EOC recognized that LEAs and headteachers might not have realized the implications of continuing the traditional practices of segregating the sexes for these subjects; that this was not just an issue of access to practical subjects, but, linked with the tendency for girls to reject maths and science, the cumulative effect was to exclude girls from access to a whole range of careers traditionally held by men.

This informal approach did bring some change. However, the issue of equal access to all subjects or options on the curriculum continued to provoke complaints throughout the 1970s and 1980s, until the National Curriculum introduced a compulsory curriculum for all pupils to 16, albeit for a short time only.

Admissions

The issue of setting quotas, in order to balance the number of girls and boys, was also addressed in 1977. Concern was expressed that, since coeducational schools could no longer discriminate between the sexes in admissions, some schools might (for demographic and other reasons) have a disproportionate number of one sex on roll. This raised questions of the psychological effect on those pupils of one sex who were in the minority group. The EOC expressed the opinion that any form of quota system which admitted pupils by sex was potentially unlawful.

A major change in education practice occurred in the late 1970s when the EOC made it known that the practice of weighting and scaling procedures in educational testing to determine 11 plus allocations was potentially unlawful. It had been traditional practice in many LEAs to adjust the scores in tests at 11 and to apply different criteria to the ranking of girls and boys. This practice had been justified by the claim that girls advance more quickly than boys in the early stages of education. The EOC believed that the application of different standards on the grounds of sex could be challenged in the county court and advised appropriate bodies to review the use of those tests in the light of the SDA.

School uniform

The EOC also made it known early on that different rules relating to school uniform could constitute sex discrimination if they produced a detriment on the grounds of sex. So, for example, a girl could claim that being refused the right to wear trousers was potentially sex discrimination. This has been a particularly contentious area of practice because, over the years, many schools have continued to maintain their right to set standards of dress which include different rules for girls and boys. While many schools have recognized the fairness and educational benefits of allowing girls to wear trousers – and major stores supply them – even now the EOC continues to receive complaints from girls who are unable to wear trousers to school.

Guidance and development work

Having established opinions on the unlawfulness of a range of traditional educational practices, the Education Section, from 1978 under the new principal Wilf Knowles, sought to engage the education sector in actively challenging sex discrimination and developing equality in schools. To initiate this, a range of guidance booklets were produced which explained the law and good practice. *Do You Provide Equal Educational Opportunities?* (EOC 1979a) was published and distributed to all primary and secondary schools and LEAs in England, Wales and Scotland in 1979. This set out the educational requirements of the SDA and emphasized the need to develop good practice in the classroom to ensure that the removal of structural barriers to equality of opportunity was not negated by teachers' attitudes. It provided checklists and examples which schools could adopt.

To complement this, *Ending Sex Stereotyping in Schools* (EOC 1979b) was developed. This source book for school-based training workshops was a practical guide to addressing sex-based attitudes and practices in the classroom. The Education Section followed this manual with financial support and involvement in training courses in a number of LEAs.

Another important focus of education work in the late 1970s was careers education and guidance. It was recognized that changing from traditional roles to an acceptance of greater opportunity in education and employment would require not only change in structures to open up the full curriculum to girls and boys, but also support and additional assistance for young people to change expectations and attitudes to broadened choice beyond schooling. To achieve this, teaching materials and resources, careers information and recruitment brochures needed to be reviewed and revised to eliminate a focus on one sex only in particular settings. The EOC received many enquiries from careers practitioners about sex-biased careers literature from its beginning. In 1979 the Education Section set up a working party to look at the whole area of careers information and to produce guidelines for producers and users of careers materials. Also in 1979, with Wiltshire LEA, the Education Section produced a set of posters for primary schools depicting men and women in non-traditional jobs. In the same year a film was made addressing non-traditional careers aspirations and the section organized a one-day conference on Non-Traditional Careers for Girls. Held in Manchester, this event was designed to encourage second and third year pupils (aged 13–14) to consider careers in craft and technology occupations and other non-traditional areas of work; 400 girls from 20 schools attended the conference.

This example of a positive action event to encourage young girls to broaden career choices was one of many which were organized across the UK by individual schools and LEAs – and by the Women's National Commission with their Training Roadshows, in the late 1970s and 1980s. There is less evidence of such events in the 1990s, despite the continuing sex stereotyping of subject and career choices. With increased attainment in all subjects, the importance of girls maximizing their career opportunities remains a significant challenge for equality and positive action provides a mechanism for encouraging change which has yet to be fully exploited.

Developing good practice through partnerships 1980–9

As the structural barriers to equality in schools were gradually removed, the task facing the EOC in its education work changed. The major obstacle to progress was now perceived to be the persistence of discriminatory attitudes and stereotyped assumptions.

Sex differentiation in the curriculum and the under-representation of girls in maths, science and technical subjects at O level and CSE were recognized as major inhibitors of progression and opportunity. It was apparent by this time that girls' perceptions of these subjects were not necessarily improved by changes in school organization to open up access to all subjects, but continued to be dictated by traditional expectations and sex differentiation from nursery onwards.

To challenge this, during the 1980s, the EOC adopted a proactive approach, identifying and supporting strategies which could counter the more subtle and negative influences on education practice and outcome. This was, arguably, the most successful and significant period for the EOC in its aim of promoting equality in education. Under the leadership of Lynda Carr, principal of the Education Section 1980–9, the EOC engaged in an ambitious and influential programme of development work. Recognizing that good teachers, sensitive to gender issues in the classroom, were the key to moving equality in education forward, the Education Section sought to develop a range of partnerships with practitioners and lead organizations to develop good practice and to disseminate this across the sector. This approach meant that LEAs, schools and teachers who were already active in addressing sex differentiation – or who recognized the need to take action – were able to gain support, knowledge and expertise from each other.

One of the first joint projects concerned with the attainment of girls in schools was the Girls Into Science and Technology Project (see Chapter 9) funded jointly by the EOC and the Social Science Research Council, and based at Manchester Polytechnic. The project team worked with the science staff of ten Manchester comprehensive schools, and intervened with positive action strategies which they believed might improve the performance of girl pupils. The pupils' progress was monitored from 1980 up to the end of their O level (or equivalent) education in 1984.

The final report on the GIST Project was published in May 1984. The interventions appeared to reduce pupils' general gender-stereotyped attitudes but to have had little effect on gender differences in attitudes to particular subjects. More importantly, the interventions did not seem to increase girls' take-up of science and craft subjects. The results of the GIST Project were disappointing and signalled for the first time the rigidity of stereotyping and the size of the task in changing girls' attitudes to science (see Barbara Smail, Chapter 9).

Joint LEA projects

At least six LEAs joined with the EOC to work on gender equality during the 1980s. These included:

- Clwyd/EOC a two year project to scrutinize the secondary curriculum and to develop teaching aids for in-service and classroom use (EOC/ Clwyd 1981).
- Cleveland/EOC two projects (1981): one to overcome the stereotyped and negative attitudes to learning of boys and girls aged 9–13, and a

second to develop equality in nursery education by classroom observation of teacher–pupil interaction and a review of materials and books; the published report was *A Woman's World* (EOC/Cleveland 1981).

- City of Manchester/Tameside/EOC two teachers appointed to increase participation of girls in science subjects by devising strategies to challenge sex stereotyping (1982).
- Croydon/EOC strategies for attracting girls into IT with production of guidelines for teachers (EOC/Croydon 1982a).
- Sheffield/EOC two projects (1983): one to intervene positively in the careers guidance programme in five secondary schools and eight primary schools to change attitudes of pupils and teachers to non-traditional work; the published report was *Breaking the Mould* (EOC/Sheffield 1983). The second, with support from the Department of Trade and Industry (DTI), was an investigation into ways of developing IT in primary schools with guidelines for teachers; the published report was *Equal Opportunities and Computer Education in the Primary School* (EOC/Sheffield 1986).
- London Borough of Merton/EOC/SCDC the Equal Opportunities in Education Development Project developed and trialed strategies to implement equal opportunities in the classroom (1985). The material produced by the project director (Kate Myers) was published by the SCDC in 1987 as *Genderwatch* (subsequently updated and published in 1992 as *Genderwatch! After the Education Reform Act*: Myers 1987, 1992) and was a vital resource for schools in auditing and developing their equal opportunities work across all curricular and broader areas of the school.

Other partnerships

Joint work with the Schools Council and the Schools Curriculum Development Council and with the support of Longman Press led to a range of curriculum guidelines in the 1980s. These included:

- M. Eddowes (1983) *Humble Pi: The Mathematics Education of Girls*
- J. Harding (1983) *Switched Off: The Science Education of Girls*
- R. Kant and M. Browne (1983) *Jobs for the Girls*
- B. Smail (1984) *Girl-Friendly Science: Avoiding Sex Bias in the Curriculum*
- R. Stones (1983) *'Pour Out the Cocoa, Janet': Sexism in Children's Books*
- A. Watts and L. Kant (1986) *A Working Start: Guidance Strategies for Girls and Young Women*
- J. Whyte (1983) *Beyond the Wendy House: Sex-Role Stereotyping in Primary Schools*

In 1982 the EOC also worked closely with the Schools Council's Sex Differentiation Project and jointly funded with the ILEA a conference 'What's In It For Boys?', which looked at the importance for boys of developing life skills and changing attitudes to women and work. (Myers and Pinkerton 1982).

EOC publications

This was also a prolific time for EOC publications and guidance for teachers. Some of the titles produced during the 1980s are listed below:

- *A Guide to Equal Treatment of the Sexes in Careers Materials* (EOC 1978)
- *Getting It Right Matters* (EOC 1982a) to explain to children the implications of sex-stereotyped choice of exam and subject options.
- *We Can Do It Now: Case Studies of Good Science and Technology Practice in Primary Schools* (EOC 1982b)
- *Women Scientists Posters* (EOC 1982c)
- *Information Technology in Schools: Working with Computers* (EOC 1983a)
- *Women Mathematicians Poster* (EOC 1983b)
- *An Equal Start: Guidelines for Those Working with the Under 5s* (EOC 1984)
  The National Nursery Examination Board (NNEB) had asked the EOC to assist in raising awareness among NNEB students of the learning implications of sex stereotyping in very young children, and the commission's work in primary schools had revealed a concern among primary school teachers that many children enter school at $4^1/2$–5 years of age with a fixed notion about which play and learning activities are appropriate for girls and which for boys. *An Equal Start* was written in consultation with Sheffield LEA's Early Learning Adviser and over 13,000 copies were distributed in the first year of publication.
- *Equal Opportunities in TVEI* (EOC 1985)
  Equality of opportunity between girls and boys was a specific criterion for receipt of funding by LEAs for TVEI. This leaflet was produced for use in teacher-training sessions as a stimulus for discussion and a guide for action.
- *Equal Opportunities and the School Governor* (EOC 1986a)
  This booklet set out the role and responsibilities of governors under the SDA and recommended good practice strategies. It was revised in 1991.
- *Talking about Equal Opportunities* (EOC 1986b)
  The leaflet, for classroom teachers and curriculum planners involved with equal opportunity issues in schools, outlined how to set up discussion groups and identified further sources of advice on gender-related topics.
- *Get Your Future Right Now!* (EOC 1987b)
  A leaflet depicting men and women in non-traditional jobs for 13–14-year-olds making option choices.
- *Positive Action in Vocational Education and Training* (EOC 1987c)
  Explained for schools, colleges and training providers the forms of positive action which could be adopted to encourage women and men into non-traditional work.

Publicity campaigns

Curricular options

In 1982, for the first time, the EOC directed its attention towards parents themselves. It had become increasingly clear that a number of factors which were outside the control of the school system played a very influential part in pupils' choice of examination subject options and subsequent careers. Among these factors were the influence of parents and peer groups. In order to make direct contact with parents and pupils the EOC decided to explain its concerns through an advertising campaign which encouraged girls and their parents to consider the advantages of qualifications in maths and science. Different types of posters and leaflets, relevant to pupils at pre- and post-option stages, were dispatched to schools. These were deliberately provocative in style, designed to generate discussion among the young people at whom the campaign was directed. Advertisements were placed in education journals and papers in order to inform teachers of the campaign's existence and early in 1983 further advertisements offering information packs were placed in a number of teenage magazines, and in two major women's magazines. The campaign budget was £65,000 and the response was very positive.

WISE

In January 1984, the EOC in conjunction with the Engineering Council launched the Women into Science and Engineering (WISE) campaign. The project attracted widespread and continued media interest throughout the year. The national press provided full coverage as did radio stations, provincial papers, children's television programmes and many specialist magazines and newsletters. A WISE bus was launched in Downing Street by the Prime Minister, Margaret Thatcher.

It was evident from early planning of the campaign that the aims of WISE were supported and endorsed by education and industry and a great deal of interest was generated. It soon became apparent, however, that despite enthusiasm for the campaign, the willingness of employers and education providers to devise special projects was, to a large extent, dependent on the availability of support from the EOC or the Engineering Council. This was particularly true of the education sector, where lack of resources meant that many schools were unable to organize and sponsor their own projects without some support from other agencies.

Many of the projects in the secondary sector took the form of WISE conferences or careers events and featured women employed in industry. A number of schools devised visits to local firms to give girls experience of the work environment, or set up further and higher education 'taster courses'.

WISE was effective in giving a profile and dynamic to work to encourage girls in science, technology and engineering. It has continued to the present day with the sponsorship of the Engineering Council. Current figures show that while only 14 per cent of students on engineering and technology courses are women, this is double the number in the mid-1980s (EOC *Annual Report* 1997).

Research

In 1984 Pratt, funded by the EOC, evaluated the effect of the Sex Discrimination Act upon practice in schools and concluded that although the pattern of curricular provision had altered substantially over the period, that of option choice was little changed. On a simple level, the association between formal equality of provision and take-up of non-traditional subject options appeared limited.

Pratt's study suggested that the feature most associated with non-traditional take-up of subject options was single-sex schooling, but the author warned that this conclusion should not be pressed too far, since many of the single-sex schools examined were, in fact, selective. The EOC sought to shed greater light on the influence of single-sex schooling on educational achievement by commissioning two further projects, a research review and a statistical analysis, which were published together in January 1984.

The research review (Bone 1983) evaluated the evidence both for and against single-sex education for girls and found that attainment was more influenced by the type of school attended than by whether it was coeducational or single sex. However, differences in the ability range of pupils in mixed and single-sex schools complicated attempts to isolate the particular effects of a single-sex education and the conclusions reached in the review were inevitably qualified ones. A detailed statistical analysis comparing mixed and single-sex schools was commissioned from Steedman (1983). Using the National Child Development Study data, she set the examination results of girls and of boys against characteristics of the pupils and their schools. Her findings emphasized the importance of allowing for these factors rather than simply ascribing large differences to mixed or single-sex schooling.

The next stage in the research programme was to study the relative attainment of children in mixed and single-sex settings in a way which took into account differences in the ability of pupils at entry to secondary school. To this end, a project was initiated which compared the performance in mathematics of two groups of pupils, one having been taught in mixed sets over five years and the other in single-sex sets. Because both groups of pupils were attending the same comprehensive school, this research had the advantage of isolating the effects of individual classroom factors from the complicating effects of school-based factors. The study found that segregated setting in itself had no effect overall on the performance of girls and boys in GCE O level and CSE examinations, although some short-term improvements were noticed. However, over the longer term there was a notable improvement in girls' mathematics performance in the school, which suggested that the awareness of, and concern about, the issue among teachers may be of greater significance than the particular setting arrangements adopted (Smith 1986; EOC 1987d).

Section 54 grants

As a complement to its research programme, the EOC supported innovative work on gender equality in education through the use of grant-awarding powers under Section 54 of the SDA. A large number of projects were funded which contributed to the elimination of barriers to full curricular access for all pupils and to the promotion of girls' participation in non-traditional subjects. Two of these were investigative projects: Valerie Walkerdine researched the discontinuity in girls' mathematics performance between primary and secondary schools (EOC 1982d) and Lorraine Culley studied the gender differences in the take-up of computer studies in secondary schools (Culley 1985). A grant was also given to assist in the development of an innovative course for boys in secondary schools: Hackney Downs Comprehensive School introduced a highly successful course entitled Skills for Living (see Frances Magee, Chapter 10). A further three projects were promotional: the Centre for Applied Research in Education at the University of East Anglia produced a booklet on sex stereotyping within primary schools: the Girls and Mathematics Association produced a newsletter and prepared a resource bibliography with the aim of improving girls' achievement in mathematics generally; and the Schools Council's Equal Opportunities in Education Centre produced a list of a thousand groups and individuals currently working in the equal opportunities field.[1] (See Val Millman, Chapter 8).

The law

During the 1980s, the Education Section continued to receive complaints about access to education. Early on, a joint policy statement with the EOC was issued by Somerset LEA in response to EOC concerns that its 'special request' system for access to curricular options contravened the SDA.

In 1984, the case of *Debel, Sevket and Teh v London Borough of Bromley* was heard in the county court. The plaintiffs were three 10-year-old girls when, in 1982, together with five other girls, they were kept in the third year junior class of their school for a second year because the top class was full. The headteacher decided to keep down not the eight youngest pupils, but the eight youngest girls. At the court hearing an agreed statement was read out in which the LEA and the headteacher admitted discrimination and expressed their regret. The girls each received a small sum in damages for hurt feelings. This case supported the EOC's opinion that quotas and balancing on the grounds of sex is unlawful. It has relevance now for reduction in primary class sizes to thirty which will result in mixed age classes in some primary schools.[2]

One of the most significant education FIs which the EOC has undertaken was that into West Glamorgan LEA. In 1987 a group of parents complained that girls and boys were being treated differently in terms of access to craft subjects. In October 1988, the EOC completed and published its report of the two linked formal investigations into six schools (two coeducational primaries, two coeducational comprehensives and two single-sex comprehensives) in West Glamorgan (EOC 1988). The investigating team found that in the primary schools the girls were taught mainly needlework while the boys experienced a variety of other crafts such as carpentry. In the coeducational secondary schools, pupils in their first two or three years were supposed to have a choice between CDT or home economics (food and textiles). However, the arrangements for making the choice resulted in practice in almost all the boys studying CDT and almost all the girls studying home economics.

In the single-sex schools, facilities did not exist for girls to study CDT nor for boys to study home economics. The EOC therefore made formal findings that the West Glamorgan LEA and certain of the governing bodies unlawfully discriminated against girl and boy pupils, and these findings, together with a number of recommendations, were reported to the Secretaries of State for Education and Science and for Wales. The Secretary of State for Wales issued a letter supporting the findings and instructing LEAs to comply with the SDA. Five other LEAs changed practices as a result. This FI established the responsibility of LEAs for curricular provision across its schools. It has particular significance now in relation to equality of access to specialist schools in an area.

In 1987, the EOC judicially reviewed the practice of Birmingham LEA in maintaining 540 boys' and 360 girls' grammar school places. The High Court held that girls were less favourably treated than boys and that the LEA was acting unlawfully. Birmingham appealed to the Court of Appeal but lost. The judgment made it clear that there was an onus on local authorities to be sure that selection arrangements, and indeed the curriculum in their schools, were consistent with the provision of equal opportunities between the sexes. Birmingham lodged a further appeal to the House of Lords. In February 1989, this appeal was dismissed.

During the 1990s, the Birmingham situation was again referred to the High Court when one of the boys' schools involved became grant-maintained and the LEA claimed that this school was no longer part of its overall provision and therefore not included in the LEA's Section 23 duties. This claim was rejected. The EOC believes that the responsibility of LEAs with regard to their duties under Section 23 of the SDA has now been established by the courts. Since then several LEAs on the advice of the EOC have agreed to change their selection procedures to eliminate potentially unlawful sex quotas.[3]

The EOC also carried out a general Formal Investigation in 1988 into the extent of gender equality work in initial teacher training. The results were 'good in parts but disappointing overall' and the EOC (1989a) recommended to the DES that the accreditation criteria should address equality. In November 1989 the DES issued revised criteria which took on board this recommendation; disappointingly in 1992 the criteria were revised again to exclude equality. The plea for enhanced equality work in teacher training to address different teaching and learning styles and strategies has been one of the key messages to government, the Teacher Training Agency (TTA) and Ofsted from the EOC during the 1990s.

Assessing the impact

Overall, the 1980s were characterized by high-profile education work at the EOC, with a principal devoted to education with specialist knowledge and understanding of the issues, a large team of staff to support proactive development work, and access to EOC funding to support projects across the UK. The impact of this work is difficult to assess. While initiatives like the Technical and Vocational Education Initiative and the introduction of GCSE undoubtably assisted in the process, there is evidence of change in the behaviour of LEAs, schools and pupils during the 1980s, which can be attributed directly or indirectly to the EOC and/or the SDA.

There were changes in curriculum structure to increase access for girls to a broader range of subjects, and statistical evidence of improving achievement even in non-traditional subjects. Equal opportunity work in some LEAs was funded and support for the work of the increasing number of LEA equal opportunity advisers was provided. Positive action to broaden subject and career choices for girls was placed on the agenda of schools, careers services and education bodies and equal opportunities was brought into the mainstream of educational debate. It is significant that there was an increase in entry for girls into maths and physics at CSE and GCE between 1975 and 1985. This suggests that the SDA and curriculum development work to change expectations and subject choice were making a difference – even before the changes to exam and curriculum in 1988 and 1989 respectively. The engagement of girls generated before these reforms can be attributed to genuine non-stereotypical choice, whereas increased engagement subsequently may be a reflection of the compulsory nature of the National Curriculum.

In 1987, the EOC surveyed LEAs to ascertain to what extent they were active in implementing equal opportunities policies and practices.

Approximately 50 per cent reported action on gender equality. To further stimulate LEA activity, the EOC set up the Education Network with every LEA represented, to disseminate information to LEA equal opportunity advisers and teachers through twice yearly newsletters and a series of seminars. The first network seminar on the Education Reform Act (ERA) was held in March 1989 and a second conference to exchange equal opportunity ideas and strategies for change was held later in the year. By the end of the 1980s, therefore, there was undoubtably high interest in and high engagement with gender equality work.

Gender equality post-ERA 1990–6

The Education Reform Act 1988 brought significant changes to compulsory education in the form of the National Curriculum, SATs and local management of schools (LMS). In its publication *Gender Issues: The Implications for Schools of the Education Reform Act 1988*, the EOC (1989b) welcomed the National Curriculum as a mechanism for securing girls' entitlement to and engagement with key subjects such as science and technology to 16, and emphasized the need to ensure that issues of gender difference were taken seriously by those who 'design and implement the National Curriculum' and that 'programmes of study, themes and syllabi are free from gender bias in order to encourage the full and active participation by both girls and boys'.

The potential of the National Curriculum to improve equality of access and outcome for girls was huge. This major change coupled with evidence of much good curricular development work in schools led the EOC to conclude in its 1989 strategy review that the large amount of time and resources devoted to influencing policy and practice in education had been successful, and that the delivery of equality in education could safely be left to the sector itself. The *Annual Report* of 1990 sums this up and describes the new education role for the EOC:

> A core curriculum is emerging and many schools and local authorities are taking measures to combat sex-stereotyping in subject and career choice. It is hoped that the National Curriculum can deliver equality, but the EOC intends to maintain a monitoring role to see if this actually happens.
>
> (EOC *Annual Report* 1990: 7)

The policy and monitoring role

During the early 1990s, the Education and Training Unit assessed and engaged with policy makers on the gender content and impact of the education reforms on practices in schools and outcomes for pupils. Apart from the clear benefit of the National Curriculum in securing access to the full curriculum for girls and boys, there was little evidence initially of other new policy developments promoting activities in schools or LEAs to move gender equality forward.

The introduction of LMS linked to the economic imperative in education, placed decision making on training issues for teachers in the hands of governors and school managers and reduced the influence of LEAs in determining and leading on good practice in schools. Many schools elected not to buy equal opportunities training, much good equality work was shelved and many LEAs dispensed with their equal opportunities advisers. At the same time, the demands of the National Curriculum with its prescriptive programmes of study and assessment placed a burden on schools and teachers which left little time for curricular development work on equality issues in the classroom.

The education reforms also heralded a new focus on performance and standards based on the emerging data provided by SATs and GCSE results. This policy development was particularly helpful in identifying the great improvement in girls' performance, particularly in non-traditional subjects such as science and technology. It also revealed the relative under-performance of boys in English at all ages and placed boys' underachievement and target-setting to reduce the gender gap on the agenda for schools. In focusing gender equality work on charting achievement data, the issues of sex differentiation and stereotyping in the curriculum which affect post-school destinations and life chances of girls and boys and the need to put in place appropriate strategies, have become less important for schools (Arnot *et al.* 1998b).

The EOC sought to explore these concerns and others through meetings with ministers. In 1990 and 1991, meetings were held with John MacGregor, then Secretary of State for Education and Science, and Baroness Blatch, Education Minister. The EOC stressed the need for training on equal opportunities for school governors to be compulsory in the light of the extension of their responsibilities under ERA to cover curriculum, resourcing and staffing matters and sought joint guidance with the DfEE. This call was rejected and instead, in 1991, the EOC revised and distributed to all schools *Equal Opportunities and the School Governor*.

Also on the agenda for the ministerial meetings were concerns around gender and the National Curriculum. Casework indicated that facilities for teaching technology in single-sex schools were inadequate and reflected traditional sex-linked skills. In addition, it had become clear that National Curriculum subject working groups were not addressing gender issues in programmes of study and in subject delivery. The National Curriculum provided a great opportunity to improve educational attainment for girls in science and technology but could only secure progression if the technical device of keeping girls in 'non-traditional' subjects to 16 was matched by strategies in the classroom to make this extended learning a positive experience for girls. The EOC stressed that equal access to the curriculum in itself would not solve sex-segregated choice and engagement in training and employment, that is equality of access does *not* guarantee equality of opportunity or outcome. It is interesting that the response from ministers was that there was no longer any potential for sex discrimination in the school curriculum and they would expect the National Curriculum to encourage girls' participation in science beyond 16. While there has been a small increase in the numbers of girls studying science to A level and beyond, the expected follow-through has not happened and it is a continuing source of concern that many girls achieve well in science and technology to 16 but the majority elect to drop these subjects as soon as the opportunity arises.

Following from the actions against Birmingham and West Glamorgan LEAs, the EOC raised, with the ministers, the possibility of joint guidance with the DfEE on LEAs' Section 23 SDA duties. The move towards increased parental choice, autonomy of schools and diversity of types of education during the 1990s resulted in renewed resistance to the application of this part of the legislation which addressed equality of access for girls and boys to schools. Twice, following the *Choice and Diversity* (DES 1992) and *Self-Government for Schools* (DfEE 1996) White Papers, the DfEE sought to amend the SDA to subordinate the LEA responsibility to 'efficient use of resources'. The EOC has strenuously resisted this and argued – successfully – for the SDA to remain intact. In the EOC's view the education system can be fair and effective in improving achievement and outcome and providing equality of opportunity only if girls and boys have equality of access to all types of schools on offer. This requirement does not create a barrier for schools wishing to change their status, or specialism, but rather offers the possibility of more schools offering an enhanced curriculum so that all pupils – and not just those of one sex – can benefit from the full range of education in an area. An ally in championing the SDA has been the Funding Agency for Schools, which has worked to deliver on its SDA duty and ensure that provision of school places in LEA areas complies with equality legislation. After resistance to joint guidance in the early 1990s, in 1997 the DfEE agreed to work with the EOC. It is hoped that this will appear in 1999 to support the newly formed Schools' Organizations Committees and Adjudicators with their work.

By 1993, the EOC, recognizing that there was a loss of impetus on equal opportunities work across the education sector, again made education one of its priority issues. The EOC was particularly concerned that the benefit of the National Curriculum in delivering equality of access to age 16, would be undermined by proposals to increase flexibility at Key Stage 4. The EOC made strong representations to Sir Ron Dearing's *Review of the National*

Table 3.1   Entries into Part One GNVQ pilot years 1 and 2, 1995–7

	Boys (%)	Girls (%)
Health and social care	12	88
Manufacturing	71	29
Information technology	67	33

Source: Figures supplied to the EOC by Ofsted

Curriculum (Schools Curriculum and Assessment Authority (SCAA) 1994) on the dangers inherent in reintroducing choice into the Key Stage 4 curriculum, arguing that if the aim of freeing curriculum time and offering vocational options at 14 was to raise achievement levels for *all* pupils, then work on challenging stereotypes needed to be applied with vigour.

Vocational options were introduced with no supportive measures to assist non-stereotyped decision making and choice and, as predicted by the EOC, the figures for participation in Part One GNVQs, the vocational option at Key Stage 4, show overt stereotyping (Table 3.1).

There is a clear message here for the current review of the curriculum by the QCA and the intention to advocate further flexibility at Key Stage 4. Renewed emphasis on developing gender equality in schools is essential to ensure that opening up choice does not increase stereotyping, reinstate a gendered curriculum and reduce the potential for equality in the workplace.

New partnerships

In 1994 the EOC confirmed its heightened profile on education matters and recognizing that DfEE, Ofsted, Schools Curriculum and Assessment Authority (later Qualifications and Curriculum Authority) and Teacher Training Agency, by this time largely determined policy and practice in schools, sought to develop joint work to give equality a profile on the education agenda. The EOC also developed partnership working with the CRE and with other key education organizations, including Further Education Development Agency (FEDA), Further Education Funding Council (FEFC) and Committee of Vice Chancellors and Principals (CVCP).[4] In 1995, EOC officers met representatives of the TTA and pressed again for the inclusion of gender as a criterion for the accreditation of courses in order to stimulate equality work in the training of teachers.

In the same year, the EOC provided detailed written evidence to the House of Commons Education Committee Enquiry into the Education of 14–19-Year-Olds, pointing out particularly the different choices and routeways on which girls and boys could now embark at 14, and the implication for equality and individual attainment beyond schooling. Also in 1995, officers met with the then Secretary of State, Gillian Shepard, and voiced concerns about differential achievements, choices at Key Stage 4 and access to specialist schools, teacher training and its poor engagement with equality issues and the need in the growing nursery sector to build equality in to the services it provided.

A meeting with Ofsted in 1995 was particularly positive and helpful in securing an ongoing commitment to the inclusion of gender equality in the Framework for Inspection. The Ofsted EO requirement has been a positive driver of behaviour on equality in schools (Arnot *et al.* 1996).

In 1996, with Ofsted, the EOC produced a joint discussion document, *The Gender Divide: Performance Differences between Boys and Girls at School*. This focused on the relative achievements of girls and boys, stereotyping in the curriculum and in post-14 choices, personal and social education, classroom management, effective schools and the legal framework for equality. Using Ofsted inspection evidence and EOC casework and research, the booklet reported that:

- Girls outperform boys from an early age in English and are more successful than boys at every level at GCSE in almost all subjects, including technology, mathematics and science.
- Despite their success at GCSE, the trend continues for relatively few girls to opt for A level courses in mathematics, science and technology, which limits potential career opportunities in those areas.
- There are differences in the way that girls and boys respond to different types of teaching; some strategies are more successful than others with each sex.
- Some schools are more effective than others in meeting the needs of both sexes and in encouraging achievement.

The booklet was distributed to all Ofsted inspectors and to schools in 1996.

A positive meeting with SCAA in 1996 led to the EOC being invited to sit on working parties on careers and guidance. Challenging gender stereotyping has not had a high profile in the advice given by SCAA (now QCA) to schools and partnership working has provided the EOC with the opportunity to convince QCA of the importance of this work and the need for support through good practice strategies for schools.

Education reform and gender equality

One of the most significant and important pieces of work in assessing the relative impact on gender equality of changing education structures and practices under ERA and other reforms, *Education Reforms and Gender Equality in Schools* (Arnot *et al.* 1996), was published by the EOC in 1996. The report considered the state of gender equality in schools in England and Wales in the decade 1984–94. In particular it assessed whether the various

changes of the late 1980s and early 1990s strengthened or interrupted previous trends and/or generated new trends towards greater gender equality.
The EOC surveyed 853 secondary schools (1 in 4), 961 primary schools
(1 in 2) and all LEAs. Some of the main findings are set out below:

Ninety-eight per cent of LEAs, 81 per cent of primary and 93 per cent
of secondary schools reported having an equal opportunities policy
which included gender. Eighty-three per cent of these school policies
were produced after the 1988 Education Reform Act.

Equality issues are not viewed as a high priority by most schools and
LEAs. Less than 10 per cent gave gender issues a high priority; approximately 30 per cent claimed to be 'moderately interested' or 'actively
involved' in developing equal opportunities policies.

Primary schools are less likely to have policies on equal opportunities
and to see equal opportunities as integral to their practice rather than
as a discrete priority.

Wide variation amongst schools and LEAs exists in the awareness and
applications of gender issues, in the interpretation of equal opportunities
and in trends in student performance.

LEAs reported low levels of involvement in introducing curriculum
reforms in schools and in influencing, particularly, secondary school
policies and practices. They claimed to have been a major factor in
supporting equal opportunities in schools through provision of specialist
services, monitoring and training functions and advisory support. This
is not a view shared by schools which typically report low levels of
LEA support for equal opportunities work.

Seventy per cent of primary and secondary schools claimed not to have
had LEA-provided equal opportunities training for senior managers,
classroom teachers of careers teachers. Only a third of school governing
bodies were reported to be taking responsibility for providing training
and for monitoring gender performance in schools.

Changes to the curriculum and examinations (e.g. TVEI, GCSE,
National Curriculum, SATs) are seen largely to have a positive impact
on promoting equal opportunities, particularly in secondary schools.

TVEI was reported to have had a positive (or even a very positive) effect
on equal opportunities by 87 per cent of secondary schools; similarly
72 per cent saw positive effects of GCSE.

Reforms concerning the monitoring of performance and standards, and
new systems of school inspections using equal opportunities criteria
have tended to focus attention on the reduction of gender difference;

two thirds of LEAs claimed that Ofsted had raised the profile of equal opportunities.

Administrative and organizational reforms, provisions to support greater parental choice, and financial changes have been seen by LEAs as having a largely negative effect on gender equality. These include the introduction of LMS, grant-maintained schools (GMS), City Technology Colleges (CTC), representing a parallel loss of power of LEAs which in some instances were actively engaged with promoting greater gender equality.

Gender is perceived as having moved *downwards* in the policy agenda particularly in LEAs and schools with a greater commitment to equal opportunities. Small shifts **upwards** are discerned, post 1988, in other schools and LEAs which for the first time have been required to address gender issues in their reporting and evaluation procedures.

New areas of concern have emerged such as boys' under-achievement. This is beginning to be perceived as a major gender issue in schools, although there is little evidence of strong parental concern for gender issues.

Gaps in equal opportunities support are noticeable despite increased development of equal opportunities policies. These include **lack** of:

- governor training;
- classroom focused INSET;
- awareness and involvement of parents and parent governors;
- awareness among headteachers and classroom teachers (particularly at primary level) of the range of policy and curriculum strategies available;
- coordinated specialist resource centres, and libraries; and
- coordinated equal opportunities networks and advisory expertise.

There are lessons for government, local education authorities, teachers and the EOC in these findings. Curriculum, assessment and inspection frameworks which address equality have been a catalyst for moving equality forward – ideally all current and new education structures, systems and requirements should explicitly mainstream equality. Additional support for curriculum development work to change policy into action planning and good classroom practice is needed to ensure that equality gains achieved by education reforms are consolidated and secured for the future.

New challenges – new opportunities 1997–2000+

An EOC review of research on differential achievement across education and training (EOC 1998) together with the Ofsted *Recent Research on*

Gender and Educational Performance (Arnot *et al.* 1998a) signals that there are still areas of education and training where girls and boys engage in different ways and underperform relative to each other.

Key gender issues

The EOC defines the key gender issues as follows.

Differences in achievement levels

Both boys and girls have improved their performance at GCSE but girls' performance has increased more rapidly than boys. Boys are performing less well than girls in most subjects and at all ages to 16. It is important to recognize that there are differences in levels of achievement between different ethnic groups and not all pupils have shared equally in the increasing rates of achievement; the achievements of African Caribbean boys are a cause of concern (Gillborn and Gipps 1996). Girls continue to gain lower level vocational qualifications than boys.

Stereotyping

The trend towards increased choice at Key Stage 4 has marked an unwelcome return to stereotyping of girls and boys into traditional subjects and work-related areas of learning. Stereotyping continues to dominate subject choice at A level, FE and HE.

Different post-school destinations

More girls than boys enter FE and the under-representation of girls on Modern Apprenticeships is very marked in some regions.

Segregated career, training and occupational choices

Disappointingly, there has been little change in the types of work that girls and boys move into, despite girls' success in science and technology at 16 and the disappearance of many traditionally 'male' industries. This has implications for pay and economic independence.[5]

Addressing the issues

In seeking ways to address these issues, consideration should be given to the following:

• Reducing choice in the National Curriculum has helped gender equality; reverting to increased choice at Key Stage 4 has seen the reintroduction of stereotyped choices; any moves towards even greater flexibility at Key Stage 4 in the National Curriculum Review should recognize the inherent danger and the need for support in the form of a programme to challenge gender-stereotyped decision making.

- Access to schools has become more complex with the development and expansion of single-sex specialist schools; rights of equality of access must be maintained.
- Focus on academic achievements and targets as a measure of standards and excellence in schools has meant that choices and destinations have become relatively less important.
- Education can improve results for one sex and/or the other, but schools need to teach young people to make the most of their ability and potential; gender is still a key determinant of destination – and opportunities.
- Focus on specific National Curriculum subjects has squeezed out living skills, rights, responsibilities, roles and 'citizenship': all these need to be part of the education of girls and boys to secure changes in behaviour to accompany changes in opportunity in education and employment.
- The turn round in girls' engagement and achievement in science and technology to 16 is a great success story; girls' progression in science and technology beyond 16 needs to be secured.
- Research on aspects of gender equality should inform policy development, for example work on tiering and setting at GCSE has clearly indicated barriers to progression (Elwood 1995).

The way forward

In the letter accompanying the White Paper *Excellence in Schools* (DfEE 1997), David Blunkett said that this 'is as much about equipping the young people of this country for the challenge of the future as it is about the Government's commitment to equality of opportunity and high standards for all'.

The election in 1997 of a government which recognizes that equality of opportunity and good education go hand in hand has added a new, positive and welcome dimension to gender equality work. The EOC has secured a commitment from the Prime Minister to mainstream equality into all policy developments and the DfEE has adopted this objective. The EOC has been responding to a raft of education consultations, suggesting to the DfEE, Ofsted, QCA and TTA how and where gender equality should be mainstreamed into new policy proposals.[6]

In order to mainstream equality effectively, it is necessary to understand the different ways that girls and boys respond to all aspects of education. Clearly there is a major role here for the EOC and others in educating policy makers about gender policy issues, current research and the need for focused strategies, in order to produce good policy which is translated into good classroom practices.

Also, the announcement that the government's Women's Unit within the Cabinet Office has identified underachievement of girls in its broadest sense as a key issue is a very positive development and will, it is hoped, lead to a heightened profile and progress on improving progression and outcomes for girls.

There are other encouraging developments. In 1999 the DfEE published criteria for the accreditation of teacher-training courses which reintroduced an equality requirement. While this is minimal and has not been reflected explicitly in the new Ofsted Framework for the Inspection of Teacher Training, the requirement can be used to press both the TTA and Ofsted for greater engagement with gender equality issues in teacher training. With renewed calls from both the EOC and the CRE for the TTA to give a higher profile to equality in order to improve teachers' classroom practice with all pupils, progress on this front may now be possible.

A further positive development is the establishment by the QCA of a Gender Equality Advisory Group on which the EOC, local education organizations, teachers and academics are represented. We hope that this group will develop into an effective mechanism for airing concerns and for influencing education policy development and curriculum guidance. This is particularly important in relation to the review of the National Curriculum.

The EOC has also commissioned research into the extent of gender equality work in the advice and guidance given to young people by the career services. We hope to bring a renewed focus on the need to develop ways of challenging gender stereotyping in subject and career choices. The research report makes policy recommendations to government about the effect of contractual requirements and targets on gender equality work, and highlights current examples of good practice.

Also, following on from the review of differential achievement, the EOC has called on ministers to support good practice guidance for schools to identify teaching strategies which will engage girls and boys and tackle differential performance and stereotyping.

The EOC has always recognized that equal access to education free from gender bias, which promotes free and informed choice, is the starting point for equality in pay, employment and society. We have also recognized the need to embed good practice and curricular development work in schools and to mainstream equality through all major policy changes.

The EOC's commitment to moving equality forward in education has been a key and consistent feature of its work over the years. Its education officers have interpreted, intervened, advised, influenced, monitored and evaluated progress, continually assessing how, who and where the EOC can press for positive change. The results in terms of girls' participation in all curriculum areas and their achievements are extremely encouraging.

Evidence of increased entry to higher education and into the professions such as law and medicine provide clear indicators of progress on equality. There is work still to be done on boys' achievements and on destinations and choices of girls and boys.

Undoubtedly there are very real opportunities for progress on achievement and stereotyping at present with equality back on the political agenda. The EOC needs to ensure that moves towards increased autonomy for schools, different types of education and greater flexibility in the curriculum, that is different education for different needs, are introduced in such a way that the principle and practice of equality in education is secured and girls and boys are encouraged to experience the full range of curricular opportunities. This requires recognition that delivering equal opportunities is about defining levels of expectation and outcome across the curriculum, which are constant for all young people irrespective of their gender or race, and that achieving these equality outcomes in education may require a range of different strategies and interventions with individuals and groups.

The EOC needs to monitor developments carefully and to ensure that the government's policy commitment to mainstream gender equality into proposals for changes to schools and the curriculum is fulfilled. Developing equality in education will, therefore, remain a high level objective for the EOC into the millennium.

Disclaimer

The views expressed in this chapter are those of the author and do not necessarily represent the views of the EOC.

Notes

1 Section 54 grants: details of all awards made under Section 54 are included in the EOC's annual reports.
2 In *Debel, Sevket and Teh v London Borough of Bromley*, the plaintiffs claimed that they had been discriminated against on the ground of their sex contrary to Section 22 (c) of the SDA. They said that they had been deprived of continuity of association with their friends and classmates, of access to higher level academic stimulation they would receive from working in the wholly fourth year class, and of the benefit of teaching which was at entirely fourth year level. They claimed they had been placed in a class where, because of the lower average age of the children, the level of educational attainment would not be as advanced as in a class of older pupils. They claimed that they would repeat work they had done the year before and that the difference in age would inevitably affect the level of presentation of material and sophistication of discussion. In addition, the girls had suffered a loss of status in the estimation of their peers, had experienced a

loss of self-confidence and felt that they had not been treated fairly. The respondent denied these negative effects.

At the hearing the respondent admitted that the acts complained of breached Sections 1 and 22 of the SDA 1975. The Bromley County Court ordered by consent that the proceedings be discontinued, that the plaintiffs' costs be met by the respondent, that each of the plaintiffs be paid £351 as general damages, and that Selmin Sevket be paid an additional sum in respect of the cost of private tuition undertaken to reduce the effects of being kept in the third year class.

3 In *Equal Opportunities Commission v Birmingham City Council (1989) No. 1*, Birmingham City Council provided 540 places for boys at five single-sex grammar schools, and 360 places for girls at three equivalent schools and, therefore, girls had substantially less chance than boys of obtaining a grammar school education. The EOC brought an action for judicial review against the LEA seeking

1 a declaration that the arrangements concerning selective education constituted sex discrimination, contrary to Section 23 (1) of the SDA read with Section 8 of the Education Act 1944 (now Section 14 of the 1996 Act) and
2 an order of mandamus requiring the LEA to consider without delay the means by which such discrimination could be removed.

The High Court upheld the EOC's complaint and granted the declaration sought. The LEA unsuccessfully appealed to the Court of Appeal and the House of Lords. The appeal was dismissed for the following reasons:

1 To establish that there had been less favourable treatment of girls in the LEA's area on grounds of sex it was not necessary for the Commission to show that selective education was 'better' than non-selective education; it was enough for the Commission to show that the LEA had deprived the girls of a choice which was valued by them or their parents: *Gill v El Vino Co Ltd [1983]* 1 All ER 398, CA and *R v Secretary of State for Education and Science, ex p Keating* applied.
2 It was not necessary for the Commission to establish that the LEA had an intention to discriminate. Whatever the LEA's motive may have been, it was because of their sex that girls in the LEA's area had received less favourable treatment than boys in regard to selective education, and so they were subject to discrimination under the 1975 Act: dicta of Lord Denning MR in *Ministry of Defence v Jeremiah [1979]* 3 All ER 833 at 836, CA, of Browne-Wilkinson J in *Jenkins v Kingsgate (Clothing Productions) Ltd* [1981] 1 WLR 1485 at 1494 and of Taylor J in *J v Secretary of State of Education and Science, ex p Keating* applied.
3 An LEA was in breach of Section 23(1) of the 1975 Act if its system of selective education was such that fewer places were provided for girls than for boys at selective schools, so that girls were required to achieve a higher mark than boys to gain entry to such schools. The Commission was not required to show the LEA were in breach of their duties under Section 8 of the 1944 Act (now Section 14 of the 1996 Act) but only that in carrying out those duties an act or omission on their part constituted sex discrimination contrary to Section 23(1) of the 1975 Act: *R v Secretary of State for Education and Science, ex p Keating* applied.

In his speech, with which Lords Keith, Roskill, Brandon and Griffiths agreed, Lord Goff said:

> [Section 25 of the 1975 Act] is . . . intended, not to outlaw acts of discrimination as such, but to press on such bodies a positive role in relation to the elimination of sex discrimination. The idea appears to have been to see that such bodies are, so to speak, put on their toes to ensure that sex discrimination does not occur in areas within their responsibility.

In *Equal Opportunities Commission v Birmingham City Council (No. 2) (1992)*, the Court of Appeal upheld the decision of the Divisional Court that:

> In performance of its statutory duties to provide grammar school places without sex discrimination, the LEA is obliged to take into account places available for boys at a grant maintained school.

In *Re: EOC and the Sex Discrimination (Northern Ireland) Order 1976 No. 1 (July 1988)*, it was held that the procedure whereby 27 per cent of boys and 27 per cent of girls who sat the 11 plus examination and were awarded non-fee-paying places of grammar school so that non-fee-paying places were awarded to boys who had obtained lower marks than some girls who were not awarded non-fee-paying places constituted discrimination under the Northern Ireland legislation. This was because it was a system under which 'on the ground of their sex certain girls are treated less favourably than certain boys'. Therefore, it was decided that it was appropriate to award places to the top 27 per cent of children regardless of their sex.

In the light of this decision, 305 additional girls were eligible for non-fee-paying places because they were within the top 27 per cent of children, 422 boys had been awarded places under the old scheme for which they would not have been eligible under the new scheme but their places had not been withdrawn.

In *Re: EOC and the Sex Discrimination (Northern Ireland) Order 1976 No. 2*, the judge had to deal with the question of whether the 555 girls who sat the 11 plus exam and who did not come within the top 27 per cent of girls but who obtained marks equal to or higher than the 422 boys had been discriminated against because they had not been awarded non-fee-paying places.

He decided that there had been discrimination because the 422 boys had achieved their places as a result of discrimination and, therefore, 'their favoured treatment flowed directly from acts of unlawful discrimination' and 'that one group are boys and one group are girls is the decisive reason why the boys have non-fee-paying places and the girls do not'.

4 The EOC, CRE and FEDA have worked jointly to produce several publications. These include:

> S. Dadzie (1998) *Equality Assurance: Self-Assessment for Equal Opportunities in Further Education.* London: Further Education Development Agency.
>
> EOC (1994) *Black and Ethnic Minority Women and Men in Britain.* Manchester: EOC.
>
> J. Powney, S. Hamilton and G. Weiner (1998) *Higher Education and Equality: A Guide.* Manchester: EOC.

5 Women employees working full-time earn on average only 80 per cent of the average hourly earnings of male full-time employees. Weekly pay rates in male-dominated sectors of industry are generally higher than those in sectors where women predominate:

Computer analyst/programmer	£498.8
Engineering technician	£460.3
Nursery nurses	£197.5
Hairdresser	£158.2
	(full-time employment)

Source: New Earnings Survey 1997

6 The EOC has responded to the following consultations during 1997–8 and copies of these can be obtained from Education and Training Unit, Equal Opportunities Commission, Overseas House, Quay Street, Manchester, M3 3HN:

Audit Commission (1998) *Changing Partners: A Discussion Paper on the Role of the Local Education Authority.*

DfEE (1997) *Investing in Young People.*

DfEE (1997) *Early Years Development Plans.*

DfEE (1997) *Higher Education for the 21st Century.*

DfEE (1997) *Excellence in Schools and Executive Summary.*

DfEE (1997) *New School Framework: Technical Consultation.*

DfEE (1997) *Database of the Education and Training Participation and Achievements of Young People aged 14–21.*

DfEE (1997) *Connecting the Learning Society: The National Grid for Learning.*

DfEE (1997) *Revision of the Requirements and Guidance for Careers Services.*

DfEE (1997) *Behaviour Support Plans: Draft Guidance for LEAs.*

DfEE (1998) *Draft Guidance on School Attendance and the Role of the Education Welfare System.*

DfEE (1998) *Future Selective Admission Arrangements for Grammar Schools.*

DfEE (1998) *Student Support in Further Education.*

DfEE (1998) *Targets for Our Future.*

DfEE (1998) *Guidance on Section 550a of the Education Act 1996: The Use of Reasonable Force to Control or Restrain Pupils.*

DfEE (1998) *Baseline Assessment: Consultation on Regulations for September 1998.*

DfEE (1998) *Local Education Authority Education Development Plans.*

DfEE (1998) *Secondary School and College Performance Tables.*

DfEE (1998) *Induction for New Teachers.*

DfEE (1998) *Draft Code of Practice on LEA–School Relations.*

DfEE (1998) *Improving Access to Information about Post-16 Learning Options.*

DfEE (1998) *The Learning Age.*

DfEE (1998) *Draft Guidance on Home-School Agreements.*

DfEE (1998) *TECs: Facing the Challenge of the Millennium.*

DfEE (1998) *Draft Code of Practice on School Admissions.*

Employment Service (1997) *New Values for the Employment Service Further Education Student Support Arrangements* (1998).

HEFCE (1998) *Widening Participation in Higher Education: Funding Proposals.*

Initial consultation on the *Higher Education Institute for Learning and Teaching* (1998).

North East Skills Agenda Consultation Document (1998).

Ofsted (1997) *Revised Framework for the Inspection of LEAs.*

QCA (1998) *Providing Opportunities through Regulations to Permit the Wider Use of Work-related Learning at Key Stage 4.*

SCAA (1997) *Work Experience: National Quality Standards.*

Social Exclusion Unit (1998) *Inquiry into Teenage Parenthood.*

References

Arnot, M., David, M. and Weiner, G. (1996) *Educational Reforms and Gender Equality in Schools*, Research Discussion Series no. 17. Manchester: Equal Opportunities Commission.

Arnot, M., Gray, J., James, M., Rudduck, J. with Duveen, D. (1998a) *Recent Research on Gender and Educational Performance*, Ofsted Reviews of Research. London: The Stationery Office.

Arnot, M., Millen, D. and Maton, K. (1998b) *Current Innovative Practice in Schools in the United Kingdom*, for the Council of Europe's Group of Specialists in Equality between Men and Women, University of Cambridge.

Bone, A. (1983) *Girls and Girls-Only Schools: A Review of the Evidence.* Manchester: EOC.

Culley, L. (1985) *Gender Differences and Computing in Secondary Schools.* Published by the author.

DES (1977) *Education in Schools*, Green Paper. London: DES.

DES (1992) *Choice and Diversity: A New Framework for Schools*, White Paper. London: DES.

DfEE (1996) *Self-Government for Schools,* White Paper. London: DfEE.

DfEE (1997) *Excellence in Schools*, White Paper. London: The Stationery Office.

Eddowes, M. (1983) *Humble Pi: The Mathematics Education of Girls.* York: Longman for Schools Council.

Elwood, J. (1995) Undermining gender stereotypes: examination and coursework performance in the UK at 16, *Assessment in Education*, 2(3): 283–303.

EOC (1976–89) *Annual Reports.* London: HMSO.

EOC (1977) *Formal Investigation Report: Tameside.* Manchester: EOC.

EOC (1978) *A Guide to Equal Treatment of the Sexes in Careers Materials.* Manchester: EOC.

EOC (1979a) *Do You Provide Equal Educational Opportunities?* Manchester: EOC.

EOC (1979b) *Ending Sex Stereotyping in Schools.* Manchester: EOC.

EOC (1980a) *Equal Opportunities and the School Governor* (revised 1991). Manchester: EOC.

EOC (1980b) *Talking about Equal Opportunities.* Manchester: EOC.

EOC (1982a) *Getting It Right Matters.* Manchester: EOC.

EOC (1982b) *We Can Do It Now*. Manchester: EOC.

EOC (1982c) *Women Scientists Posters*. Manchester: EOC.

EOC (1982d) *Girls and Mathematics: The Early Years*. Manchester: EOC.

EOC (1983a) *Information Technology in Schools: Working with Computers*. Manchester: EOC.

EOC (1983b) *Women Mathematicians Poster*. Manchester: EOC.

EOC (1984) *An Equal Start*. Manchester: EOC.

EOC (1985) *Equal Opportunities in TVEI*. Manchester: EOC.

EOC (1986a) *Equal Opportunities and the School Governor*. Manchester: EOC.

EOC (1986b) *Talking about Equal Opportunities*. Manchester: EOC.

EOC (1987a) *Briefings on Men and Women in Britain: Management and the Professions*. Manchester: EOC.

EOC (1987b) *Get Your Future Right Now!*. Manchester: EOC.

EOC (1987c) *Positive Action in Vocational Education and Training*. Manchester: EOC.

EOC (1987d) *Separate Beginnings?* Manchester: EOC.

EOC (1988) *Formal Investigation Report: West Glamorgan Schools*. Manchester: EOC.

EOC (1989a) *Formal Investigation Report: Initial Teacher Training in England and Wales*. Manchester: EOC.

EOC (1989b) *Gender Issues: The Implications for Schools of the Education Reform Act 1988*. Manchester: EOC.

EOC (1990–7) *Annual Reports*. Manchester: EOC.

EOC (1995) *Inquiry into Education and Training for 14 to 19 Year Olds*. Manchester: EOC.

EOC (1998) *Gender and Differential Achievement in Education and Training: A Research Review. Research Findings*. Manchester: EOC.

EOC/Cleveland (1981) *A Woman's World*. Manchester: EOC.

EOC/Clwyd County Council (1981) *Equal Opportunities and the Secondary School Curriculum: Report of the Project*. Manchester: EOC.

EOC/ILEA /Schools Council (1982) *'What's in it for Boys?' Report of Conference held on 19 November 1982*. Manchester: EOC.

EOC/London Borough of Croydon (1982a) *Information Technology in Schools: Guidelines of Good Practice for Teachers of IT*. Manchester: EOC.

EOC/London Borough of Croydon (1982b) *Information Technology in Schools: Report of the Project*. Manchester: EOC.

EOC/Ofsted (1996) *The Gender Divide: Performance Differences between Boys and Girls in School*. London: HMSO.

EOC/Sheffield (1983) *Breaking the Mould*. Manchester: EOC.

EOC/Sheffield (1986) *Equal Opportunities and Computer Education in the Primary School*. Manchester: EOC.

Gillborn, D. and Gipps, C. (1996) *Recent Research on the Achievements of Ethnic Minority Pupils*. London: HMSO.

Harding, J. (1983) *Switched Off: The Science Education of Girls*. York: Longman for Schools Council.

Kant, R. and Browne, M. (1983) *Jobs for the Girls*. London: Schools Council.

Myers, K. (1987) *Genderwatch: Self-Assessment Schedules for Use in Schools*. London: Schools Curriculum Development Council.

Myers, K. (1992) *Genderwatch! After the Education Reform Act*. Cambridge: Cambridge University Press.

Myers, K. and Pinkerton, G. (1982) Equal Opportunities: 'What's in it for boys'. Report of conference funded by EOC and supported by ILEA and the Schools Council, 19 November.

Pratt, J., Bloomfield, J. and Searle, C. (1984) *Option Choice: A Question of Equal Opportunity*. Slough: NFER-Nelson.

Smail, B. (1984) *Girl-Friendly Science: Avoiding Sex Bias in the Curriculum*. York: Longman for Schools Council.

Smith, S. (1986) *Separate Tables? An Investigation into Single-Sex Setting in Mathematics*. London: HMSO.

Smith, S. (1987) *Separate Beginnings?* Manchester: EOC.

Steedman, J. (1983) *Examination Results in Mixed and Single-Sex Schools: Findings from the National Child Development Study*. Manchester: EOC.

Stones, R. (1983)*'Pour Out the Cocoa, Janet': Sexism in Children's Books*. York: Longman for Schools Council.

Watts, A. and Kant, L. (1986) *A Working Start: Guidance Strategies for Girls and Young Women. A report based on a seminar held by the School Curriculum Development Committee, EOC and Further Education Unit*. York: Longman for SCDC.

Whyte, J. (1983) *Beyond the Wendy House: Sex-Role Stereotyping in Primary Schools*. York: Longman for Schools Council.

Chapter four

Equal to the task? The role of the NUT in promoting equal opportunities in schools

Ruth Blunt

By the elevation of the teacher we elevate the value of education and accelerate the progress of civilisation.
(J.J. Graves, NUT president 1870,
cited in Bourne and MacArthur 1970: 9)

Introduction

In this chapter, I trace the National Union of Teachers' contribution to
equal opportunities in chronological order. First and briefly, initiatives
before the Sex Discrimination Act in 1975; second, between the SDA and
the Education Reform Act 1988; and third, post-ERA. Finally, I conclude
with a ten-point plan for progress.

Good for teachers – good for pupils

The story of the NUT begins over 100 years before the Sex Discrimination
Act. The principle which underpins all of the NUT's work dates back to its
inception in 1870. The above quotation from the inaugural speech of
Mr J.J. Graves (they were all 'Mr' in those days), the first president of the
NUT, underlines the philosophy that there should be no conflict between
the interests of teachers and the interests of children.

The NUT has always had a strong dual commitment to equality. This has
been and is manifested through its fundamental commitment to equal educational opportunities for all pupils and students in all schools and colleges
as well as its network of support on conditions of service issues for its
members. This dual commitment is as old as the union itself.

Early campaigns for women's equality: before the Sex Discrimination Act

Gender equality was an early concern of the NUT. A key focus in the first part of the twentieth century was the campaign for equal pay for women teachers. NUT annual conferences discussed equal pay as long ago as 1904 and adopted equal pay as policy in 1919 after a referendum. The policy was not universally popular, however, and a group of men left the NUT in protest and formed the National Association of Schoolmasters.

It took many years before the campaign succeeded, with equal pay for women teachers being phased in between 1955 and 1961, well in advance of the introduction in 1970 of equal pay legislation nationally. (In practice, however, equal pay is a principle which has yet to become a reality. Because of the under-representation of women at senior levels in the profession, the average pay of women teachers is lower than that of men. In 1997, the average pay of women teachers was £21,130 while that of men was £22,880 (*TES*, 5 February 1999: 7) – one of the many issues still to be addressed.)

Between the First and Second World Wars, many local authorities operated marriage bars which prevented married women from entering the profession. A woman teacher who married while in employment was forced to leave her post. The NUT fought such bars locally and in many cases succeeded in lifting the ban. The marriage bar was finally outlawed in 1944 as part of the Education Act. During this time there was a reaction against women in senior management posts. According to Barbara Lloyd, a past-president of the NUT, 'there was a reluctance on the part of men to serve under women headteachers and a popular slogan between the wars was "no masters under mistresses" then' (Lloyd 1996: 5).

The NUT was one of the first trade unions to appoint an officer with responsibility for gender equality. Sarah Griffiths, appointed in 1925 as the Woman Organiser, served for over 30 years. She was replaced in 1959 by Olwen Morris, who held the title of 'the Woman Official' until 1965. After a few years' gap, Jean Farrall was appointed in 1971 as the Woman Official, a title which changed to 'the Women's Official' and then, in 1985, to Head of Equal Opportunities. Jean Farrall held this post until 1987.

Race equality: before the Race Relations Act

Over the years, it became apparent that there were other areas where inequality and discrimination needed to be tackled. In 1967, the union published its first document on multicultural education. It was called *The Education of Immigrants* and although its language was a product of its time, it recognized the need for all children 'to secure the full benefits of education' and that this was 'a matter which concerns all teachers' (NUT 1967: 1).

Between the SDA and the ERA 1975–88

There were many important developments during the years between 1975, when the Sex Discrimination Act became law, and 1988, which brought the Education Reform Act. Once again, these were underpinned by the dual commitment to achieving equality for teachers and for pupils. A third theme, that of equal representation at all levels of the NUT itself, emerged. Barbara Lloyd, NUT past-president, outlined the position.

> Equal pay was won, at least in theory, and it seemed then that gender problems were resolved. It took some time for us to realise just how much more work remained to be done in the field of appointments and promotions, in the curriculum and in the way in which girl pupils were treated and, of course, within the Union itself.
>
> (Lloyd 1996: 6)

The three themes – equality for teachers, equality for pupils and equality within the NUT itself – form a common thread throughout its work since the mid-1970s.

NUT equality structures: the late 1970s

Structures within a trade union may seem rather esoteric but, looking back, it seems that establishing the right structures enabled proper priority to be given to equal opportunities policies. In 1975, the year of the Sex Discrimination Act, the NUT's national executive established a committee to consider specific equal opportunities issues related to 'the child at school and to the teacher of that child'. Among the topics considered were career opportunities, maternity provisions, part-time service and sex bias in children's books.

Promotion and the woman teacher: 1980

The year 1980 saw the publication of *Promotion and the Woman Teacher*, a report of a research project undertaken jointly with the Equal Opportunities Commission (NUT/EOC 1980). The report found that women teachers faced difficulties in gaining promotion and that women faced discrimination. The discrimination identified was broken down into three main types: straightforward sex discrimination, discrimination against older teachers and discrimination against married women. The report concluded that:

> We are brought inescapably to the belief that the overwhelming need for women teachers is through a promotion structure that is flexible enough to take account of the varied ways in which women order their lives and which considers them not on the basis of their age, nor of their

marital status, nor of their maternal capacity, but solely as teachers on the basis of their professional competence alone.

(NUT/EOC 1980: 54)

With hindsight, these conclusions seem unsurprising. At the time, however, they gave voice to thousands of women teachers who knew that they did not have a fair deal. Also significant was the collaboration between the NUT and the EOC.

Working at local level: the 1980s

An important development was the establishment of local working groups on equal opportunities. By 1980, at least 70 such groups had been identified, a clear indication of the concern not only of individual members about their career prospects but also of local associations about the issues raised within *Promotion and the Woman Teacher*. The NUT's branches, known as local associations, were also urged to appoint equal opportunities officers. A suggested job description was drawn up to highlight the tasks which an equal opportunities officer could undertake. These included encouraging participation by all groups of members, providing information on campaigns, ensuring that equal opportunities issues were addressed in negotiations with local authorities and supporting members in relevant casework.

The women's development initiative: the 1980s

An exciting initiative of 1981 was a residential workshop at the NUT's National Education and Training Centre at Stoke Rochford Hall in Lincolnshire. The workshop led to the organization of a day conference held in London in 1983, involving more members on a delegate basis. It was recommended that a positive role for women should be developed within the NUT, that women should have access to equal opportunities for career development in the education service and that appropriate steps should be taken to enable individual teachers to become more aware of their curricular responsibilities in developing equal opportunities.

Training for women members began with a popular four-day residential course in June 1983. At the time though, there was a great deal of debate about whether women-only training would be of value. Two of the women involved in the programme in its early days described the debate.

> Initially it was argued that changing the attitudes of individual women would make little overall impact. Indeed it was argued that the effort to change attitudes would divert energy from more fundamental changes in structure and organisation. Some regarded women's training as patronising; they argued that it adopted a deficit model which emphasised women's lack of skills and placed the responsibility for change on women

rather than more properly on men. Since men hold positions of power and influence, the argument goes that men have the prime responsibility for change; if attitudes and behaviour require modification, then men rather than women should be the focus of such training. Others also expressed concern that although women's training might enable some women to take on greater responsibility, attitudes and priorities in the Union would remain largely unchanged unless the male ethos is challenged.

(Shipton and Tatton 1989: 194)

Over the years, it has become apparent that the women's development courses have been successful in encouraging women to become more involved in and informed about the NUT and its work. The training also has enabled women to decide on their own professional priorities, to recognize their skills and to develop professionally and personally, by equipping them with strategies which can be practised including assertiveness and presentation skills. Women's development courses continue to be run successfully by the NUT.

The Advisory Committee: the 1980s

The 1984 annual conference of the NUT adopted as policy a memorandum entitled 'Equal opportunities in education' which reaffirmed the commitment to work towards equality for teachers, pupils and within the union's own structures. The memorandum urged local associations to negotiate equal opportunities policies and practices with their local authorities.

Significantly, the memorandum also established an Advisory Committee for Equal Opportunities which included lay members with expertise on equal opportunities as well as members of the national executive. The first chairperson of the committee, Barbara Lloyd, recalled the early days:

Those elected to that first committee were so enthusiastic, so committed. I can still see the look on Fred Jarvis' face [then General Secretary] when he came to the first meeting. I saw three types there – those like myself who had come to these issues through our trade union background; those who used the Union to promote ultra-feminist views and those who used gender issues to promote their own political views. (I don't say this disparagingly). The important thing was that we gelled and we got through a lot of work.

(Lloyd 1995)

Developing anti-racist training: the 1980s

The NUT was a pioneer of anti-racist training. A commentary on two pilot racism awareness workshops organized in 1983 is indicative of the union's strategies-based approach.

[The workshops] were designed for teachers who wished to develop an awareness of the operation of racism in society in general and in the education system in particular at an institutional and personal level. The aim was to provide participants with information and skills to help them to make an effective contribution to anti-racist strategies in their own schools and local areas, in support of Union policy. Participants found that the course strengthened their commitment and awareness and, in some cases, members have already reported the setting up of local workshops based on the Union's model in their own schools and local associations.

(NUT 1984: 88)

The challenge of ERA: 1988

The Education Reform Act 1988 presented the NUT with a new challenge in relation to equal opportunities. Shirley Darlington, Assistant Secretary for Equal Opportunities from 1988 to 1994, identified the difficulties:

As teachers struggle to find their way through a plethora of paperwork, government circulars, statutory instruments and orders, a jungle of new jargon, statutory attainment targets, programmes of study, assessment arrangements, curriculum working group reports and non-statutory guidance, how are they to keep alive their ideals and the vision of creating equality of opportunity for all their pupils? . . . The aspects of educational equality of opportunity currently under threat from policy makers whose main concern appears to be with producing an elite through a competitive market forces ethos are many and various: the professional challenge to teachers is to retain a sense of optimism and a commitment to quality education for all our children. Good education cannot be divorced from a concern for social justice.

(NUT 1989a: 3)

Lesbian and gay equality: the end of the 1980s

Lesbian and gay activists had campaigned for at least ten years for the NUT to adopt policy on this area of equality. It was not until 1988, perhaps kick-started by the homophobic Section 28 of the Local Government Act 1988, that the annual conference resolved to reject all discrimination on grounds of sexual orientation. It is interesting to note that a significant number of delegates opposed the new policy. At the first conference held specifically on the topic of lesbian and gay equality in 1989, there was a great deal of anger, some of which was directed at the resurfacing homophobia of society in general.

Delegates also expressed anger at the NUT itself. This is illustrative of a not infrequent tension between the pace at which individual members wish to progress and the pace at which the union, as a large organization, actually manages to move.

Disability equality: the end of the 1980s

Although the union's work on children with disabilities and special educational needs was well-established, it was not until 1989 that the annual conference agreed policy on equality for teachers with disabilities. The input of disabled activists was a decisive factor in securing the agreement of the policy. Conference called for steps to be taken to increase the recruitment and retention of disabled teachers, for flexible work practices, adaptations to buildings and the establishment of a working party, to include lay members with disabilities. The working party has had a major influence on the DfEE which now recognizes that 'the employment of disabled teachers can make an important contribution to the overall school curriculum in terms of raising the aspirations of disabled pupils and educating non-disabled people about the reality of having a disability' (DfEE 1993: 4).

The Opening Doors campaign: the end of the 1980s

The NUT's Opening Doors campaign to encourage returners into teaching developed from the work of previous years. It coincided with the government's identification of the 'pool of inactive teachers', unfortunately referred to as 'the PIT'. The NUT called for measures to ensure that returning teachers had access to flexible working arrangements such as job sharing and to training, including 'keeping-in-touch' schemes.

Towards Equality for Girls and Boys: the end of the 1980s

Towards Equality for Girls and Boys, a pack of materials for use in schools, set down a marker that educating for equality was part of good education.

> To provide good quality education we must ensure that all pupils get a chance to fulfil their potential. This means ensuring equal opportunities are available for everyone regardless of sex, class, racial group or ability range. This is good educational practice and for this reason, if for no other, the issue for equal opportunities should be a matter of concern to all teachers.
>
> (NUT 1989b: 1)

The guidance also highlighted to NUT members their professional responsibility and their power within a school to promote equality.

These guidelines emphasise the role of the teacher in this process [promoting sex equality in education] and suggest ways in which you can promote gender equality through your teaching and interaction with pupils and others to ensure that educational institutions offer greater equality of opportunity. The daily life of the school is directly influenced by the attitudes, actions and expectations of its teachers. It is your degree of commitment to countering sexism in schools on a day-to-day basis which will largely determine whether the classroom practice and the ethos of individual schools are truly supportive of both sexes.

(NUT 1989b: 2)

Fair and equal: moving into the 1990s

Concerns raised by NUT members about their experiences in applying for teaching posts indicated an urgent need for fundamental and wide-ranging reviews of procedures for appointment, promotion and career development. The NUT's (1991) pioneering publication *Fair and Equal* had made recommendations for the establishment of clear appointments procedures by local authorities.

With the advent of local management of schools at the end of the 1980s and the devolution of a range of powers to school governing bodies, this advice was developed for use by headteachers and governors. The dual commitment to teachers and pupils was evident in the document *Fair and Equal* (NUT 1991).

Equal opportunities procedures are not only important in offering a fair chance to every applicant but also important for the school as a whole. It is important to bear in mind that staff are a vital resource for any organization. Fair appointment and promotion procedures enable schools to draw on the talents of existing staff and attract applications for vacancies from a wide range of teachers. Good procedures also promote confidence and lift staff morale, thus enhancing the educational goals for the school. It is important that pupils have positive role models in order to counteract stereotyping. A school which operates an equal opportunities policy in relation to appointments and promotion will be better able to promote equal opportunities for pupils (NUT 1991).

An increasing problem at this time was the misuse of fixed-term contracts, the vast majority of which were held by women.

New debates on gender equality: the 1990s

The focus of debate nationally shifted in the 1990s, most notably with the surfacing of concerns about boys' achievements. The NUT's approach has been to welcome and celebrate the rising levels of achievements of girls, to point out that boys' achievements have also improved and to set the debate in the context of the continuing inequality in the outcomes of education leading to inequalities in the labour market. The NUT has argued against a knee-jerk response to concerns about boys' achievements and has urged that the debate should be kept broadly based.

> There are dangers in the debate on girls' and boys' achievements. One trap which could be fallen into is that of arguing that the focus on raising girls' achievements has led to a neglect of boys' achievements. Boys' educational performance should be viewed as an equal opportunities issue requiring its own strategies, maintained resources and expert staff. Attention should continue to be focused on the need to raise girls' achievements in all curriculum areas while at the same time addressing all areas of boys' achievements.
>
> (NUT 1998: 2)

The NUT was quick to refute any claim of a relationship between the gender composition of the teaching profession, that is, predominantly female, with concerns about pupils' achievements, referred to by some commentators in terms of boys' 'underachievement'. The union has restated its belief that it is educationally important for children throughout their school lives to see women and men teachers taking a range of roles throughout all the curriculum subjects and in senior management positions in schools.

Continuing race equality work: the 1990s

The anti-racist training of the 1980s has now evolved into a course on 'School improvement and race equality' which aims to consider the implications of the school improvement movement and to help to ensure that race equality is central rather than marginal to initiatives arising from the school improvement philosophy.

Black teachers and teachers from minority ethnic groups are under-represented in the teaching profession. The NUT has continued to campaign for greater recruitment of black teachers into the profession and, looking at its own structures, to increase the involvement of black members at all levels. The union has also campaigned consistently to protect funding to meet the specific educational needs of minority ethnic pupils. While seeking to protect the jobs of teachers employed under Section 11, now the Ethnic Minority Achievement Grant, the union has argued the educational benefits of the fund for all children.

Moving forward on lesbian and gay equality: the 1990s

During the 1990s, the NUT's reputation for its work on lesbian and gay issues has grown considerably. The establishment of a task group, whose members include lesbian, gay, bisexual and transgendered teachers, was the most significant factor in increasing members' confidence in the union's commitment to this issue. Guidance to schools, entitled *An Issue for Every Teacher*, highlights how teachers can educate children to respect and celebrate diversity (NUT 1999).

Policy was significantly strengthened by the annual conference of 1996 which affirmed the right of lesbians and gay men to decide for themselves whether or not to 'come out' at school and offered the NUT's full support to any member who chose to do so. The policy was agreed overwhelmingly with only a handful of delegates in opposition, a measure of the shift in thinking since the debate of 1988.

An inclusive approach: the 1990s

After years of debate, the annual conference agreed in 1996 a policy towards children with disabilities and difficulties, which was firmly inclusive in its approach. The union has argued that inclusion is a process, not an end product, which involves a change in the ethos of a school to include children with a wide range of educational needs.

The NUT successfully collaborated with the charity Scope on the Within Reach campaign. A study was commissioned to investigate the costs of promoting access to schools for children with physical and sensory impairments. The study was so influential that, in 1995, the government established the Schools Access Initiative, a fund for which local authorities can bid in order to make adaptations to make their schools more accessible to disabled children.

A whole school approach: the 1990s

Equality of opportunity is a priority for the NUT and not something to bolt on or add on. The union firmly recommends a whole-school approach to equal opportunities. Equality of opportunity in schools involves focusing on each person's individual needs and allowing all members of the school community the opportunity to develop to their full potential. Doug McAvoy, General Secretary, summarized NUT policy:

> For many years, the Union has advocated a whole school approach to equal opportunities, that is, one which involves all members of the school community in its development and implementation. The Union recommends that every school should have an equal opportunities policy, associated procedures to ensure that the policy is implemented and monitoring arrangements to assess the policy's effectiveness.
>
> (NUT 1996: 2)

NUT policy is clear that equality is an issue for every teacher. Education against prejudice and discrimination is an essential part of every teacher's role.

Lessons learned: a ten-point plan for progress

Writing this chapter has given me a welcome opportunity to reflect on the achievements since the mid-1970s. In my view, the strengths of the NUT can be built upon in order to ensure that progress towards equality continues during the next 25 years. I have drawn up a ten-point plan for progress. Central to my plan is the premise that what is good for teachers is good for pupils.

Acting on trade union principles

Collective bargaining has underpinned the trade union movement's approach to determining workers' terms of employment. Although teachers' unions lost their right to negotiate nationally on pay with the abolition of the Burnham Committee in 1987, some agreements have been negotiated nationally with teachers' employers, for example, on improved maternity benefits. At local level, the NUT has successfully negotiated agreements with LEAs, for example, on job sharing, adoption leave and the employment of disabled teachers.

Listening to teachers

NUT members offer a wealth of experience and expertise. The union must listen to its members and involve them at all levels. There is no substitute for the experience of the teacher at the chalk-face. The NUT's campaign against age discrimination is an example of how listening to members has influenced national policy. Although older teachers and entrants to the profession have irreplaceable knowledge and skills, they have reported that they were not appointed to posts because they were seen by schools as too expensive.

Reasserting professionalism

Since the late 1970s, teacher morale has sunk to a very low ebb. Many teachers report that their professional judgement has been undermined. An important role for the NUT is to reassert its members' confidence in their professional judgement.

Training NUT members

Since the early days of the women's development and anti-racist training programme, NUT training has moved from strength to strength. All of the training is firmly based on trade union principles. Active learning methods are used and participants are encouraged to draw upon their own experience and to recognize and build on their skills. New courses introduced in the 1990s include a black members' course, a 'Moving into management' course, a disability equality course and a course for part-time teachers, supply teachers and recent returners.

Many members, having attended training organized by the NUT, report that their schools have adopted, for example, equal opportunities policies or procedures for tackling harassment. Course participants are encouraged to realize that it is possible to take steps to achieve equal opportunities. Taking one step is still better than doing nothing at all.

Policy guidance

With over 200,000 members, the NUT is in a position to have a major influence throughout the education system in England and Wales. The union can provide for its local associations the policy guidance and briefing materials which will enable them to be more effective in negotiating with local authorities and supporting individual members on workplace and professional issues, including appointments procedures, harassment and race equality funding. All members are provided with up-to-date information in an equality bulletin sent directly to schools and in *The Teacher* magazine.

Flexibility

The NUT must respond to a changing agenda. New issues may arise from outside sources or from members. An example is that of equality for transgendered teachers and pupils. In 1998, informed by the experiences of transsexual members, the NUT strongly opposed government proposals to allow employers to treat transsexuals differently from other staff.

Supporting members

All unions prioritize the protection of their members. The NUT has a network of regional offices in England and, in Wales, NUT Cymru provides support and guidance to members who experience legal and professional difficulties, including cases of harassment and discrimination. In addition, many hundreds of voluntary local officers and school representatives advise and assist members.

Promoting debate

The NUT's annual Easter conference is always a focus of media attention. A number of debates at annual conferences have resulted in strong union policy, for example, on lesbian and gay equality, on anti-racism and on equality for disabled teachers. Although receiving little media attention, three other annual conferences provide an opportunity for free and frank discussion of equal opportunities issues. These are the equal opportunities conference, the black members' conference and the Pride in Education conference, which addresses issues relating to lesbian, gay, bisexual and transgender equality. Speakers have included practising teachers, academics and politicians.

Influencing the processes of education

The NUT plays a leading role in influencing education policies at national and local levels. It is represented on major national educational bodies. Drawing on the experience of its members, the union makes representations to central government on all matters affecting teachers in schools and seeks to influence education legislation. At local level, NUT representatives participate in various policy making, negotiating and consultative bodies. The challenge for the future is to ensure that equality issues are explicit in education policy and practice at all levels. Influencing the school improvement agenda, the National Curriculum review and teacher education will be a priority.

Providing leadership

NUT members look to the union for leadership on policy issues. It would have been difficult, for example, for many teachers to press for the inclusion of lesbian and gay equality in their school's or LEA's equal opportunities policy, if the NUT had not given strong leadership.

Final thoughts

As a long-term member and now as an employee of the NUT, I feel a genuine sense of pride in its achievements. There is no room for complacency, however. The next 25 years doubtless will bring new challenges and new tensions. There is bound to be heated debate on many issues. None the less, I am optimistic that the NUT will be equal to its task.

References

Bourne, R. and MacArthur, B. (1970) *The Struggle for Education 1870–1970*. London: Schoolmaster Publishing.
DfEE (1993) *Physical and Mental Fitness to Teach of Teachers and of Entrants to Initial Teacher Training*, Circular 13/93. London: DfEE.
Lloyd, B. (1995) Keynote speech, NUT Equal Opportunities Conference.

Lloyd, B. (1996) Reclaiming equal opportunities: an NUT perspective, *Education Review*, 10(1): 4–8.

NUT (1967) *The Education of Immigrants*. London: NUT.

NUT (1984) *114th Annual Report*. London: NUT.

NUT (1989a) *Education Review*, 3(2): 3–4.

NUT (1989b) *Towards Equality for Girls and Boys: Guidelines on Countering Sexism in Schools*. London: NUT.

NUT (1991) *Fair and Equal: Guidelines for Promoting Equal Opportunities in the Appointment and Promotion of Teachers*. London: NUT.

NUT (1996) *Equal Opportunities: A Whole School Approach*. London: NUT.

NUT (1998) *Girls' and Boys' Achievements: A Policy Statement*. London: NUT.

NUT (1999) *An Issue for Every Teacher: Guidance on Lesbian and Gay Equality in Education*. London: NUT.

NUT/EOC (1980) *Promotion and the Woman Teacher*. London: NUT/EOC.

Shipton, S. and Tatton, B. (1989) Once your eyes are opened: initiatives in women's training by one teacher union, in H. De Lyon and F. Migniuolo (eds) *Women Teachers: Issues and Experiences*. Milton Keynes: Open University Press.

Part II

Local education authorities

Chapter five

An episode in the thirty years war: race, sex and class in the ILEA 1981–90

Frances Morrell

Introduction

In July 1981 the Inner London Education Authority formally instructed officers to examine the issue of achievement in schools from the vantage point of working-class children, black children and girls and develop proposals designed to improve the performance of those groups. This policy initiative fused over time with the equal opportunities personnel programme being developed in parallel by the Greater London Council (GLC) to produce a revolutionary prototype strategy for schools. Controversial and contested at the time, the policy framework that emerged was in many respects the forerunner of the reformed education policy of central government today. The context for this action was the thirty years war over education policy which started in 1968 with the publication of the first Black Paper and which ended with the election of a Labour government pledged to take forward the policies – National Curriculum, tests and independent inspectorate – legislated by the Conservatives.

This chapter is in the nature of a whodunit. It will ask and answer three sets of questions. First, why was this unique prototype developed at the ILEA and nowhere else, and why at that particular period? Second, what was the prototype in its final form, and what were its strengths and weaknesses? Third, to what extent did the prototype correspond to that of national government today and to what extent does it differ? In conclusion, the chapter will identify some of the lessons, relevant to the present day that can be learned.

Why did it happen?

In the elections of May 1981 the Labour Party captured two of the largest and most powerful institutions in the two-tier system of subsidiary legislatures which at that time comprised local government in England and Wales. They were the GLC and its independent but symbiotically linked partner the ILEA. Immediately after the election a constitutional *coup d'état* took place. Left-wing councillors led by Ken Livingstone voted *en bloc* to capture the leadership and key positions on the GLC and the ILEA. GLC councillors set to work drafting radical programmes based largely on manifesto commitments which had been prepared after wide consultation in opposition.[1] They were spurred on by the perceived failure of the 1974–9 Labour government to implement its election manifesto, particularly those sections dearest to the hearts of the party faithful.

At the other end of the County Hall corridors, at the ILEA the policy initiative concerned with achievement in schools was a part of this radical surge, though it was little noticed at the time. The most controversial manifesto commitment on education had been the traditional pledge to provide *even cheaper* school meals. There had been no mention in the ILEA manifesto of an approach to achievement in schools which took as its starting point the social class, gender or ethnic origin of the children concerned. Nor had such a policy been publicly debated during the election campaign. Where had it come from, why was it introduced and why did it enjoy such a high priority and wide degree of support?

Central government

Central government sets the parameters within which subsidiary legislatures operate. And central government itself is often a conduit for external pressures. Three streams of policy affecting education had been inherited by Margaret Thatcher's government from the preceding Labour administration. First, the need for a loan from the International Monetary Fund in 1976 entailed a substantial programme of public spending cuts. These cuts appeared to signal a conversion of Labour – or at least its Prime Minister James Callaghan and Chancellor Denis Healey, to a monetarist economic analysis. When Margaret Thatcher was elected in 1979 she was determined to conquer inflation by controlling the money supply and drastically reducing public spending. Over time this became a government programme of disinvestment in public education.

Also in 1976, Shirley Williams, Secretary of State for Education, and James Callaghan, the then Prime Minister, launched a Great Debate about the quality of the education service. 'The Labour Movement has always cherished education: free education, comprehensive education, adult education, education for life', said James Callaghan, at Ruskin

College, Oxford, in October 1976 (quoted in Morrell 1989: 93). He continued:

> The fields that need study because they cause concern are the methods and aims of informal instruction, the strong case for the so called core curriculum of basic knowledge . . . what is the proper way of monitoring the use of resources in order to maintain a proper national performance, the role of the Inspectorate in relation to national standards . . . and the need to improve relations between industry and education.
>
> (p. 94)

The Great Debate revealed doubt at official level about the effectiveness of traditional Labour approaches to the education service. Alternative courses of action were beginning to be canvassed. As part of this process the issue of value for money became connected with the separate concern with reduction of spending for economic reasons.

Third, following American practice, the 1974–9 Labour government had enacted the Sex Discrimination Act and the Race Relations Act, which was an amendment and extension of the earlier 1968 Act. This legislation was a response to pressure from women's groups and ethnic minority groups which had been a distinctive feature of political life in the 1960s and 1970s. Two institutions, the Commission for Racial Equality and the Equal Opportunities Commission, were established to help further the goals of the legislation.

Under the Acts, discrimination of all sorts was outlawed. However, most of the 'known world' of equal opportunities focused on issues of employment opportunities. The reasoning for all this was clear enough. Position in the labour market sat at the nexus of all or most of the major socio-economic and cultural indicators. The only statutory codes produced under the Act related to employment. The specific employment standards which the policy sought to promote were principally those enshrined in two statutorily based Codes of Practice published respectively by the EOC and the CRE. Both codes had been endorsed by Parliament following presentation by the Conservative government. They represented the minimum essentials of good personnel practice. The GLC manifesto contained a commitment to implement an extensive equal employment opportunities programme throughout the GLC and ILEA. This was the response of the London Labour Party to demands on it from ethnic minorities and women.

The researchers

In making the case for an educational initiative based on class, race and sex, members drew on research findings. These suggested that the traditional guiding principle of education provision also known – confusingly – as equality of opportunity was flawed. Equality of opportunity in education was a system management policy designed to ensure equality of access to all children irrespective of family income. This involved the total funding of education out of taxes and rates, with taxes levied not according to a person's use of such services but according to ability to pay. The service was intended to be free at the point of use. This *economic* equality of opportunity lay at the heart of ILEA's approach to the allocation of resources. But research was gradually revealing that economic equality of opportunity was not enough. The publication by the National Children's Bureau (Davie *et al.* 1972) of *From Birth to Seven* in the early 1970s was a sensation at the time because it provided evidence on this point.

The NCB's massive longitudinal study had taken every child born in the week of 3–9 March 1958 and followed them in great detail throughout their entire school lives. The information from such studies gave a pretty clear picture of some of the learning processes inside schools with particular reference to variations in performance between social classes and girls and boys considered as groups. For example it showed that in most primary schools by the age of 7 children from poorer homes would have fallen behind in their reading age by a year. The gap would have widened by the age of 11 and by 16 the qualifications achieved by different social groups would vary considerably. In a revealing quotation, ILEA's experience too reflected the view put forward by Rowe (1970: 6) that 'the most important predictors of a child's success are not his intelligence but his parents' class'. There was little real disagreement about the finding that children as groups do tend to follow some rather similar and predictable tracks in school. The question that was raised was *why* these patterns existed and what educational conclusions should be drawn from them.

The policy communities

Two major strands of thought, overlapping but not complementary, can be discerned in the activities of policy communities at this time. One derived from the work of Professor Hayek, chairman of the Adam Smith Institute and author of *The Road to Serfdom* (Hayek 1994), written in London during the Second World War and first published in 1944. The Hayekian approach was a root and branch challenge to the welfare state. Attempts by the state to deliver social justice would require a form of bureaucratic planning which would turn citizens into clients of the state, into latter day serfs. The Selsdon Group's second manifesto in 1977 argued that 'What the public wants should be paid for by people as consumers rather than by taxpayers . . . the function of government should be not to provide services but to maintain the framework within which markets operate' (Selsdon quoted in Morrell 1989: 17).

A different counter-revolution against the prevailing orthodoxy of the educational world was being led by a small group of British academics associated with a famous series of polemical publications known as *The Black Papers*, with the Conservative theoretical journal the *Salisbury Review* and with individual pamphleteers. Among the leading figures was Dr Rhodes Boyson, originally a London headteacher, then a Member of Parliament, Brian Cox, Professor of English at Manchester University, and Roger Scruton, Professor of Aesthetics at Birkbeck College, London. They argued in effect that society was arranged into social classes with different incomes and resources because children were born with different levels of intelligence which the educational process could not affect. In general, it was suggested, intelligence was hereditary and corresponded to social class. 'There are two principal reasons why working class children on average do worse than middle class children,' wrote Richard Lynn (1971: 28) in the second *Black Paper*, 'One is that they are innately less intelligent on average and the other is that their families provide a less suitable milieu for scholastic success. Neither of these will be changed to any appreciable degree by abolishing independent and grammar schools'. The second *Black Paper* states:

> For generation after generation going well back before the days of Dick Whittington there has been an appreciable amount of social mobility. Bright children from the poorer classes forge their way upward and duller children from the higher classes drift downward. Class differences become inevitable in any civilised society.
>
> (Burt 1971: 53)

Educational efficiency pointed to a school system organized along stratified lines with differential expenditure – a selective system rather than a comprehensive one.

At this period, both the Adam Smith Institute and these campaigners whose slogan was summed up in the word *standards*, had the ear of central government, led by Prime Minister Margaret Thatcher. The policy changes that their counter-revolution had produced had to wait until 1988 for implementation.

The bureaucracy

ILEA's bureaucracy was unusually well placed to process the instruction from members of the authority to investigate a policy approach based on the relationship between social class, gender or ethnic origin and performance. Its management of the thousand institutions that made up the ILEA was based on similar principles. The ILEA school system was comprehensive, which meant that allocation of places in secondary schools was planned according to a banding system which involved testing every child during the final year at primary school and classifying each child in broad ability bands – in practice a form of social planning.

ILEA was multiracial and multilingual: 184 different languages had been counted as the family tongues of young Londoners. Some of the most socially deprived areas in the UK were to be found in Inner London. Resources were distributed to the authority's schools according to the Educational Priority Index (EPI). The EPI was based on the principle that schools should be given extra funding to help them combat social disadvantage among pupils which could be expected to lead to possible educational disadvantage. To this end, information on pupils' eligibility for free school meals, family size and structure, parental occupation, ethnic background, English fluency, classroom behaviour and mobility was collected on some 85,000 primary and secondary pupils in all of the authority's schools. A formula combining the schools roll and the EPI index score of each pupil governed the allocation of resources to each school. An outstanding and well-funded research department collected and analysed the information. An ILEA inspectorate reported on the quality of the education provided – with the support by 1981 of the multicultural inspectorate, established in response to pressure from black parents and teachers.

The decision by members of the authority to investigate the relationship between pupils' achievement and social class, gender or ethnic origin could have been seen as a logical development of the departmental agenda. But not all officers at the outset were persuaded of the usefulness of the initiative.

First, it came from members, not from the officers themselves. This was not the way that the ILEA was accustomed to doing things. Worse, the members had only just been elected and therefore had, in the eyes of officers, little direct experience. Second, the underlying thesis was not concerned with remedying deficiencies in *children* but in institutional arrangements. This suggested criticism of the administration. Third, the ILEA tradition, particularly that of the inspectorate, was pastoral. Inspectors were there to give support to teachers, not to appraise performance of schools and request improvement. Fourth, the initiative was political. Yet though it was political, it had not been mentioned in the ILEA manifesto. Fifth, some aspects of the policy that developed were challengingly radical – for example the anti-racist policy when multiculturalism was the norm. This meant braving right-wing and even social democratic criticism – and while officers were genuinely non-political, some were more non-political than others. Finally, the policy was quite new. No other local authority had adopted such a comprehensive strategic approach.

The ILEA officers seemed at first to share the characteristics of the powerful permanent bureaucracies of Whitehall, having 'a monopoly of information, the ability to tone down, blunt or delay initiatives, and [the ability to] . . . marginalise political advisers and initiatives in a rapidly moving flow of short term problems and issues' (Rhodes and Dunleavy 1995: 25).

Over time a new consensus emerged between officers and members and between the authority itself, and those responsible for its component institutions. Finally, the ILEA took ownership of the policy, which provided the strategic framework for its activities for the last decade of its existence and an enduring legacy.

The core executive

It has already been suggested that this chapter is partly a whodunit. Borrowing the language of the genre, were any of the usual suspects *primarily* responsible for the introduction and development of the policy? The answer is that they provided necessary but not sufficient conditions. Central government was preoccupied at this time with reducing public spending for economic reasons. This raised questions about value for money of the education system. The air was thick with influential cries for reform of the education service largely from the policy communities of the radical right. Academics had demonstrated the link between class, gender and ethnic origin and performance – but the work was little known within the Labour Party, and the implication of the findings was contested. The Labour government 1974–9 had put in place an equal opportunities legislation but Labour had lost the 1979 election and for its successor led by Mrs Thatcher, equal opportunities was not a priority. ILEA officers at senior level were at first reluctant to take the untried policy forward, but their subsequent contribution to its development was critically important.

The Race, Sex and Class policy initiative was introduced because a core group of members had the motive, means and opportunity and acted together to carry out their goals.[2] What had they in common beyond the fact that all save Ruth Gee were newly elected that year, and had all voted with Ken Livingstone in the *coup d'état* of 1981? First, they were elected and not appointed, and therefore subject to direct pressure within their constituencies.[3] Background may have played a part: all had grown up in working-class families. Ideology was certainly significant. All were active members of the traditional left of the Labour Party. Perhaps the most significant factor was experience. These members were well informed about current debates within education and equal opportunities and understood the need for reform. They were also experienced in public life. I had acted as an adviser to the NCB at the time of the publication of *From Birth to Seven*. Subsequently I had spent five years in government as policy adviser to the Secretary of State for Industry and afterwards the Secretary of State for Energy. I was also a qualified teacher and had a child in an ILEA school. Steve Bundred, Ruth Gee and George Nicholson had been or were existing elected members of local councils before joining ILEA and Ruth was also a qualified teacher with children in ILEA schools. John Carr, who worked for the CRE, had an extensive knowledge of and contacts in the

American equal opportunities communities thanks in part to his having been sent to the USA by Peter Mandelson in 1979 to study US race relations policy. Mandelson was the chair of the British Youth Council and Carr was a co-opted member of its Race Relations Advisory Committee. Finally, these members enjoyed the support of key groups within ILEA.[4] What was the policy in its final form and what were its strengths and weaknesses?

What did we do?

Challenging cultural assumptions

A key feature of the Race, Sex and Class initiative was its challenge to cultural assumptions. First and foremost, it challenged the Labour movement assumption that ever-increasing expenditure and an ever-diminishing teacher–pupil ratio were of themselves the keys to improving performance. It challenged the assumption – defended by a section of London teachers – that working-class children did not want to achieve in the middle-class terms of good public examination results. It also challenged the assumption that racist and sexist attitudes within the staff room, classroom or playground were either acceptable or permissible. It challenged the assumption of the ILEA senior managers that a good enough job was being done by the authority so far as academic standards were concerned. The preoccupation with improvement in achievement led to an emphasis on accountability which challenged notions of leaving matters to the professionals. It challenged the assumption that children's educational experience could be isolated from the mores of the school community inhabited by the child: an educational message was sent, it was argued, if for example all the academic staff were white and all the cleaning staff were black, or if all the senior teachers were male and all the junior teachers were female. Finally, by working closely with representatives of parents and governors as well as teachers it challenged the Old Labour trade union traditions of the party. In all this, left-wing members of the ILEA had, surprisingly, something in common with the radical right campaigning for improved standards, and with the Great Debate launched by James Callaghan. Its approach could almost have been seen as New Labour before its time.

Members first sought to establish the validity of their claim that a problem existed to which a solution needed to be sought. At members' request, a seminar was held at the Royal Festival Hall in October 1981. The head of each school in the authority accompanied by at least one member of staff was invited to attend. A paper was presented by the authority's Director of Research and Statistics, Dr Peter Mortimore, to an audience of 5000 London teachers. This examined research evidence in the area of school achievement and examined the reasons most commonly put forward to explain differential performance.

It represented on behalf of the authority a new attempt to create a coherent policy on race, gender and class in relation to academic achievement. Recognizing some of the shortcomings of the label 'social class' Dr Mortimore was nevertheless able to conclude that 'for all these criticisms, social class still seems to measure something and is the only tool we have for seeing if there are group differences in achievement in our education system'. 'The demonstrated relationship between social class, culture and ethnicity, and sex differences in achievement highlighted in that presentation are now more readily understood, thanks to a series of papers during the decade which analysed actual outcomes of pupils and students to set against the received wisdom of the times' (ILEA 1990: 17). By asking that this event be arranged, members had nailed their colours to the mast, and launched the policy at the same time. It required 'an examination of the relative pattern of attainment between children of different classes and groups which remained obstinately untouched by different strategies' (Morrell 1983).

A process of consultation within the ILEA followed. Presentations were made by myself and William Stubbs, the officer responsible for the schools sector in ILEA to specially arranged meetings of parents in all the ten ILEA divisions. I argued at these meetings that unless those who supported comprehensive education reformed it for themselves, it would be reformed from outside in ways that its supporters did not like. Prophetic words. Three further one-day conferences were held as part of a programme of consultation.[5] Meetings were held with black and ethnic minority groups across the authority. A series of policy publications in the Race, Sex and Class series followed.[6] Together these papers provide a summary of the historical background and of the state of understanding in the mid-1980s of the effects of racism and sexism. They include clear recommendations on planning and implementing the policies for equality of opportunity and included many of the conventional features of an equal opportunities employment policy which was being implemented by the GLC. How effective were these policies? In the words of one observer,

> The ILEA avoided the worst pitfalls in connection with their racism and sexism policies because the response was left firmly in the hands of the schools themselves and as might be expected the responses varied. Because of the industrial dispute it was several years before all schools had decided what to do. In the end the culture of London schools had begun to change. It had become normal to expect schools to be sensitive to race and to take active steps to counter racist behaviour, innuendo, and abuse. This did not of course banish all incidents of racist behaviour ... but anti-racism had to some degree at least become part of the

formal consciousness of the schools. This represented a genuine achievement for the Authority that had invested so much of its credibility
in confronting the prejudices of Londoners.

(Maclure 1990: 221)

In attempting to address the problems of educational achievement the ILEA
also embarked on a process of self-appraisal.[7] Alongside this, a series of
research reports, including research by Dr Peter Mortimore and his colleagues, provided incontrovertible evidence that the leadership, management and organization of schools and the commitment of each teacher to
the achievement of each pupil made a significant difference to the outcomes
for individuals. The findings of the ILEA Junior School Project, a longitudinal
study of nearly 2000 children from 7 to 11 years of age in 50 junior schools,
came to three major conclusions. First, there were marked differences
between the schools in their effects on pupils' progress. Second, the differences were substantial and affected all groups. Third, that the variation was
bound up with the management of the school. The policies that developed
from these initiatives reflect key elements in today's national education
policies. But policies rightly directed at eliminating variation in performance
between schools deal with one aspect of underachievement, namely that
resulting from differential provision, they do not tackle relative underachievement visible in the results of social groups in the best of schools.

Changing the structure

Culture is embedded in structure: groups protesting against discrimination
often encapsulated their case in a similar proposition. Women argued that
the personal was the political, black and ethnic minorities said that racism
was power plus prejudice. The Race, Sex and Class initiative involved
changes to the power structure of the ILEA.

Equal opportunities

An Equal Opportunities Sub Committee was established with two sub-
sidiaries, an ethnic minorities section and a caucus of women members. The
Equal Opportunities Unit was established centrally to promote and develop
policy in the field but no constituency had selected a black candidate for
a winnable London seat. In an unprecedented move, the ILEA decided to
remedy this by holding elections among black parents in each division of the
ILEA to provide black and ethnic minority representation on the authority's committees. The Equal Opportunities Inspectorate was established to
offer specialist advice in the nursery, primary, secondary and further and
higher education sectors. School governing bodies were advised to pay regard
to their composition in terms of representing their school communities.

Quality and standards

The need to deal with the variation in the quality of schools with similar intakes arose out of the findings of the ILEA Research and Statistics Department and was responded to in the Hargreaves (1984) and Thomas (1985) reports. Quality of leadership and staff governor training was recognized in the emphasis given in both reports to such training. Both reports referred to the importance of home–school links, and stressed the importance of coherent school policies to which staff could with conviction bend their efforts. They powerfully reinforced concerns about teachers and parents in partnership to promote the quality of each child's learning.

The secondary report proposed the restructuring of fourth and fifth year courses with a core curriculum of English, maths and science, built around the concept of units of study. These represented an attempt to bring more purpose and coherence to the crucial examination years. In addition the report recommended a better balance between theoretical and practical work and promoted a more active partnership with pupils in their own learning.

Monitoring and accountability

A concern with monitoring and accountability was another aspect of the restructuring. David Hargreaves was appointed chief inspector and set about reorganizing the inspectorate,

> increasing its capacity to inspect and building up the resources needed to recognise the schools that were under performing. Using the indices of performance developed by its research department the ILEA was better informed about the relative quality of its schools than any other local education authority and the inspectorate's job was to provide the follow up and support needed to act on this knowledge using tasks groups of inspectors based in schools . . . [this approach] began to show real progress by the end of the decade.
>
> (Maclure 1990: 216)

Prior to the ILEA elections in 1986, I authorized the publication of the first ever 'league table' showing the public examination results of schools ranked in terms of added value.

Finally, the Equal Opportunities in Employment policies actively set out to remove all unlawful obstacles to employment within the authority. This included a contract compliance policy initially introduced by the GLC but applying to the ILEA which required firms wishing to sell goods and services to demonstrate that they were already complying with the provisions of the anti discrimination legislation, or that they had plans to bring themselves into compliance. The standards that they were asked to comply with were those set out in the two statutory codes promulgated under the Sex Discrimination Act and Race Relations Act.

How successful were we?

In less than a decade from the introduction of the policy programme described above, the GLC and ILEA had been abolished. It is difficult to assess the strengths and weaknesses of the policy framework from any kind of long-term vantage point. Certainly, it created a major cultural shift in the attitudes and expectations of educators towards girls and ethnic minorities. Looking back to the terms of Callaghan's Great Debate and forward to the Great Education Reform Act, it is possible to see that the ILEA prototype went at least some way to satisfying some of the concerns of central government in 1976 and in so doing provided a model for central government in 1988 and beyond. It provided a coherent strategic framework for reform and the independent inspectorate under David Hargreaves began a programme of school improvement based upon it. Most important of all, the policy developed credibility with parents and members of the teaching profession.

Having said that, there were areas of unresolved confusion. Some ethnic minority groups for example did not accept some of the arrangements recommended to ensure equality of educational opportunity for girls. Some areas of equal opportunities in employment such as safeguarding against discrimination on grounds of sexual orientation did not translate straightforwardly into educational policy based on proven relationship between class, ethnic and gender groups and patterns of achievement in the classroom. The key weakness was the necessary neglect of social class. The decision was made to prioritize the elimination of variation in performance between similar schools. This was obviously the correct course of action since a badly managed and underperforming school affects the futures of all the students within it. In consequence the core issue raised in *From Birth to Seven* was not investigated. This was the relationship between underachievement and social class visible in even the best performing school – and the interaction between social class and other group identities. Arguably the biggest single obstacle to achievement in school remains unresolved.

A comparison with government policy today

At the European Secondary Heads Association (ESHA) Conference held in November 1998 at Maastricht, Professor Michael Barber, head of the Standards and Effectiveness Unit at the Department for Education and Employment, gave a presentation which included a description of the characteristics of world class education systems which it was naturally hoped the schools system in England and Wales would gradually come to acquire. Like the ILEA reformers of 1981, Professor Barber grounded his argument for reform by reference to research findings – but rather than referring to domestic longitudinal findings, Professor Barber drew on international comparisons. The Third International Mathematics and Science Study (TIMSS) 1995 had showed that England and Scotland were below the international average in mathematics and in literacy when compared with other English-speaking countries. After reviewing these and other findings, Professor Barber and his colleagues identified seven characteristics of a world class education service.[8] How similar is the present-day approach to that of the ILEA – and in what significant way does it differ?

There are a number of similarities. Professor Barber's understanding is that of the ILEA reformers, namely that a number of schools within the system are underperforming and that this can be remedied to produce both a higher and more consistent level of student achievement. His primary yardstick is that of international comparison which blurs the issue in particular of underperformance of social groups. His second assumption is that the elimination of variation of performance between schools rests on the provision and maintenance of good leaders in every school – one of the key findings of the ILEA research quoted earlier, and central to ILEA's policy approach. Third, he emphasizes school autonomy within a framework of a standard curriculum and shared goals and values. Fourth, he is in favour of targeted resources, and detailed monitoring of the operation of the system. Finally, he emphasizes equal opportunities with particular reference to the performance of ethnic minorities as revealed in the standardized testing systems. It is fair to say that Professor Barber's fluent and strategic overview bears a close strategic resemblance to the policy framework that was evolved at ILEA during the 1980s. But there are differences. The most striking omission is that of social class – and that is where New Labour differs. If it is referred to at all it is in the guise of poverty or social exclusion. Whether the literal reclassification of certain groups within society will enable effective measures to be taken to eliminate underperformance by those groups is the vital question that remains for education policy after the new consensus has been established.

The publication of the first *Black Paper* in 1968 broke the consensus around the management of the state education system. Three decades later the consensus has been re-established with the education policy of Tony Blair's New Labour government. A number of milestones can be discerned along the road to agreement. The radical right who campaigned for a market system and for standards were influential in moulding the Thatcher government's Education Reform Act 1988. James Callaghan's Great Debate launched in 1976 began a process of re-evaluation in both the Labour Party and at official level in central government. Riots in US cities in the late 1960s acted as catalysts for the legislation by the US government which encouraged and influenced the equal opportunities legislation of the 1974–9 Labour government – itself under similar though less dramatic domestic pressure. The ILEA reform programme begun in 1981 can claim to be a fourth milestone along the way.

Notes

1 The best known GLC policy was the promise to reduce fares on London Transport but there were a range of other progressive proposals relating to housing, the environment, and investment in London's then rapidly failing economy. Equal opportunities in employment within the GLC was given some prominence particularly in relation to the London Fire Brigade, a uniformed service which at the time of the 1981 election employed 6000 white men, no women and no ethnic minorities.
2 The proposal that the strategic goal of ILEA should be to investigate and remedy underachievement in schools was first put to the ILEA Labour Group by Frances Morrell, then deputy leader and chair of the Schools Sub Committee. She was supported by the then deputy chair, Andy Harris, and Schools Committee members Ruth Gee (Hackney Councillor from 1979 and from 1982 borough member for Hackney and deputy leader of the ILEA but at that time a co-opted member) and George Nicholson (then deputy chair of the GLC Planning Committee, later its chair and also a member of the Schools Sub Committee). John Carr (chair of the Staff Committee of the GLC and therefore responsible for the ILEA's equal opportunities personnel policy) and Steve Bundred (deputy chair of the GLC Police Committee and later chair of finance of ILEA) also played important roles.
3 'The members of ILEA had no option but to react to the immediate concerns which affected their constituents. It is to the credit of the members who devised the 1983 strategy that they exposed their own electoral positions and also placed 'on the line' the capacity of ILEA to respond to the everyday needs of the many communities of inner London. In such actions the importance of a healthy system of local government is demonstrated' (ILEA 1990: 60).
4 The two representatives of the teaching unions on the Schools Sub Committee were strong supporters of the achievement in schools policy from the outset. The addition of the commitment of Charlotte Gibbons, of ILEA's Parents Central Consultative Committee, and Alison Kelly, of the National Association of Governors and Managers (NAGM), created a powerful momentum within ILEA ensuring that the issues were discussed, papers written and training provided for parents and governors.
5 The three one-day conferences were on multi-ethnic education (November 1981), on the education of girls (March 1982) and on the outcome of consultations with ethnic minority groups (April 1983).
6 Publications in the Race, Sex and Class series included *Achievement in Schools* (1983), *Multi Ethnic Education in Schools* (1983), *A Policy for Equality: Race* (1983), *Anti Racist Statement and Guidelines* (1983), *Multi Ethnic Education in Further Higher and Community Education* (1983) and *A Policy for Equality: Sex* (1985).

7 A committee was established under the chairmanship of David Hargreaves to consider the curriculum and organization of secondary schools with special reference to pupils who are underachieving. Its report was entitled *Improving Secondary Schools* (1984). A committee chaired by Norman Thomas was established to identify and recommend those whole-school strategies which appear to enforce the confidence and achievement of pupils of primary school age particularly those from working-class backgrounds. Its report was *Improving Primary Schools* (1985). A committee chaired by John Fish was established to review the range, quality and coherence of provision to areas of special educational need in the authority (in primary, secondary, and special schools and in supporting institutions and services and in the context of post-school provision) particularly in the light of the Warnock Report, the Education Act 1981 and the authority's initiative to promote good opportunities and combat underachievement of children from all backgrounds (ILEA 1985).

8 Professor Barber's seven characteristics of a world class education service:
- Extensive school autonomy within a policy framework which lays down curriculum, qualifications, quality assurance procedures and standards for teacher training.
- The capacity to disseminate best practice in order to achieve consistently high standards across a system. Measures included major training programmes for primary teachers in literacy and numeracy, best practice databases, the publication of model teaching schemes of work and investment in teachers' professional development.
- The capacity to innovate and manage change. Measures include a system maintaining cohesion through shared values rather than bureaucratic regulation, and quality assurance arrangements that provide regular feedback on performance of individual schools, and improving the quality of education research.
- A committed highly flexible workforce with particular measures to provide training for school leaders including training in preparation for taking on leadership, training in the first two years after taking up a leadership position and training for serving headteachers to offer refreshment and renewed inspiration.
- A commitment to equal opportunities which involved providing a high quality education for all children regardless of their background and educational needs. Measures include monitoring through national testing systems of the system's impact on different ethnic groups or on girls and boys, and expectation of high standards of all pupils.
- A society which values education.
- Consistent investment with resources.

References

Burt, C. (1971) The mental differences between children, in C.B. Cox and A.E. Dyson (eds) *The Black Papers on Education 1–3*. London: Davis-Poynter.

Davie, R., Butler, N. and Goldstein, H. (1972) From Birth to Seven. London: Longman.

Hargreaves, D. (1984) *Improving Secondary Schools*. London: ILEA.

Hayek, F.A. ([1944] 1994) *The Road to Serfdom*. Chicago: University of Chicago Press.

ILEA (1985) *Educational Opportunities for All?* (The Fish Report). London: ILEA.

ILEA (1990) *Equal Opportunities Policies in the ILEA: A Final Review of Initiatives and Implementation*, official paper. London: ILEA.

Maclure, S. (1990) *A History of Education in London, 1870–1990*, 2nd edn. London: Allen Lane.

Morrell, F. (1983) Introduction, in *Achievement in Schools*, Race, Sex and Class series no. 1. London: ILEA.

Morrell, F. (1989) *Children of the Future*. London: Hogarth Press.

Rhodes, R.A.W. and Dunleavy, P. (eds) (1995) *Prime Minister, Cabinet and Core Executive*. New York: St Martin's Press.

Rowe, A. (1970) Human beings, class and education, in D. Rubenstein and C. Stoneman (eds) *Education for Democracy*. Harmondsworth: Penguin. Quoted in ILEA (1990) *Equal Opportunities in the ILEA: A Final Review of Initiatives and Implementation*, official paper. London: ILEA.

Thomas, N. (1985) *Improving Primary Schools*. London: ILEA.

Chapter six

Now you see it, now you don't: gender equality work in Brent, 1982–8

Hazel Taylor

Equal opportunities: a local policy initiative

The vocal concern of the late 1970s and early 1980s which manifested itself with the Sex Discrimination Act 1975 also expressed itself through a demand to change the achievement, representation and status of girls and women through interventions in schooling. In 1981, the chair of the Education Committee of Brent Council, at that time Labour controlled, became the first politician in the UK to be prepared to act on the arguments of feminists within the local party that, to work effectively on the equal opportunities agenda, structures needed to be set in place with appropriate resourcing. He persuaded his colleagues to have the vision and courage to create a post of Equal Opportunities Adviser to work alongside the existing Adviser for Multicultural Education in the Education Department, the first such post nationally. The avowed intention was that both postholders would act as major change agents, and have enough structural power to be able to do so. The equal opportunities post was strongly opposed by the Conservatives on the council, who threatened to remove it if they won the local election in May 1982. I was appointed in February 1982; when I began work in May, Labour had a tiny majority and within a year had lost control.

The political turbulence of its birth lasted for the life of the post, from 1982 to 1988. More attention was devoted in Brent to the progress of the policy for multicultural education than to gender. This initially allowed the gender work to develop strongly, but as the two strands of the equality agenda came together, the work with women and girls, both black and white, was attacked and hindered. This chapter focuses on the elements of the gender work which were most effective, and relates them to the current scene, with its vocal concern about boys. It also reviews the ways in which two initially separate initiatives were interrelated.

The story is of an attempt to implement a coherent LEA policy in a situation where the surrounding conditions for successful implementation were absent – the officers of the authority were subject to continuing political uproar, and the internal arrangements were similar to those of many LEAs in the 1980s – a lack of clear focus on what its role might be in relation to the management of schools, or in relation to the outcomes from those schools. In focusing on what was achieved, I make no claims for the longevity of the work in the context in which it was done, but I do believe that many of the strategies adopted were ones which have lasting value in managing change, and that the work and the attention it attracted contributed to an overall emphasis on paying attention to recognizing girls' needs which led to the increases in their achievement which are now recorded. In the very different climate of the 1990s, many of the strategies are still relevant.

What did we mean by equal opportunities?

One of the issues which beset work on gender equality was that of definitions. The debate about anti-sexist work as opposed to equal opportunities work was a lively one. Anti-sexist feminists believed equality would be achieved only when the values base of the society was shifted to one where there was an equal balance of power and influence between men and women, and predicted that a focus on representation and achievement alone would lead to a situation where more girls might achieve well, but would continue to be denied genuinely comparable life experiences and opportunities. Those taking an equal opportunities position argued that if girls were given opportunities to achieve at school (and this was always measured through examination results) then they would be present in the adult forums where lifestyle, opportunities and political policy decisions were formulated, and could look after their interests there. The jury is still out on whether 'Blair's Babes' will vindicate this position or demonstrate its weaknesses. The Brent work took an anti-sexist stance, and it is from this perspective that I shall address the success and lessons of the initiative. The Brent approach to equal opportunities insisted that while everybody would never be the same, equality needed to be achieved in enabling access to opportunity. That had implications for identifying barriers that got in the way of access, such as prevailing social attitudes to the roles of girls and women; lack of prior skill acquisition, particularly for girls in technology; values which limited aspirations; and presentation of learning opportunities through material which excluded girls and women or focused on interests they did not relate to. We were helped in our focus on values by the public debate about feminism in the 1980s; this ensured an external climate which, while it produced vocal opposition to any challenge to the status quo, also encouraged many women to involve themselves in action for equality, which was stimulating and stretching.

Developing gender equality: a case study in change management

Strategic planning

The Brent initiative attempted to bring about change through using a complex range of change management strategies operating at different levels within the authority. I drew up a strategic five-year plan which identified the key target groups for change, the key tasks to be performed and the training to be carried out to create the capacity to carry through the changes. It also identified the evidence to be collected to enable the outcomes to be monitored and evaluated. In that respect it was like a 1990s development plan, already existing on an LEA-wide scale. It lacked the sharpness in definition of outcomes of plans a decade later, and the monitoring system was not properly set up in the time available before the initiative was overtaken by the changes determined by the 1987 and 1988 Education Acts, but it provided a very powerful framework for identifying the resources needed, directing those available, and keeping the focus clear. The plan was built on the recognition that work needed initially to focus on primary schools, as the seeds of inequality and underachievement were sown there in the school system, though before that in the development of the nature of gender identity. It identified that

- it was important to build on and strengthen the existing commitment and support of teachers and others who identified with the initiative and gave their energies willingly to promoting it
- the quality of that willing endeavour had to be good if the activities were not to be used to ridicule the whole thing
- it was necessary to tackle various aspects of change at the same time to be effective
- both bottom-up and top-down strategies needed to happen simultaneously
- both pressure and support needed to be applied for change in practice to occur.

In many ways the change management style was impressively up to date, informed as it was by the findings that schools make a difference of the seminal *Fifteen Thousand Hours* (Rutter *et al.* 1979) and the developing documentation of systems of school-based review and teacher development, particularly the projects supported by the Schools Council (Oldroyd *et al.* 1984) and The Open University's (1982) *Curriculum in Action* pack. It demonstrated elements brought to general attention in the work of Michael

Fullan (1982) and later identified in the work of the International School Improvement Project (ISIP: see van Velzen *et al.* 1985) though I was not aware of these at the time.

Pressure and support

The actual work, then, used a mixture of top-down pressure (an authority policy with a time scale for implementation in schools) with support (an extensive programme of in-service training, development of curriculum materials and classroom support from advisory teachers) and bottom-up pressure, from committed and enthusiastic teachers who formed pressure groups within their schools and authority wide and encouraged change from below. They in their turn supported each other, through the creation of complex and elaborate networks which sustained themselves as personnel changed. There was a continual debate about values, essential to sustained change, and the bottom-up pressure groups ensured that however systematic the LEA plan might have been, it would not be too systematic for the change to become 'innovation without change at the fundamental level' (Reid *et al.* 1986). However, the LEA plan was in reality the adviser's plan, and lacked the necessary backup from the authority as a whole to have real teeth, especially in the light of the shifting power alliances of the hung council, and the increasing dominance of the focus on race within Brent. The schools of course realized and, in some cases, exploited the micropolitics to avoid genuine change.

Advisory teachers and action research

There were several strands of the change management strategy which were particularly effective in creating the pre-practice changes necessary in teachers' attitudes and understandings, genuine change in classroom practice, and in the status and power of women teachers. I established a team of advisory teachers, who were on two-year secondments from Brent schools, and who themselves were able to develop an in-depth understanding of what anti-sexist education might look like, and how to begin to achieve it. In the absence of existing guidance, we created our own vision then worked back from that to discover what practice would enable the outcomes we identified. There was considerable emphasis on action research to test out hypotheses and identify how and what learning was taking place in classrooms, and on classroom observation as the key means of collecting evidence. As I wrote for an early collection of articles on developing practice, *Girl Friendly Schooling*, 'Only close observation can reveal that the cause and effect of teachers' and others' action in schools is frequently quite different from the assumptions commonly made about it' (Taylor 1985a: 112).

There were several elements to the action research. The Gender and Learning course (a 15 session, 45 hour programme equivalent to a Masters level module) included a requirement for all course members to undertake a piece of action research in their own schools, preferably in their own classrooms. It was supervised by the adviser who tutored the course, written up, published by the LEA and circulated among its schools. The two books of projects, *Seeing is Believing* (Taylor 1984) and *It Ain't Necessarily So* (Taylor 1985b), reflect in their titles the emphasis on not making assumptions about what is happening, or accepting simplistic efforts to change. The advisory teachers also directly acted as researchers with teachers, either working with small groups on a particular issue, or with a school researching an identified concern. In each case, the quality and amount of work produced in a very short period demonstrated the value of using advisory teachers to work in this way. They are more flexible and available than consultants from HE, close to classrooms, and have quick access to other services and people in the LEA to help progress work as problems emerge. One small group coordinated by an advisory teacher researched the use of construction kits in nursery and primary classrooms, producing an informative report, *Design It, Build It, Use It* (Taylor and Hartley 1986) which fostered non-sexist technology education in primary schools. Another research project, *Breaking the Circuit*, on the teaching of electronics in a junior classroom, produced clear evidence for developing good practice in developing science skills in boys and girls (Taylor 1985c).

In-service training

A comprehensive programme of substantial in-service training, either school based or with planned follow-up activities, also underpinned the management of change. Gender equality was addressed with school managers, subject teachers and new teachers at the same time as specific expertise was developed by the change agents within schools. It was the length and complexity of the training programme that made it effective. It did not rely on cascading, but sought to involve directly more and more teachers in active participation in an ongoing staff development programme linked to policy implementation.

Research projects

There were also over the six years of the initiative, four major research projects where an advisory teacher worked with a primary school to investigate areas where there was little national evidence to guide the development of practice. One, into the development of infant girls' confidence as mathematicians, was written up as a contribution to *Girls Into Maths Can Go* (Taylor 1985d) and contributed to national understanding, while another, a study of the use of time by boys and girls in a junior classroom observed over a year and painstakingly analysed, was published in Brent as *About Time* (Cooper 1987) but received no wider audience. Research was an important feature of the Brent work which had an effect in changing practice locally, but had little effect nationally because there was no emphasis on gaining wider publication. This reflected the pressure to maintain a constant pace of work with schools which left little time for external activities such as national dissemination.

Ownership of change

The emphasis on the local audience also had a lot to do with the commitment to another important element of the success of the work locally, which was a belief in the importance of ownership of change by those who are doing it. Ownership has become a buzzword for successful change implementation, with many different assumptions made about what brings it about. In Brent, we defined ownership as being created when people who had to implement change were able to play some part in determining what that change would be. That meant that in order to implement the LEA's policy for gender equality, each school was asked to develop its own, more detailed, policy and to engage in debate with the staff about what should go in, addressing the values clarification essential to bringing about real rather than cosmetic change. It meant that the authority's guidelines to support policy making in primary schools, *Steps to Equality* (Brent Education Department 1985), was produced by a working party with wide representation from schools and from teachers at all stages of their careers, serviced by the adviser but chaired by a teacher, so that when it was sent to all schools for reference, it reflected national as well as local thinking, and particularly reflected local commitment to anti-racist as well as anti-sexist practice. It meant that those involved learnt by doing, by reviewing their existing knowledge and understanding in the light of new ideas, and producing a concrete outcome which demonstrated where they had moved on to. A model of effective learning for children and adults was thus being put into practice to create genuine improvement. Teachers also developed ownership through creating classroom materials, whether it was booklets to support the teaching of texts in secondary English classes, or a photo pack of women in non-traditional jobs to support humanities work (Collins 1984), the one resource which became nationally available. Ownership created powerful commitment and generated a lot of energy which then went into classroom or school implementation. The willingness of teachers to attend after school meetings to work constructively together showed the effect of giving people power to influence their own work content, and indeed to behave like professionals in the degree of control they had. In spite of strong local commitment to the union action of the mid-1980s, activities continued long after others had stopped. While centralization of the curriculum and increasingly of the manner of its delivery might appear to be necessary to ensure entitlement for all pupils, there are real dangers that lack of ownership may lead to unthinking implementation.

Attention to process

Attention to process was another key feature of the work. Stemming as it did from a commitment to particular inclusive values, which would be challenged and refined frequently, the work not only involved teachers in its development, but also paid attention to meaningful consultation which did not avoid checking out the views of those who might otherwise be invisible, like pupils, or who might challenge prevailing beliefs, like black teachers who challenged the ethnocentrism of the dominant views of women's roles. It meant that everyone's contribution was acknowledged, that there was no culture of individual stars, and that the respect for each individual that is central to equality of value was signalled. That respect for process was not universal in the LEA, and we learnt to hold our own within the power struggles that threatened at times our very existence.

Management development

One of the issues which became very clear in the course of attempting to develop work in schools was that without competent management at all levels in a school, little could be achieved through authority initiatives or by change agents within the school. The importance of a whole-school approach with commitment and leadership from the top was clear long before its inclusion in lists of school effectiveness characteristics. From an anti-sexist perspective it was important to focus on the issue of the under-representation of women in management posts in the schools, and to do something about it. There needed to be effective women managers as role models for pupils and for other women teachers, and for a school to be effectively managed and demonstrating a commitment to gender equality, a gender balance in its management team was a necessity. Management development was essential. One of the most effective elements of all the gender work was the Women and Management course, which ran twice a year over several years, changing with time. It aimed to encourage women teachers to believe that they could be managers, to provide them with information and skills to enable them to carry out management roles, and to equip them with skills to apply successfully for senior posts. The programme was planned by a group of women, and combined experiential activities with presentations, group work and personal action planning. An evaluation of its medium-term effects (Taylor 1988) identified that it had powerful effects in developing ambition and confidence in the participants, and that a very high proportion of them (73 per cent) obtained promotion very rapidly after attending it. Participants also reported using the networks developed on the course to provide support once in a new post, and to replicate that web of contacts which had been identified as so important in men's progress up the corporate ladder. Many of those networks still exist, with women now in a far-flung range of senior positions in education across the UK, in headships, higher education and government agencies.

Collecting and using data

Another strand in the change management strategy was the use of school-based working parties who among other activities played a very large part in collecting detailed data about the situation of girls and boys in the school. They compiled figures showing the breakdown by gender of option groups, exam entries and results, participation in extracurricular activities, computer clubs and so on. They also analysed staffing structures to show the different positions held by men and women teachers. All these data were invaluable in providing clear evidence about a situation which may have been denied, and in providing the means for measuring change. Nationally available data were often dismissed in a school as being irrelevant to their particular situation, and the school-based data removed that defence. The data were collected at LEA level and were being developed to provide evidence of policy implementation when the project ended. This was a clear forerunner of the national data now collected, with the regrettable difference that national data still do not include ethnicity, thus making it very difficult to identify variable performance within genders by ethnic group and concealing the much smaller difference in gendered performance by black and Asian pupils (Gillborn and Gipps 1996).

Anti-racist, anti-sexist working

What of the attempted fusion of anti-sexist and anti-racist work in Brent? A great deal of energy was spent in the process of attack and defence of each position which could otherwise have been spent on working together, though it is too rational to suggest that this would have been possible in a situation where both groups were struggling to define an identity in a minority position. In Brent, anti-sexist work came under valuable close scrutiny from the increasing numbers of black and Asian women who were addressing gender equality in their own lives and perceived the Eurocentric bias of the debate. Working in the LEA with the largest ethnic minority population in the UK, we found ourselves facing a reversal of the national pattern where ethnicity was largely ignored. Work with girls was attacked, largely by men, as a diversion from work on the more fundamental issue of racism; it was pointed out that even underprivileged white women had more power than black people, and that black women were caught between their ethnic and their gender identities and doubly penalized. That racism is still a more pervasive and intractable injustice than sexism for women managers in the 1990s has been confirmed by Davidson (1997).

The change strategies of the two initiatives were sharply different. The gender work was essentially incremental and sought to avoid polarization in spite of its anti-sexist and increasingly anti-racist stance, while the race work was driven by a power-coercive approach that created confrontation rapidly. The gender work appealed more readily to more teachers: very many women regardless of their politics could find some common cause with it and recognized gender inequalities, whereas there were few black teachers to create an immediate pressure and they were more marginalized and divided by the system than white women. But the LEA put far more resources into its anti-racist work, and it was that which attracted the worst and most persistent media attacks. This highlighted another apparent contradiction, that work with an absolute minority (ethnic minorities) is more threatening than work with half the population (women), either because the essential 'otherness' of ethnic minorities is more profound and therefore more threatening than that of women, in which black women are invisible, or because ethnic minorities, largely represented by men, are perceived as more potentially powerful than 'only' women.

In any event, our experience was that as we became more effective in schools in creating interest, getting action taken, publishing findings, holding well-attended and well-received events, making alliances with black women and changing as a result, we were more and more attacked by the anti-racist workers, and more and more required to subsume our work in theirs in such a way that it became harder and harder to identify gender as a specific variable in inequality. By 1987, the gender work had all but disappeared as a discernible strand, while resources were reduced. When the post was removed in 1988 as part of a major LEA budget cut, the focus had already gone.

Gender equality in the 1980s to gender equality in the 1990s

But for so much of the gender work, there was a direct continuation into 1990s national policy – school effectiveness, a common curriculum, management development, detailed performance monitoring, and increasingly successful girls from all ethnic groups. The emphasis on addressing pupils' achievement from the centre through the National Curriculum and the other measures which have accompanied it has removed some inequalities of access to the curriculum, but access to the entitlement still needs to be more mediated by a pedagogy that recognizes differences in learners. The 1980s debate about how to address the different needs of girls in relation to their class or cultures, in order to address the best way of maximizing achievement through recognizing the starting points for learning, needs to be revived in relation to the current debate about boys. The collection of data in schools is now much more sophisticated and any underachieving group can be easily identified. The 1980s experience revealed that unravelling the genuine picture about girls' participation in science required painstaking analysis of different curriculum patterns; now it is important to make sure that comparisons by gender of results do not produce overgeneralized conclusions that do not hold up when a points score system of analysis is applied, or when gender differences are analysed in relation to ethnicity and socio-economic status.

The great value of those action research projects that focused on detailed observation, the trialing of a small change, and then re-evaluation, has been recognized in the small fund available from the Teacher Training Agency for classroom action research. It is a shame that there are such constraints on the topics eligible for funding that an interest in underachievement because of difference, whether of gender, class or ethnicity, is not currently likely to attract support.

The whole current pattern of centralizing education, while having benefits, has balancing tensions that limit its success. The gender work in Brent was so helped by the enthusiastic commitment of many teachers who today have neither the spare energy to work at something that is not prescribed, nor the enthusiasm created by ownership to involve themselves in those aspects of current priorities where they might be able to find a space to look at a personal concern. The pressure to implement givens, often at a level of carrying out a particular sequence of activities, makes attention to a process that respects the individuals involved very difficult. This is not a precious observation, but one which reminds that self-esteem and morale are strongly connected to an experience of being valued by being able to contribute to a worthwhile creation and being genuinely able to influence its shape. While there is satisfaction to be gained from that precise use of high-order skills which is required by effective classroom teaching, the lack of time for attending to one's emotional involvement and reflecting and debating about the whole process of teaching shifts the nature of the experience and provides less reward for the practitioner. Low self-esteem among teachers is due not only to the climate of public blame, but also to the added stress from lack of control over both time and job tasks. If groups of teachers in the 1980s all over the UK helped to create a recognition that there was a national problem to be addressed over the aspirations and achievement of girls, then what issues of current concern to minorities of practitioners are going unexplored because of the lack of space to look at them? The current concern about boys is popularly presented as a result of neglect while girls received additional attention. In this context it is interesting to go back to those action research projects of the 1980s and rediscover that the teachers involved were as anxious to enable boys to apply themselves to their work for their sake as they were to allow time for interactions with girls. In the *About Time* project (Cooper 1987), for example, the change strategies included circle time assertiveness training to reduce aggressive communication from both boys and girls, and to increase confidence in unassertive boys and girls. A later project where the advisory teachers worked specifically on training classroom teachers to do assertiveness training with their classes, again explicitly focused on the benefits to everybody of developing personal effectiveness. The distracting behaviour of some boys always was, in Brent, seen as a limiter to their own achievement and therefore something to be addressed. Similarly, it was recognized that while girls might be disadvantaged by their lack of early skills in using construction kits, boys were disadvantaged by their difficulties in discussing their feelings, and that both needed to be recognized in the selection of teaching styles. It seems that one of the current difficulties for teachers lies in the conflict between a theory of effective teaching and learning which recognizes that teachers need to know about and work with the individual needs of the learner, and the increasing prescription of a tightly defined curriculum, for example, for the literacy hour, in which there is little room for variation. Undoubtedly there is room for a crisper, more demanding delivery, but this must not be at the expense of recognizing and catering for difference.

The emphasis within Brent on extending girls' and women's aspirations achieved directly measurable success for those participating in the Women and Management course, and contributed to the national increases in entry by young women into higher education and the professions. That emphasis on high aspirations was encouraged for all girls, not just those perceived as middle class or from supportive homes. The range of work open to boys was seen as wide and relatively unproblematic. Small inroads were being made against the prejudices against male nurses and early years teachers; those there were were warmly welcomed as they provided role models both for boys and for the breaking of stereotypes. Girls' entry into manual trades was also progressing slowly when the political changes, the recession and the decline in manufacturing of the late 1980s radically changed the nature of much employment that was still predominantly male. Whereas girls and women have had to adapt and extend their understanding of what femininity embraces, and were helped in this by the cultural climate created by feminism, many boys now have to extend their understanding of masculinity to meet the economic and social demands of these times. But the structural debate is perhaps a harder one, as women as a group regardless of difference within their gender by class and so on, have the experience of subordination to men, whereas for boys the experience is one where some men have constantly done well and exercised a wide range of power and continue to do so, whereas others have had power in more limited ways and now have little in relation to work (Mac an Ghaill 1994). The Brent experience suggests that to make such a shift requires a groundswell of public debate and pressure for a change in values, and that a debate focusing only on difference in exam performance is not enough. The men who are working on this area within education need the support of women who should not feel threatened, and should also ensure that the efforts to enable school success for all boys do not result in a return to disadvantage for girls. Inclusive education is still an achievable dream.

The 1980s work where individual LEAs were free to identify their own priorities for change has given way to a far more centralized focus of resources on areas identified by government as important. That is fine as long as the values underpinning those central decisions respect and value difference. But how can difference be explored except in a system that allows more diversity of practice? And how can diversity of practice ensure that social justice is consistently addressed in our education system?

References

Brent Education Department (1985) *Steps to Equality: The Report of the Primary Gender Equality Working Party.* Brent: Brent Education Department.
Collins, F. (1984) *Working Now.* Brent: Curriculum Development Support Unit.
Cooper, L. (1987) *About Time: A Study of Gender Differences in Classroom Interaction in a Primary School.* Brent: Curriculum Development Support Unit.
Davidson, M. (1997) *The Black and Ethnic Minority Woman Manager: Cracking the Concrete Ceiling.* London: Paul Chapman.
Fullan, M. (1982) *The Meaning of Educational Change.* Toronto: OISE Press.
Gillborn, D. and Gipps, C. (1996) *Recent Research on the Achievement of Ethnic Minority Pupils.* London: HMSO.
Mac an Ghaill, M. (1994) *The Making of Men: Masculinities, Sexualities and Schooling.* Buckingham: Open University Press.
Oldroyd, D., Smith, K. and Lee, J. (1984) *School-Based Staff Development Activities: A Handbook for Secondary Schools.* York: Longman for Schools Council.
Open University (1982) *Curriculum in Action: Practical Classroom Evaluation.* Milton Keynes: The Open University in association with the Schools Council.
Reid, K., Hopkins, D. and Holly, P. (1987) *Towards the Effective School.* Oxford: Blackwell.
Rutter, M., Maughan, B., Mortimore, P. and Ouston, J. (1979) *Fifteen Thousand Hours: Secondary Schools and their Effects on Children.* London: Open Books.

Taylor, H. (ed.) (1984) *Seeing is Believing*. Brent: Curriculum Development Support Unit.

Taylor, H. (1988) The use of single sex career development courses in reducing the under-representation of women in school management. MSC dissertation, University of East London.

Taylor, H. (1985a) Inset for equal opportunities in the London Borough of Brent, in J. Whyte, R. Deem, L. Kant and M. Cruickshank (eds) *Girl Friendly Schooling*. London: Methuen.

Taylor, H. (ed.) (1985b) *It Ain't Necessarily So*. Brent: Curriculum Development Support Unit.

Taylor, H. (ed.) (1985c) *Breaking the Circuit: Girls, Boys and Electronics*. Brent: Curriculum Development Support Unit.

Taylor, H. (1985d) Experience with a primary school implementing an equal opportunities enquiry, in L. Burton (ed.) *Girls into Maths Can Go*. London: Holt, Reinhart and Winston.

Taylor, H. (1998) The use of single sex career development courses in reducing the under-representation of women in school management. MSc dissertation, University of East London.

Taylor, H. and Hartley, B. (eds) (1986) *Design It, Build It, Use It: Anti-Sexist Guidelines for Using Construction Kits with Children 3–11*. Brent: Curriculum Development Support Unit.

van Velzen, W., Miles, M., Ekholm, M., Hameyer, U. and Robin, D. (1985) *Making School Improvement Work: A Conceptual Guide to Practice*. Leuven: Acco.

Chapter seven

Did it make a difference? The Ealing experience 1987–9*

Kate Myers

An introduction to the perspective

Tim Horton

The issue of 'gender' in education has been a sustained interest for practising teachers for a number of years . . . The issue has many manifestations. In the 1960s and 1970s the chief matter of note was the content of books but research and development, together with the emergence of a wider women's movement, has broadened the focus to include language, role models and assessment. While public research grants in most western countries were not generous to this area of concern in the 1980s, courses of many kinds sprang up and aroused a good deal of interest from men and women.

One of the areas that has been alleged to be most impervious to change is the upper echelons of administrative/advisory services which, despite all the changes to the system, filter and sometimes determine the direction of education for most young people. Attempts to recognize the lack of women in senior positions in educational administration have been made. In *Perspective 3*, Kate Myers, now senior inspector for the London Borough of Ealing, gives an account of her attempt to alter matters at the levels of both *policy and practice*.

She describes several strands of policy within the authority that she and her immediate colleagues saw as valuable within an overall strategy. She sets out priorities [in the early part] of her account. It is first necessary to understand that Kate's experience was substantially grounded in earlier

* The first part of this chapter was written in 1989, while Kate Myers was the Inspector for Gender Equality in the London Borough of Ealing. It was written for an Open University Course E271 *Curriculum and Learning* and is reproduced with the kind permission of The Open University.

work in directing a Schools Curriculum Development Council/Equal Opportunities Commission (SCDC/EOC) initiative.[1] One outcome of this work
has been the publication of *Genderwatch* – a set of self-evaluation schedules
widely disseminated among the teaching profession (Myers 1987). A novel
approach, which she sought to introduce in Ealing, was the linking of
schools in order to encourage 'peer evaluation' of the school-level appraisals.
She describes the progress of this strand of her work . . .

Gender

Some years ago with help from the DES and ILEA, I visited the USA to
observe the work of their sex equity centres. These centres are federally
funded on 'soft' money (i.e. grants that have to be reapplied for regularly
sometimes against open competition) and they serve vast regions. The funding system ensures that key personnel spend a disproportionate amount of
time attempting to get themselves refunded, and the constant uncertainty
about the future of the centres makes long-term planning difficult and encourages staff with career plans to look for more secure prospects. Serving vast
regions promotes a 'flash and dash' approach and centre staff have to strive
hard to create and maintain relationships with huge numbers of teachers,
principals and school administrators. Nevertheless, two centres in particular impressed me greatly. The staff in both Washington, DC and Ann Arbor,
Michigan, were knowledgeable, were generous with their time and taught
me an enormous amount about effecting and managing change. One of the
centres specialized in producing high quality, informative and useful materials
for teachers. The other centre worked as closely as geographical distance
would allow with the school districts it served, adopting a needs assessment
approach. This involved the centre staff working with school district personnel to set goals, supporting the schools in their efforts to achieve these
goals and helping them evaluate their success.

When the opportunity arose some years later to work in the London
Borough of Ealing it seemed it might be possible to put into practice some
of the lessons learned in the USA. I was appointed to a permanent post (as
equal opportunities organizer) and so should not have to spend time or
energy securing funding.

My appointment was made by a new council with a manifesto commitment to equal opportunities. Equal opportunities was viewed as a 'loony
left-wing' initiative and Ealing was increasingly being described in that way
(along with Haringey, Brent and ILEA) by the media. I took up my post
in January 1987 a few days before the council was due to consider the
final draft of the Education Committee's sex equality policy. This policy
had received attention from the national press as it assumed that issues of
sexuality merited consideration within a sex equality policy. The enormous

(and largely orchestrated) public outcry that followed resulted in the offending clause being changed (high schools and colleges were now charged with developing respect for others, including homosexuals) and the rest of the policy being unchallenged. Given this context and the publicity surrounding equal opportunities work it is perhaps not surprising that, although I was greeted with great courtesy by colleagues, I sensed a considerable amount of suspicion about my role and how I would operate.

Influences upon me

I had read and been influenced by Michael Fullan's (1987a, 1987b) work on change . . . and thought it important to start small and establish good practice and credibility as quickly as possible.

The 'swamp theory' (adapted from original ideas from the Counselling and Career Development Unit, University of Leeds) was also a formative influence and seemed highly relevant to the current situation. The idea is that it is a waste of your time and energy (and perhaps your life) to use valuable resources rescuing your colleagues stuck in the far end of the swamp. You will only find yourself sinking with them. It is much more 'cost-effective' to concentrate on those nearest the firm land who will help you try to reclaim it.

I was sure that sharing and support are very important in this field. Working on equality issues can be very stressful and isolating and it is essential to establish personal and professional support networks. First, people undertaking this work often find that the issues do not stay confined to the classroom and start to affect their everyday lives. This can put a strain on relationships if the people they share their lives with are not similarly affected. Second, colleagues can feel very threatened by equal opportunities. People who are threatened react in a variety of ways including ridiculing, marginalizing and being aggressive towards those they perceive as being responsible. It can be extremely stressful being on the receiving end of this. Third, although many LEAs have equal opportunities policies and legitimized working in this field, many have not. Even within LEAs that have policies, there are headteachers who are not convinced of the issues, and it is extremely difficult trying to effect change in this area without support at the top.

In my view good equal opportunities practice is synonymous with good education practice (one cannot exist without the other). Women are not a homogeneous group and may suffer disadvantage because of their race, class, disability and sexuality as well as their gender. I felt that the issues of inequality cannot therefore be treated in isolation. There is no blueprint for success; equal opportunities is a process rather than a product and although the process is important the wheel does not need to be constantly reinvented – good practice can be shared.

What I wanted to achieve

My priorities therefore were to

- seek out the good practice and support already in existence
- initiate and encourage good practice
- publicize and coordinate good practice
- establish support networks
- establish an understanding that good equal opportunities practice equals good educational practice.

There was an expectation in schools and colleges that I was going to come in to tell them what was wrong and instruct them to make changes. Partly in order to overcome this expectation, I felt that it was important to resist the considerable pressure that was put on me to start my job by 'inspecting'. An external evaluation of an institution is invaluable when properly negotiated by those within the institution and the external evaluators. An LEA inspection involves follow-up work and if the school is going to 'hear' and be able to work on the suggestions made, particularly in a sensitive area like equal opportunities, it seems important that those involved have some credibility in the field and in the authority. It therefore seemed crucial to try to establish credibility by the strategies outlined above before embarking on inspections.

Dealing with structures

Another pressure that I was initially less successful in resisting was attendance at meetings. My post was designated as 'organizer': this was explained as half-officer, half-inspector. (The reality turned out to be, of course, a whole officer and a whole inspector.) My diary was filled with over 40 meetings in the first term and, although it was pleasing that it was felt necessary to have a gender equality perspective at all these gatherings, it also made it difficult to make vital links with colleagues in schools and colleges and to work towards the goals I had set myself.

Fortunately, the LEA had realized that the task of implementing its sex equality policy was impossible for one person on their own and had made provision along with the organizer's post for two advisory teachers – one primary phase and the other secondary. This left a gap in the support we could offer to further education and it was agreed to fund from grant-related inservice training (GRIST) an advisory lecturer post, filled in September 1987.

Attempting to work in a feminist, collaborative way as a team within a hierarchical structure is fraught with problems which we have still not fully resolved but continue to try to work on. Issues around race become particularly pertinent when black and white women are trying to work together on issues of gender equality and have resulted in frustrating and painful moments for many members of the team. Nevertheless the original members of the gender equality team and those that have subsequently joined, all have a strong commitment towards equality in education and a desire to work through the tensions together.

In order to seek out the good practice and support that already existed in Ealing, soon after I took up my post I wrote to all schools and colleges asking the interested ones to invite me in. This initiative did not provoke an overwhelming response and, although I did get some invitations from the curious and the courteous, I had to ask inspectorate and officer colleagues for further recommendations. I was very keen to establish a contact in each establishment and felt that this should be someone with a coordinating role for equal opportunities. The evaluation of the SCDC/EOC's equal opportunities project that I had been involved with had indicated that the ideal coordinator was someone with commitment towards the issues (although not necessarily to begin with a very detailed knowledge about the theory, as this could be taught), interpersonal change skills, ability to handle stress and access to the authority structure. I therefore proposed that the head-teacher/principal of each establishment should be ultimately responsible for implementing equal opportunities and should appoint a member of staff to carry out the day-to-day work, reporting directly to the headteacher. I was instructed, however, not to write to schools to ask them to do this because the internal arrangements for the allowance structure were a matter for the headteacher. As these coordinators were going to be the target group for in-service training and key 'change agents' a solution had to be found. Schools were subsequently asked *who* their named person was for equal opportunities (making the assumption that they would all have someone nominated and did not need to be told to do so). Fortunately no one seemed to object to this. To begin with, a few headteachers and principals nominated themselves for the role but this became increasingly rare, and most institutions now have a member of staff with specific responsibility for equal opportunities.

Giving a focus

One of my original priorities was to establish an understanding that good equal opportunities practice equals good educational practice, and vice versa. In order to do this it seemed important to remove the work as far as possible from the image some of the media had bestowed upon it. Just one example of this is the way the *Sun* newspaper reported a residential conference on equal opportunities for *invited* headteachers. The idea was to give all headteachers the opportunity of joining one of the courses, intentionally run far enough away from Ealing for them to be able to be relieved of the minutiae of running a school for a few days and have time to reflect on the issues at hand – common practice in many authorities. No headteacher was instructed to go; in fact a few did decline the invitation. At no time as far as anyone can recollect was the issue of books discussed in detail and there was certainly no discussion, let alone a suggestion, about banning books. The first time I had heard of 'Robin Redbreast' was when I read in the *Sun* that the LEA was supposed to have banned it, presumably because the breasts of robins are sexist. I have still not come across an actual copy (the article is reproduced here).

Loonies ban sexist Robin Redbreast!

by John Kay

The children's book Robin Redbreast has been outlawed by schools in a Labour-run borough – because loony Lefties say the 'breast' in the title is sexist.

Copies have already been removed from some junior-school libraries in Ealing.

And the Janet and John stories have also been given the boot – because the child characters are white.

Council bosses in the West London suburb – home of Labour leader Neil Kinnock – ordered heads to ban books of 'a racist or sexist nature.'

A Tory councillor claims the heads were taken to Brighton for secret three-day sessions on which books should be kept in schools.

Policy

One junior-school head has already removed 21 SACKFULS of books – including Robin Redbreast and Janet and John.

> *A teacher at the school said: 'Robin Redbreast was considered sexist because of the word breast. It's a disgraceful decision.'*

A council spokesman denied there was a blacklist of school books.

He said: 'We have an equal-opportunities policy about race and sex, and heads know of it. It is up to them to apply it in the choice of school books.'

But Tory leader Councillor Martin Mallam said: 'The council has equal-opportunities staff touring schools advising on books.'

(*Sun*, 17 May 1987)

One way of starting to change the image of our work seemed to be to establish links with other authorities and undertake joint work. Key people involved in the SCDC/EOC's equal opportunities project were now working in Merton, Hounslow and Ealing and were prepared to develop strategies that were tested in the project. The SCDC agreed to trawl other London boroughs to see if any of them would be interested in joining an Equal Opportunities Consortium. Enfield, Haringey, Redbridge and Waltham Forest became part of the group. A central coordinator was appointed and was based at the Institute of Education in central London. (See Diana Leonard's Chapter 11 for more information on this initiative.)

In Ealing the Education Committee's approval was given to join the consortium. We decided to support about 20 schools with the resources we had available. The consortium was to be based on the same model as the earlier SCDC/EOC's project, and in setting up the project in Ealing several points from the evaluation of the original project were taken into account.

Evaluation pointers	Our attempted resolution
Approaching schools There were some initial misunderstandings about the purpose of the SCDC/EOC project and the commitment required by the school. This caused delays in getting the project launched in some institutions.	All Ealing schools were trawled seeking genuine volunteers to be involved. All those that showed interest were visited by the equal opportunities organizer and the implications for joining the project were fully discussed.
Role of the coordinators Coordinators were given no time or remuneration for undertaking a considerable amount of extra work.	Extra cover was given for each coordinator for half a day a week.
Some coordinators were given equal opportunities responsibility without any negotiation.	Schools were advised that the role of coordinator should be openly advertised and were provided with a specimen job description.
Lack of in-house support for some coordinators.	Schools were advised that coordinators should have direct line management to the headteacher (or deputy in high schools).
Role of headteachers Some headteachers felt deskilled compared with their coordinators, who responded to in-service training provided and grew in confidence during the year.	In-service training was offered to headteachers.

All schools were invited to join the project. Twenty-one schools responded and were visited; twenty schools subsequently became fully committed members of the project (seven first, six middle, two combined, two special and three high schools).

The following is extracted from the Ealing progress report on the project:

Schools were all allocated a particular Advisory Teacher ... and the method of working with schools by the Gender Equality Team was one of school self assessment. All the Project schools were committed to addressing the issues of Equal Opportunities but only the people working within the institution knew which issues were of real concern to colleagues and in what order or priority issues should be tackled.

(Ealing Education Service 1988)

In Ealing the project heads meet regularly for their own in-service needs which they plan with support from the gender equality team. Each spring term the project schools are invited to contribute to a progress report.

In 1988 an additional twelve schools joined the project, and we attempted to 'twin' them with schools from the original group. Twinning did not prove to be a great success partly because of the time involved. In addition schools had been linked on the basis that some were old and therefore experienced members of the project and others were new and would therefore benefit from this experience. This may well have been true but it did not take into account the issues that were important to each institution nor the needs and experience of the coordinators and headteachers involved. However, several schools did make informal links with feeder schools or schools geographically near, and some have now formalized these links and have arranged for joint staff in-service training, visits, and so on.

I have mentioned how useful it was to have central resources available to support initiatives. One of the earliest provisions the newly elected council made in 1986 was to add 11 per cent to each school's capitation budget specifically targeted towards equal opportunities. Schools have now had this extra allocation for three years and it has proved an extremely effective strategy. It enables colleagues who were desperate to improve the quality of their resources, to do so. Even more importantly, it perhaps encouraged an awareness in others who did not previously realize that their resources were not appropriate or adequate.

What the gender team provides

The gender equality team has facilitated central and school-based in-service training and sought out appropriate externally run courses. The earlier in-service training had two thrusts. The first was to help colleagues become familiar with the issues, then comfortable and confident enough to tackle them. Target groups have included teachers, headteachers, support staff, inspectors and officers. Courses have ranged from single-issue sessions to groups of Ealing teachers taking a module on race and gender towards the Institute of Education's diploma and others as a local group following The Open University's Masters course in gender.

The second thrust was to support women in their career development, both those who wished to apply for promotion and those who were already in positions of responsibility, hence the professional development course for black women teachers and the conferences for women headteachers and deputies. Nationally, women – and in particular black women – are under-represented at headship and the higher allowance levels. Adopting equal opportunities recruitment policies and facilitating in-service training for under-represented groups is legal and indeed essential if the pattern is to change. However, women already in positions of responsibility can face particular problems, and the opportunity to meet other women in similar situations can be extremely beneficial.

The advent of the Education Reform Act 1988 has added a third thrust to our in-service provision: to ensure that equal opportunity issues are kept on the agenda. Although the notion of pupil entitlement to a national curriculum could well further equal opportunities, the curriculum content of the national curriculum, the teaching styles adopted, and assessment and publication of results may not. The local management of schools weakens the power of the LEA, and so it is crucial that headteachers, principals, teachers, lecturers and governors are themselves convinced of the issues and committed to implementing them.

We have always attempted to avoid the 'bolt-on' approach to equal opportunities. By consistently demonstrating that good equal opportunities practice equals good educational practice we have hoped to encourage a perspective whereby equal opportunities is seen as something that affects all aspects of school life. However, it is easy to understand if teachers facing the current enormous pressures for change feel that they have no time for equal opportunities. Our strategy has therefore been to encourage colleagues to include equal opportunities issues as a matter of course in all in-service training delivered (including governor and local management of schools training) and to focus on particular aspects of the Education Reform Act and equal opportunities in the in-service training that the gender equality team offers to the coordinators and the project heads.

I have seen my role as a member of the inspectorate team as supporting colleagues to take on gender equality matters within their phase, issue or subject responsibility. Some colleagues were doing this long before my arrival and some others have since been very willing to explore the issues. Recent appointments to the inspectorate (including a chief inspector) of people from boroughs that have firm equal opportunities philosophies have very much strengthened our joint experience in this area. Initiating and encouraging good practice have been important parts of the work of the gender equality team.

For three years, we invited Ealing schools to complete an equal opportunities development plan. This has been adapted from *Genderwatch!* and encourages the staff to review what has happened so far, to set precise goals for the coming year and somewhat more flexible long- and medium-term ones. When setting their goals schools also have to consider how they will evaluate their progress. The pro forma for these development plans has been refined every year and schools are now asked to discuss them with their link inspector. In-service training development plans are similarly being produced and we are moving towards creating institutional development plans which will have a specific section devoted to equal opportunities but will also include equality issues throughout.

In September 1988 my role changed from being an organizer to a general inspector. Having established that there was no blueprint for success, that schools have to decide themselves the areas they need to pursue, and that self-evaluation is an extremely important part of the process, it seemed timely and appropriate to get involved in formal inspections. Like many other authorities we needed to examine the range and type of inspection we could offer. Full inspections and reviews now include discussions with single-sex groups of pupils and staff (with same-sex inspector).

Reflecting on the developments

I have attempted to describe the methods that the gender equality team has used to seek out the good practice already in existence, to initiate and encourage good practice and to establish support networks. In order to publicize and coordinate this good practice we have produced a variety of publications which range from typed and duplicated pamphlets to professionally printed ones. They all have the purpose of sharing good practice and validating some of the excellent work being undertaken by teachers in our schools.

Ealing Education Department has recently been restructured and there is a firm commitment from the new director to deliver a high quality service to all our pupils and students regardless of their race, gender, class, sexuality or disability. Recent comments by ministers, particularly Angela Rumbold, have indicated ministerial approval for authorities that have equal opportunities policies and implement them. It seems we are at last moving away from the 'loony left-wing' image. It remains to be seen what effect the community charge and the pending local elections will have on the work we have started in Ealing.

Postscript

Tim Horton

Kate Myers completed her account in April 1990. The May 1990 elections in Ealing saw an alteration in the political composition of the authority. Ealing became the only local education authority where Labour Party control switched entirely to the Conservative Party. The Conservatives in fact won fourteen seats from Labour and two from the Liberal Democrats. Commentators stated that the borough saw a collapse of traditional Labour support. In a year when across the UK as a whole there had been an ebbing of Tory support, Ealing represented an area of good news for the party in control at Westminster. Newspapers made much of the borough in the following week, when the 'gender issue' also achieved prominence. The two newspaper articles reproduced here show how the *Sunday Times* and *Daily Star* dealt with the political transition. The gender equality team has now been disbanded.

Red Flag comes down in Ealing's Kremlin

by Frances Rafferty and Maurice Chittenden

THE Union Jack flew over Ealing town hall yesterday from the pole where the African National Congress emblem and the Red Flag used to fly.

The Conservatives claim that their surprising but decisive local election victory in the west London borough – home to Neil and Glenys Kinnock – has returned it to British rule.

The council's race unit, set up by the defeated Labour administration, is unable to complain: it is now being hurriedly scrapped. Going, too, are the self-defence lessons for lesbians, the housing advice service for gays, and the research into the oppression of Irish women in west London.

This week the new Tory rulers will be delving into filing cabinets and probing every corner of a town hall annexe where those Labour political appointees were based. It was leased for £5m and known locally as the Kremlin.

They will not find the KGB. They will, however, find lists of "change agents" appointed to schools to enforce Labour councillors' former views on racism and sexism.

They will also unearth the records of the animal rights officer who campaigned to close pet shops and a "bunny park" in a children's playground.

Last week, crates of files relating to Labour's suburban Utopia were consigned to the bins as the new Tory leader, Martin Mallam, a 37-year-old insurance broker, wheeled in the celebratory champagne.

The Tories' mission this week is to identify 200 workers they claim were employed for left-wing political purposes on salaries of up to £30,000. These officers, serving such causes as the women's committee and the gay and lesbian working party, will be sent to services such as housing and planning or made redundant.

Last week Mallam toured the town hall and its annexe meeting staff. Handshakes were reserved for those "with a proper job".

His party won 17 seats, nearly all from Labour, in the election. "People were fed up with Labour's loony left antics and their past record of putting up the rates by as much as 65% a year," he said as he inspected his new domain.

The new leader did not venture into the spacious open-plan offices of the race unit, where 20 people once worked from desks decorated with potted plants and posters of Nelson Mandela. Mallam has already axed their posts and impounded their files. The staff are supposed to be on extended leave. Instead, they sit at desks with nothing to do.

Nalgo, the local government union, threatened to call all 4,000 council staff out on strike if there are compulsory redundancies. "It is racist and provocative the way the race unit has been singled out and closed," said Chris Morey, the Ealing branch secretary.

The Tories promise good housekeeping and competitive tendering for council services. It will be good news, of sorts, for the Kinnocks: their poll tax of £435 each will be cut next year to £370.

At least £2 per head will be saved by axing grants to such organisations as the Southall Black Sisters and the police monitoring group. Neena Patel, of the Black Sisters, which has been receiving £80,000 a year from the council to offer an advice service, said: "It is our only source of income. We will have to close."

The gay and lesbian unit will close with the loss of two posts. Another 40 jobs will go in the economic development unit, which was intended to encourage industrial growth. Mallam claims it has only bought one set of workshops. Labour says, however, that it has also set up a scheme with a merchant bank to help small businesses.

(Sunday Times, 13 May 1990)

REVEALED – THE SECRETS OF LONDON'S 'KREMLIN'

By KERRY ALLOTT

THEY used to call Neil Kinnock's town hall the Ealing Kremlin. But thanks to the spectacular Tory win in the London borough where the Labour leader lives, the loony lefties are being booted out.

Sanity returned to the council last week as the voters gave their verdict on the regime that had Hilary Benn, son of

Council workers face sack as Tories tackle the loony leftovers

MP Tony Benn, as deputy leader and education chairman.

And the change to Conservative control spells the end to specially-staffed units to deal with gays, lesbians and race.

The Tories say that the savings they make by axing them — and by reclaiming £9 million in rent arrears — will help chop the £435 poll tax to £370 next year.

Judgment

Dozens of workers are reported to be doing political jobs for Ealing council.

There was a driving instructor for women and an animal rights officer. The loony lefties set up education gender teams, women's committees and teams to advise council departments on women and disability.

Now they all face Judgment Day . . . on May 22.

Councillor Martin Mallam, the 37-year-old high-flying leader at Ealing, has ruled that they are costly and unnecessary.

He says: "There were about 40 jobs for the boys under Labour rule.

"We're making it very clear to all the staff that so long as they are good efficient officers they have no need to worry."

But people who don't pull their weight under the Tory regime will have to leave. "All the units Labour set up to deal with gay and women's issues will have to go," he says.

"We're determined to become efficient. Some staff will have to go.

"A third of the workers here are agency staff, which is an expensive option.

Mystery

"We will certainly be making cuts there."

Separate advice teams attached to council departments were inefficient, he says.

But with the return of sanity one of the great mysteries of Ealing will have to remain unsolved.

No one outside the clique that ruled the borough seems to have any idea what the "education gender teams" actually did.

Mr Mallam confesses: "I haven't got a clue."

'What did education gender teams do?'

Second thoughts

For the purposes of this book I asked a few of the key players involved in the equal opportunities initiatives in Ealing to look back and reflect on the experience and key issues of the period.

Hilary Benn, Deputy Leader and Chair of Education, Ealing Council, 1986–90

Looking back, I have a number of impressions of the time. To begin with, the political climate was rather different; in particular it was febrile and more ideological than today. Linked to this was the media hysteria. 'Loony leftism' was a given perspective through which local government was reported, often with complete disregard for the facts. For example, the famous 'Robin Redbreast' story was completely untrue, but it became received wisdom. There were also sections of the media which were anxious to tarnish the reputation of the borough where Neil Kinnock, then Leader of the Opposition, lived.

However, it is also true to say that we failed to pay sufficient attention to the way we presented some of our policies, and in public life you cannot blame anyone else for that! Having lost the election in 1990, we bounced back four years later and have just won another term in office.

Time also moves on. What raised eyebrows then is routine and mainstream now. To some extent, change was more difficult because we did what we did when we did, although we were by no means the first. Ealing, as an authority, lagged behind others, including many of its own schools, in terms of policy and practice. Change was needed.

But most of all, what strikes me is how the debate about gender equality, and equal opportunities, has moved on since. Gender equality is much more firmly entrenched within education now, and the big issue today is actually boys' underachievement. That is not to say that problems like the glass ceiling have been overcome – far from it – but there has been real progress. There is also a much firmer emphasis now, and rightly so, on raising standards for all and measuring our success in doing so. I watch the debate about school inspection with interest, having as Chair of Education in 1989 taken the decision to make Ealing's own inspection reports public. The genie of openness and accountability will not go back into the bottle, and it should never have been there in the first place.

As to the lessons, the most important is a very simple one. Successful change is about taking people with you. The things that worked in Ealing, as Kate Myers' description of the success of her team shows, were those that involved and engaged teachers, heads and governors. A local authority must give a clear lead – that is its role – but without ownership, words in a policy statement mean little. Supporting people in discovering how they can review and change their practice is also essential, and offering financial support is a very practical way of doing this. Resources do help oil the wheels of change. But the most important lesson of all is that the issue we, along with many others, grappled with – namely how to enable as many pupils as possible, whatever their background, to achieve to their full potential – remains the key task for the education service as it faces the challenge of the new century.

Penny Clayton, Headteacher, Ravenor School, Ealing

'Don't expect to get it, they've always had a man.' These were the kindly meant words of a male LEA inspector shortly before the interview for my first headship. The school was tough – set in a high-rise housing estate in the London Borough of Ealing. In spite of beating the male opposition and securing the post, his words lingered throughout those first years of head-ship as I felt I had much to prove. A woman with ten years' teaching experience, an 18-month-old son and the distinct possibility of having more children seemed to be a risk not usually taken. Certainly the meetings of headteachers in Ealing at that time appeared to be largely populated by white men in suits. Out of school I was running a working mothers' group and discovering that a wide range of employed women were facing attitudes and work practices prejudicial to their promotion and well-being.

The invitation to join an equal opportunities project proved irresistible. The deputy head and I were already evolving our own methods of leading the school in a fair and equal manner but were keen to learn more. She became the school's project coordinator and the excitement began. The word 'excitement' is used wisely as through awareness-raising training we were able to be proactive and creative, to reconsider many aspects of our work, to challenge assumptions which affected practice and begin to make a real difference at pupil level. Our natural style of management gained credibility and we had the strength to lead by empowering others rather than by the systems and management tools gleaned from other courses.

Within a couple of years most schools had meaningful equal opportunities policies. These policies were not created through pressure from roving or indeed raving loonies but from schools personnel themselves questioning their own practices, curriculum content and resources. The project coordinators were skilled in helping schools manage change and were gentle in their approach. The difficult part was shaking off the negative, hysterical messages being perpetrated by the press threatening to damage relationships between the school and its community. Employees in Ealing were used to the cycle of political swings and extremist doctrine affecting their work but this time the gulf between what was happening in schools and what was being reported in the media was wide indeed. The discomfort was increased with the knowledge that something inherently fair and just was being regarded with such fear and suspicion.

However, for most of Ealing's teachers, headteachers, inspectors and officers, the commitment to equality in their schools developed a life of its own so that changes in political power had little effect. Recruitment practices across the authority became clear, fair and largely faultless. New teachers actively selected Ealing because of its reputation for equal opportunities; only those with a commitment and true understanding secured jobs. Staff who moved away realized just how far forward Ealing had gone when they discovered themselves in LEAs with practices seemingly light years away. Staff that remained shared a common bond and worked to consolidate the developing ethos in Ealing of quality and equality for all.

At school level, equal opportunities permeated every aspect of school life. The advent of the National Curriculum supported the notion of entitlement for all. Girls assumed their right to play rugby and football and to take a fairer share of the playground space. In the school where I currently work, primary pupils play an active role in decision making through School Council and will always challenge stereotyping and unfairness. Resources are always selected or rejected with reference to equality of opportunity. The greatest observable difference, however, is in the confidence, competence and high achievement of the girls. The girls from Asian backgrounds in particular indicate growth in self-esteem, overtly displaying pride in their cultural backgrounds, taking active roles in the life of the school and generally reaching their true potential. This has been a steady development since 1989. Successful though the project in Ealing undoubtedly was, there remains much to be done, such as part-time employees having equal access to training, appraisal and other employment benefits. A further current concern is the comparative deteriorating standards of the achievement of boys, together with their greater incidences of exclusion, unacceptable behaviour and placement on special needs registers. Questions must continually be raised about the best ways to ensure both boys and girls have the opportunity and the motivation to achieve their true capabilities.

Alan Richardson, Chief Inspector, Ealing

It is difficult to recall what the prevailing attitudes were in 1989 and which issues prompted the intensive activity that was undertaken in the area of equal opportunities in Ealing. The whole educational climate was very different then: it was immediately before the introduction of the National Curriculum with teachers having much greater freedom to develop the curriculum and teaching approaches, to be more adventurous and being given greater encouragement to be so; this was certainly the case in Ealing. Locally, a new administration was elected with a strong commitment to equal opportunities and to the taking of positive steps to turn this commitment into action to change attitudes and practice. It is clear in retrospect that the conditions were right to make real strides in equal opportunities.

The approach that was promoted is best summed up by the phrase 'good practice in equal opportunities is good practice fullstop'. The statement was repeated frequently, made a real impact and survived, being regularly quoted in discussion of all aspects of equal opportunities. There was also an attempt to ensure integration of approaches towards equality of opportunity for different groups. Although not always successful, this was particularly important as there were other teams working in the areas of race equality and disability within the borough. Consistency of approach has become a basic principle in approaching equal opportunities in the LEA.

Certainly some early steps in, for example, handling non-sexist language were ridiculed by some but came to be seen as important indications of attitudes and are now widely accepted. Humour was a useful deflection of confrontation. A sign in one high school – 'Mistresses' Cloakroom' – was parceled up as a gift and presented with some ceremony to the Inspector for Gender Equality prior to an inspection. Now gender-neutral terms are the norm.

The introduction of a gender equality team of a significant size, led by a senior officer, itself had an effect on ways of working within the Education Department. Its internal organization and functioning led others to question their practice. The 'project' approach, a basic strategy which the team adopted, is now widely accepted as an effective means of targeting resources and achieving specified objectives. Working initially with schools who were committed and prepared to try new approaches, establishing success and then encouraging others to join, rather than concentrating on those schools thought to be most in need of support, was highly effective. The size of the committed group grew as the benefits of the work being done was increasingly recognized. In time, for the less committed or sceptical schools, at least there were both clear expectations of what they should be doing and examples of good practice to support them.

It is easy to take for granted the progress that has been made. What have become legal requirements in relation to the appointment of staff have long been an integral part of appointment procedures in the LEA. Few, if any, schools would now be unable to provide a thorough analysis of pupil performance data by gender and describe the strengths and weaknesses that are revealed. In the much more frequent and systematic observation of classroom practice that now occurs, the different impact on boys and girls are an important feature reported upon; the same would be true for interactions in playgrounds and social areas of the school. Teachers have, over time, increasingly become aware of the need to take account in their lesson planning of the individual needs of pupils, and among other factors, of the difference in preferred learning styles of boys and girls. Few schools have 'token' equal opportunity policies: usually they are documents which result from much debate and repeated redrafting. It is difficult to judge the contribution of the gender equality initiatives to these particular developments. There is certainly now less overt work on 'equal opportunities' in whatever form. The positive view is that a further phase of development has been reached in which the issues are considered as a natural component of any discussion about education. The heads and teachers who are still in Ealing and who worked with the project in whatever way have continued to influence the thinking and practice of more recently appointed staff in schools.

Although there was some formal evaluation of the early stages of the project, there has been none in relation to the long-term effects. There is clear evidence in pupil performance data of improved results of girls in some subject areas and increased take-up of some subjects. Now that girls are outperforming boys in most aspects of the performance tables published annually, there is a clear need to focus on aspects of improving boys' achievement. Work with boys was proposed within the project but was not developed to any extent. As to the changes in attitudes, the changes of teaching and learning styles and generally the quality of the experience of school, most staff working in schools as well as the LEA's inspectorate would recognize the strides that have been made.

Certainly positive impact has been apparent in a number of areas of the work of the project. From time to time those who have worked in Ealing for long enough will say rather wistfully that we will need to have another period of intensive work on equal opportunities issues – to review and develop the work ten years on. With the present preoccupation with the many initiatives currently being promoted by central government, it would be timely to look at current practice to ensure that the responses to these initiatives do take account of equal opportunities. The Education Development Plan currently being produced includes a priority which would perhaps have been surprising in 1989 – raising the levels of attainment of boys.

Kate Myers, Inspector for Gender Equality 1987–90

It seems a lot longer than a decade ago when the work described above took place. Much of what we now take for granted was still extremely controversial in 1989. The notion that boys and girls should have access to the same curriculum had had legislative support for only a few years and there were many examples in schools of this just not happening. My main memories of this time are the excitement of working on this initiative that had political (local) and much school-based support; working with stimulating and committed people, both colleagues in the advisory team and heads and teachers in schools; trying to ensure that equal opportunities was seen as a professional issue and dealt with in that way; being ridiculed by the media and consequently having to be ultra-careful about everything that was said, written and done; the occasional feeling of being attacked on all sides and not being able to please anyone (too soft and liberal for the 'hard' left and too extreme for the right); and finally tensions between people working on equality issues, particularly about race and gender. Rereading the piece has reminded me about introducing change;

the personal cost of being involved in equality issues; and the importance of institutionalizing change.

When I took up the appointment, heads and teachers in Ealing were used to an autocratic and top-down management style. I think I was right to resist perpetuating this model of change and initially to avoid getting involved in inspections. I am sure that what did work in Ealing did so because we worked hard to get the commitment of those involved and initially worked with the enthusiasts bringing in others when credentials were established.

This is always a tension for policy makers – not least so for our current government. Children have only one opportunity of schooling and there is little time to wait around until the reluctants and recalcitrants are convinced. However, unless those charged with implementing the change are convinced about it, they will find ways to subvert or marginalize it.

Near the beginning of this chapter I mentioned how people can feel threatened about equal opportunities issues and how some of them react. Looking back, I think that the personal cost to many of those engaged in these issues may have been underestimated. The main focus of my current work is school improvement. Usually it is possible to leave these issues behind when dealing with personal relationships, watching television, visiting the cinema or an art gallery. Equality issues do not tend to separate in that way and manage to permeate everything you say and do. The professional becomes personal. I remember many teachers talking about the consequence of this on their personal lives; they were changing and growing and in some cases their partners were not.

As the postscript from Tim Horton says, the Labour Party lost control in May 1990. The gender equality team was disbanded the day after the election and our posts redesignated. This result was not anticipated and so we had made no plans for this eventuality. As can be seen from the newspaper articles, many of the incoming politicians were derisory about equal opportunities issues. For a while the resulting ethos was a bit like John Cleese's *Fawlty Towers* sketch about the Germans. Equal opportunities were not to be mentioned. Posters were hurriedly taken down, conversation was cautious and we were forbidden to use the term 'equal opportunities' in committee papers or reports. Nevertheless, many of the practices that had been introduced under the umbrella of equal opportunities (such as interview procedures and curriculum initiatives) proved popular with the schools and were retained and improved upon by many.

I have no doubt that during this period there was a change in the mind-set and aspirations of many heads and teachers, some of which can be put down to the work of the gender equality team. Unfortunately I have no evidence of this nor of any impact that this work had in the classroom and on the aspirations of pupils. We have no evidence because we did no systematic evaluation. Technology and the climate were different. There were no baseline measures, no pupil/parent/staff attitudinal surveys, and although we did have some self-evaluation as part of the development plans and action research cycles, apart from inspections, there was no external evaluation. This is what I would have done differently with the benefit of serendipitous hindsight.

Acknowledgements

Members of the gender equality team have included Hilary Claire, Roz Davy, Liz Dibb, Pat Keel, Helen Marchington, Sybil Naidu, Kathleen Pepper, Diane Raey and Hilary Soper.

Grateful acknowledgement is made to the following sources for permission to reproduce material in *Perspective 3*:

Allott, K. (1990) 'Revealed – the secrets of London's "Kremlin" ', *Daily Star*, 10 May 1990, Express Newspapers plc; Kay, J. (1987) 'Loonies ban sexist Robin Redbreast', *Sun*, 17 May 1987, The Sun/Rex Features; Parrott, S. (1990) *Featherstone High School, Equal Opportunities – Progress Report March 1990*; Rafferty, F. and Chittenden, M. (1990) 'Red flag comes down in Ealing's Kremlin', *The Sunday Times*, 13 May 1990, © Times Newspapers Ltd 1990.

Note

1 In 1985–6 the SCDC and the EOC jointly funded a pilot project called Equal Opportunities in Education. Most of the work for this project took place in the London Borough of Merton in eight targeted schools (all phases including special). The project was externally evaluated by Dr Ian Jamieson and Mary Tasker of Bath University (1986) *Final Evaluation Report of the SCDC/EOC Equal Opportunities in Education Development Pilot Project in the London Borough of Merton*, available from the EOC.

References

Allott, K. (1990) Revealed – the secrets of London's 'Kremlin', *Daily Star*, 10 May.
Ealing Education Service (1988) *London Boroughs Project on Equal Opportunities: Ealing Progress Report 1987–88*. London: Ealing Education Service.
Fullan, M. (1987a) Managing curriculum change, in *Curriculum at the Crossroads*. Report of the SCDC Conference on Aspects of Curriculum Change, Leeds University, mimeo.
Fullan, M. (1987b) Implementing educational change: what we know. Paper presented for the World Bank, Washington DC.
Kay, J. (1987) Loonies ban sexist Robin Redbreast!, *Sun*, 17 May.
Myers, K. (1987) *Genderwatch: Self-Assessment Schedules for Use in Schools*. London: Schools Curriculum Development Council.
Rafferty, F. and Chittenden, M. (1990) Red flag comes down in Ealing's Kremlin, *Sunday Times*, 13 May.

Part III

Projects

Chapter eight

Was there really a problem? The Schools Council Sex Differentiation Project 1981–3

Val Millman

Introduction

The late 1970s and early 1980s were exciting times for those of us wanting to introduce educational changes that would promote greater sex equality in schools. They were also testing times, both personally and professionally, for those seeking to challenge the status quo as well as for those who were in positions to defend it. Painful choices sometimes had to be made and there were few precedents to draw on. In 1978, a woman colleague at my secondary school instigated the first educational case under the new Sex Discrimination Act and I participated as a witness, giving evidence against the headteacher to the Equal Opportunities Commission. My colleague did not win her case, but all of those affected by it, both locally and further afield, had learnt some early lessons about the impending process of change.

In 1981 I was looking for a new job and had put in a couple of applications for head of faculty posts (after, perhaps not surprisingly, failing to gain further promotion in my own school!). I then spotted an advertisement for a job as Development Officer for the Schools Council Equal Opportunities Project and applied immediately, against the advice of many colleagues who saw faculty head posts as much more prestigious. I was surprised and thrilled to be offered the post and excited at the prospect of working with the project staff whom I had met at the interview, an enabling process which had given me a taste of things to come. The project ethos and working practices were key to the success of the projects; they were inclusive, supportive, imaginative, energetic, challenging and purposeful – and, on top of all this, there were opportunities for fun and laughter.

In this chapter I shall describe some of the Schools Council project initiatives with which I worked over the following two years and reflect on where they may have taken us since then. My focus will be on the role played by such projects in bringing about change in relation to gender issues in schools together with an examination of preconditions for such change and the change strategies themselves. This will inevitably be a personal perspective shaped by my Schools Council work and by my years of working on equality issues in Coventry LEA. I hope, however, that it will be both recognizable to those who were there at the time and accessible to those who wish to make sense of, and draw from, what we learnt and experienced.

First, I briefly set the national context for educational change in relation to sex equality in the early 1980s. Then I give a flavour of the rapid escalation of interest in this change that took place between 1981 and 1983. I follow this with a more detailed examination of the significance of strategies adopted in Schools Council projects and an analysis of project features which were key to its success. Finally, I offer some comparative reflection on conditions for change that exist in schools of the late 1990s.

The context for educational change

There were a number of factors that accounted for the emergence of concern in Britain about sex equality in education in the late 1970s and early 1980s. The post-war educational agenda had consistently focused on equality of educational opportunity, but this had mainly been defined in terms of social class. By the 1970s, the US Civil Rights Movement and the British Women's Movement had stimulated concern about sex-differentiated employment patterns and the reasons for women and minority ethnic groups clustering in a narrow, lower paid sector of the labour market. Educational concerns focused on the relatively few 'black' people and women in senior positions, the latter numbers further dwindling as more schools became coeducational. Discrepancies between subject choices and examination results of boys and girls also appeared more marked in coeducational schools even in newly emerging technology subjects. These discrepancies were now being publicly highlighted, particularly as boys' qualifications apparently had higher labour market currency than girls'. In 1979, the European Economic Community (EEC) published a draft resolution 'concerning measures to be taken in the field of education to improve the preparation of girls for working life and to promote equality of opportunity for girls and boys in society' (quoted in Millman and Weiner 1985: 12).

An increasing body of academic research on sex differences in employment and in education was becoming available from Britain and beyond. This included data from the DES, HMI, LEAs as well as action research findings from education pressure groups within unions and political parties, school groups and individual teachers.

While the introduction of legislation in the mid-1970s on pay and discriminatory practices was helpful in preventing individuals from experiencing overt discrimination, the main importance for education of the new sex discrimination law was to alert society to dangers of unconscious bias and stereotyping. The EOC offered the following guidance:

> The Sex Discrimination Act cannot remove all the influence of tradition, custom and prejudice, but it will help to ensure that no-one suffers from unlawful discrimination in formal education and training . . . If true equality of opportunity is to be achieved for girls/boys then it is essential that during the schooling process boys and girls receive the same educational opportunities, to fit them for equal access to further and higher education courses, training and employment opportunities.
>
> (EOC 1982: 1)

A time of educational change 1981–3

Despite a developing context of concern about sex equality issues outside of education at this time, when the Schools Council project, Reducing Sex Differentiation in Schools, began in 1981, there was still relatively little official interest in achieving equal opportunities between the sexes in schools. (A detailed outline of project developments can be found later in this chapter.) There were, however, emerging teacher-initiated debates in various parts of the country and some political initiatives, mostly in inner and outer London LEAs. There were also a number of teachers, mainly women, trying to bring about changed practice in schools, where traditional and sexist attitudes were common and sex-differentiated administrative and teaching practices were routine. In many cases these teachers were working with little in-school support and were labelled as 'bra-burning feminists' or 'disruptive loonies' with 'a chip on their shoulders'. At this time, there were no published classroom materials or training resources which could counter the sex-stereotyped curriculum materials and teaching approaches that were in common usage in school classrooms. While most teachers firmly believed that they treated all pupils without prejudice or bias, much of what was happening in classrooms was characterized by the assumption that girls and boys should have differential educational experiences.

In 1981, it was clear that the Schools Council project would have to gain, maintain and sustain support from a wide range of interest groups from regions with different histories and cultures in a very short period of time. While the recent equality legislation and EOC were both important sources of legitimacy for sex equality work in education, there was, at the start of the project, no easily shared language, knowledge base, history or vision which could help to build alliances across the range of disparate, and sometimes polarized, perspectives of key partners in this process of change.

Widespread raising of awareness of the problem of sex differentiation in schooling and its effect on educational and employment outcomes for girls and boys was therefore of paramount importance. Existing evidence would have to be systematically collected and analysed and its implications for changed educational practice closely scrutinized and widely publicized.

By 1983, little change had taken place in pupil attitudes and educational and employment outcomes evidenced some two years earlier. While some schools were developing, piloting and evaluating strategies for reducing sex differentiation, there was still widespread evidence of resistance to change within the media and within the educational and political establishment in many parts of the UK. When, in 1983, the Conservative government announced the closure of the Schools Council, it appeared unlikely that national equal opportunities in education initiatives would continue in the future.

The seeds of change towards greater sex equality in schools, however, had been sown in fertile ground, not only by Schools Council initiatives but also by many others seeking educational change. By the early 1980s there was prolific evidence of a growing awareness of the problem of sex differentiation in schools and of a variety of approaches to tackling it. Many teachers, whose confidence and creativity had previously been sapped by isolation and hostility, now felt empowered to promote change in an increasingly legitimate area of education. A new language was entering educational debates and there was a more informed and coherent view of changes that were needed.

The rapid growth in interest in the Schools Council projects over this short time was indicative of expanding developments in different parts of the UK. In its two years of existence, the Schools Council project mailing list grew to 4000. A resource centre was established housing a comprehensive bank of educational data, research studies and classroom materials. There were case studies of tested strategies for curriculum and institutional change and recorded findings of school-based action research. Around 850 projects working on sex equality in schools were listed in a contact directory that was distributed to teachers' centres across the UK and a resource pack containing pupil and teacher materials was distributed to 500 interested organizations. Over 1000 teachers had registered their names on a computerized equal opportunities network and alliances were rapidly being forged across a range of political and professional organizations. There were regular requests for speakers at educational courses and conferences, and also frequent enquiries from parents, governors and students, as well as from newspapers, television and radio. Increasing numbers of LEAs were showing active support for sex equality development work and a few were appointing staff with this designated brief. Despite ominous noises from the Conservative government, the possibility of positive change was being vigorously signalled.

Background to the Schools Council sex equality initiatives

The Schools Council

The Schools Council was an independent organization, founded in 1964, funded equally by central and local government. The council's committees included teachers, representatives of central and local government, churches, parents, industry and further and higher education. Its main tasks were to keep under review and to promote the development of the curriculum, teaching methods and examinations.

The Schools Council supported, financed and coordinated various research and development projects based in schools, teachers' centres, local authorities and institutions of higher education in England and Wales. The council also published teaching materials and guidance based on these projects. The council was well recognized and respected by the education profession and provided a significant forum for exchange of educational thinking.

The Schools Council's commitment to sex equality in schools

In 1979, the Schools Council expressed its commitment to 'the elimination of sex stereotyping and promotion of equality between the sexes'. It established a Sex Differentiation in Schools working party, with Lesley Kant as its lead officer. The working party's brief was to examine the problem of sex bias in education and consider ways in which the council could be influential in the furtherance of sex equality. The EOC was represented on this committee in addition to the usual bodies represented on Schools Council committees.

During the next two years a number of practical activities were initiated by this working party which had 'reducing sex differentiation in schools' as its central theme. These included the following:

- The Sex Role Differentiation Project – a project to initiate research and development work with teachers. Gaby Weiner was appointed as half-time coordinator from 1981 to 1982. I then took over the role of coordinator until the project ended in March 1983. Kate Myers joined the second year of the project on an ILEA-funded full-time one-year secondment to identify and coordinate anti-sexist work undertaken in ILEA and to initiate and support new developments.
- The Equal Opportunities in Education Project – a project to establish an information base and contact centre for teachers and other educationalists. I was appointed as development officer for two days a week from 1981 to 1983, jointly funded by the Schools Council and the EOC.
- The Girls Into Science and Technology (GIST) Project – a research project part-funded by the Schools Council to identify intervention strategies that could encourage girls to take science and technical craft options after

the third year. Judith Whyte, Alison Kelly and Barbara Smail's research was closely associated with other Schools Council equal opportunities projects. (See Barbara Smail's Chapter 9.)

- A joint Schools Council / EOC venture to commission and publish curriculum booklets following the EOC's (1982) pamphlet *Do You Provide Equal Opportunities?*.
- Links with other relevant projects, organizations and LEA initiatives such as Brent, ILEA and Sheffield, and assistance in disseminating their developments.

The Schools Council Project: Reducing Sex Differentiation in Schools

The main thrust of this project's work was to respond to the stated needs of practising teachers by

- exploring ways in which the issue of sex differentiation could be presented to their colleagues who were either unaware of the processes which reinforce sex differentiation and stereotyping in schooling or resistant to changing their practice
- providing information on resources, strategies and contacts for teachers who were already developing their own means of dealing with the problem.

It was decided to direct the work of the project along three interconnecting paths. The first of these was initiating, supporting and developing teacher group work in local education authorities, a number of which had already expressed an interest prior to the project coordinator's appointment in February 1981. The second was collecting examples of existing good practice, using these to build up a bank of materials that could inform both the newly established teacher groups and any others who might be interested in undertaking work in this area. Third, four issues of a regular newsletter were planned, for disseminating the project and other relevant initiatives. The project's newsletter proved to be a powerful vehicle for building new alliances and networks.

Developing teacher group work

The project aimed to support groups of teachers working in a variety of contexts from independent 'women in education groups' to LEAs which were either 'starting out' from first principles or were seeking help with coordination and development. The project offered teachers' groups different levels of support according to their needs and priorities.

The main aims of teacher group work were

- to identify, develop and promote practice which would lead to the reduction of sex differentiation in schools
- to raise, at school, local authority and national level, awareness of sex equality in education as an important contemporary issue
- to produce guidelines and materials for use by teachers in schools.

Primary and secondary teacher groups were initially convened by LEA officers and advisers in Enfield, Leicestershire, East Sussex and Clwyd LEAs. They worked closely with the project coordinator to identify and support a one-year programme of research and development work. The groups became a rich source of expertise and an important forum for stimulus and support. (LEAs joining the project later were supported in a more limited way in running day conferences, carrying out small-scale surveys and producing local reports for discussion.)

The teacher groups' work moved through the following stages:

Choice of issues and topics

Teachers needed initially to identify elements of school life that were most likely to influence differential perceptions and performance of girls and boys and which they were in a position to investigate effectively. Action research case studies included the following aspects of both the 'overt' and 'hidden' curriculum:

- textbooks and classroom displays
- departmental practices
- option choice take-up
- patterns of examination performance
- teacher attitudes
- boys' and girls' attitudes and interests
- pupil career aspirations
- employers' attitudes
- primary reading schemes
- staffing patterns
- the 'hidden' curriculum, such as registers, assemblies, uniform, extracurricular activities
- classroom interaction and relationships
- curriculum content
- careers education and guidance
- language use

While data from all of these areas had the potential to inform change strategies addressed at both girls and boys, most teachers chose to focus on the school experiences of girls. Some also explored 'race' dimensions of school experience. However, although the problem of 'race' and sex discrimination was often rooted in similar practices, most teachers found that initial change strategies needed to be discretely focused on individual dimensions of equality.

In-depth studies

Having identified an area of investigation, teachers had to choose a suitable research method. The advice of the project coordinator and the support of LEA staff were invaluable at these early stages. Teachers were usually undertaking this work in their spare time and could not afford to become side-tracked or submerged with irrelevant data. They were also assisted in gaining some theoretical understanding of equality issues although the change strategies that emerged from their studies reflected no single theoretical approach. Exploring attitudes as well as behaviour was considered by most teachers to be central to embedding long-term change.

Many of the existing research instruments had to be adapted, sensitized or redesigned by teachers to meet the needs of this new area of study. Selected research methods included pupil questionnaires, structured interview schedules, information request pro formas, checklists and schedules, and classroom observation methods using audio and video tapes.

Involving teachers in carrying out school research proved to be a powerful route to curriculum innovation and, indeed, sometimes to whole school change. Objective teacher observation and school-generated research data on sex differentiation were considered to be both useful to participating teachers and worthy of serious consideration by colleagues, despite occasional methodological imperfections. Some sceptical colleagues became 'converts' to reducing sex differentiation after viewing current practice through 'new eyes'. Often staff relationships were strengthened by this common focus of interest, although personal and professional differences were sometimes heightened and perspectives polarized.

Analysis, documentation, dissemination and discussion

Data gathered from in-depth studies was analysed, shared within the teacher groups and described in reports and guidelines. These records of school practice were presented to school staff and LEA colleagues and described in the final project report (Millman and Weiner 1985). They represented a significant contribution to a relatively new area of knowledge at this time and they were often used as the basis for decisions about further research, in-service training programmes and policy developments. Some teachers also conducted nine and eighteen month follow-up studies to assess the longer term impact of their research findings on school practice and on pupils.

Project support for existing teacher groups was also available. Assistance was given to already developing teacher groups; this included expertise, small-scale funding, information and contacts which succeeded in helping groups to become self-functioning and independent. For example:

- a group of teachers based at the Berkshire LEA teachers' centre wishing to publish primary classroom materials
- a group of probationary PE teachers in Liverpool seeking recognition for their work on equal opportunities
- a London Women's Education Group (WedG) seeking additional transitional funding to promote its awareness-raising programme for teachers, lecturers, parents and students
- the Girls and Mathematics Association (GAMMA) needing help in becoming more securely established and better able to undertake national awareness-raising work around girls and mathematics.

Through supporting these sorts of groups, interest in sex differentiation in schools often spread to LEAs and other organizations and institutions which had not previously been involved.

Collecting examples of existing good practice

Teacher group work identified many examples of effective change and good practice in promoting equality of opportunity in schools. Most change was 'bottom-up', initiated by women teachers in low positions in the school hierarchy. Despite high levels of personal energy and professional interest, they found it difficult to achieve sustained change without active support from senior staff and whole-school commitment.

Change strategies that were tested included the following:

- establishing parents' groups to raise awareness
- developing 'positive action' strategies to encourage increased take-up and improved performance by girls in technological options
- setting up new curriculum initiatives, for example a Skills for Living course in the all-boys Hackney Downs School (see Frances Magee's Chapter 10)
- developing and implementing a whole-school equal opportunities policy and guidelines
- attempting to redress inequalities in school staffing patterns, for example by providing positive adult role models for female staff
- appointing a teacher to take responsibility for equal opportunities
- allocating resources to departmental equal opportunities initiatives
- establishing systems for ongoing monitoring of girls' and boys' option choices, examination performance, career destinations and participation in extracurricular activities

- consulting boys and girls on their attitudes and interests and recommending relevant changes.

Disseminating the project and other relevant initiatives

The Schools Council provided significant legitimacy at local and national level, both with educationists and with parents, even where initiatives were not directly related to project teacher group work. Dissemination of school developments was an essential aspect of project work at a time when many senior staff in schools and the majority of LEAs did not recognize that there was a problem of sex inequality in schools, and did not take seriously teachers' attempts at curriculum innovation in this area. There remained strong currents of resistance to the project by both women and men working in education. These were typified by a letter sent to Gaby Weiner from a primary headteacher:

> Obviously from your writing you are an intelligent person, thoroughly involved with a desire to neuter the sexes. I really don't think this is a good idea . . . let's be reasonable! Women generally enjoy looking after their children and providing a loving home – it's the same with cats and dogs (or should I say, cats and bitches?) Fathers generally become the willing providers – ever heard of the birds and the bees? . . . Why not pack up your troubles and prejudices. Get married – raise a traditional family and be happy.

Such attitudes were frequently reinforced by the media, who often helped to misrepresent the educational aims of the work and undermine educationists working on sex equality issues. Early in the project, a School Council Equal Opportunities in Education Information Centre was established to assist with project dissemination and form the focus of a contact and communication network. In addition, the centre built up a bank of relevant data, research findings and resources for use within and beyond the project. At the end of the project, the centre published an *Equal Opportunities in Education Directory* which contained details of local projects, lists of interested teachers and classroom materials. This information, which was also held on the Schools Council computer system, provided an important basis for future networking. As the project progressed, dissemination also took place through a series of newsletters, project contributions to courses, seminars and conferences, the publication of school curriculum and in-service training materials, and the distribution of resource packs to 500 interested schools, organizations and teacher trainers.

The series of four project newsletters constituted a pioneering, comprehensive and practical collection of resources and information about national and international developments in the field of equal opportunities in education. They were always much in demand not least because they gave isolated teachers, particularly in primary schools, access to a network of like-minded professionals. The final project report (Millman and Weiner 1985) identified two critical stages through which teachers and educationists needed to pass in order to achieve real equal opportunities within the education system:

1 Recognition that, despite a general belief among teachers that they do not discriminate between pupils on grounds of gender, girls and boys leave school with differential qualifications, career aspirations and self-perceptions partly as a result of their school experience. Achieving this recognition demands widespread awareness-raising.
2 Implementation of changed practice in schools in order to challenge the restricted aspirations and stereotypical views held by many pupils.

Changed practice does not automatically follow raised awareness of sex equality. It was often fiercely resisted by men and women who had strong reactions to this personally and professionally sensitive area of education. However, although it would be a number of years before the impact of changed school practices on pupil performance could be measured, there was much evidence that the Schools Council project helped many involved in the educational process to move school practice forward, further and faster than would otherwise have been the case.

Key features of the two-year project

The Schools Council sex equality projects both influenced and reflected wider educational developments taking place in the early 1980s. Their evident effectiveness resulted not only from 'being in the right place at the right time' but also from the following project features:

- individuals committed to sex equality in schools, mostly women, in influential positions
- an explicit project focus on sex equality while also keying into other emerging educational initiatives
- an enabling rather than prescriptive project approach, providing teachers with support they were unable to access in individual schools and the opportunity to share their learning with others
- a framework which gave direction but also encouraged creativity
- an emphasis on the increasing legitimacy of this area of change
- a recognition of the value of both top-down and bottom-up approaches to change
- energetic and imaginative project dissemination to spread awareness and stimulate change, for example through 'peer' pressure between schools, between LEAs, between unions and between other organizations

- an emphasis on working collaboratively with a wide range of organizations within and beyond education, capitalizing on energy and commitment wherever it was to be found
- a recognition of the importance of securing a database to underpin developing practice and to monitor change
- finding ways of making academic research processes and findings accessible to and useable by educational practitioners.

The feelings of many who had been involved over the two-year project period can be summed up by the following letter written in November 1983:

> Thank you so much for the pack of project materials you sent me. I know that I shall find them very useful in my work. It is a pity that the Sex Differentiation project had to come to an end at a time when there is so much work still to be done. We shall just have to keep plugging away in our own patches.

After the funded projects ended in 1983, a number of strategies were devised to try to secure the continued national coordination of work on sex equality in education. Discussions were held with the EOC to identify potential ways forward and support was received from Joan Lestor, Opposition Spokesperson on Women's Rights and Welfare, who, in December 1982, tabled a parliamentary question in the House of Commons about project evaluation and continuation. Jo Richardson, MP, Joan Lestor's successor, also wrote to the School Curriculum Development Committee, the replacement body for the Schools Council, urging the SCDC to 'take these issues on board when identifying programme priorities.' It was sometime later before the SCDC jointly funded an 18-month project with the EOC which culminated in 1986 with the publication of *Genderwatch* (Myers 1987; Myers 1992). However, there was no explicit focus on these issues by national educational bodies that were subsequently established.

Where are we now?

We are now seeing renewed concern about the differential educational achievements of girls and boys, albeit with the focus now firmly on underachieving boys. School inspection teams are required to report on comparative attainment of girls and boys and we are seeing high-profile Ofsted publications on gender being sent to schools. The present Labour government now expects LEAs to identify strategies for raising boys' achievement in their statutory Educational Development Plans.

Most of the intervening years have been bleak times for those of us continuing to work on gender equality in schools. Not only was there an absence of any national equality focus but also there was a relentless onslaught on anything that could be characterized as 'politically correct', a loss of dedicated 'equality' resources and a rapidly changing educational agenda that left no room for such 'irrelevancies' as gender equality.

Leaving aside consideration of the wider social, political and economic context for educational change at the start of the new millennium, it is interesting to reflect on the following structures, policies and practices that are in place in many schools today, as compared to the 1980s. They point to significant opportunities for generating and managing change in relation to gender which, for most schools, is currently focused on raising boys' levels of attainment.

- 'Raising boys' achievement' is seen as a whole-school priority.
- There is recognition of the need to change the whole-school culture and ethos rather than merely 'tinker around' at the edges of selected curriculum areas.
- Many senior management teams are committed to actively leading change in this area.
- There are men in senior positions who can act as positive role models for boys.
- Target-setting strategies legitimize a focus on individual and group attainment and achievement.
- 'Positive action' is a legitimate phrase in the 'change' vocabulary.
- The crucial influence of teacher expectation on pupil performance is recognized.
- 'Sex stereotyping', 'sexist attitudes' and 'macho' behaviour mostly are now accepted as operating against boys' interests.
- A language is in place that legitimizes and enables debate around issues of boys' 'underachievement' to be part of schools' mainstream agendas.
- Structures are in place in many schools to enable change strategies to be implemented, for example equal opportunities working parties, equal opportunities coordinators.
- Information management systems are in place which can facilitate analysis of boys' – and other groups' – performance across the curriculum.
- There is increased emphasis on monitoring and accountability.
- Relevant research on classroom organization and teaching and learning is becoming readily available.
- Single-sex grouping is increasingly accepted as a potentially appropriate teaching strategy.
- An increased national emphasis on literacy enhances access of boys to initiatives such as summer literacy schools.
- An increased national concern about equipping boys for technical jobs of the future is increasing the emphasis on key skills such as team work, communication and presentation skills.

- Newly published resources show girls and boys in a range of contexts and roles.
- Whole-school change processes and strategies are better understood by more people.
- There is a 'conventional gender wisdom' in schools which facilitates communication, albeit oversimplistic.

Many of the above are now regarded as 'normal' practices. In the early 1980s, when teachers were proposing 'positive action' for girls, many such practices represented major challenges to the school system. Indeed, many of the change strategies which were ridiculed and resisted at that time, now form the bedrock of recommended strategies for raising boys' achievement. Backed by national policy, sophisticated information systems and increasingly accountable for improving pupil performance, schools are apparently well placed to set about raising boys' attainment.

Detailed discussion about the current national focus on 'underachieving boys' is beyond the scope of this chapter and is well covered elsewhere (Weiner *et al.* 1997). However, those involved in implementing current change strategies might wish to consider the following factors that have been identified through reflection on the Schools Council work on sex differentiation:

- The importance of a coherent change strategy that addresses the learning needs of both girls and boys who are at risk of not achieving their potential.
- The need to use working definitions of educational achievement rather than focus solely on educational attainment.
- The importance of recognizing and planning for long-term changes in attitudes and behaviour.
- The value of enabling bottom-up and sideways-on change strategies as well as top-down ones.
- The creative energy released in teachers by both collaborative working and by experiencing professional ownership of change.
- The importance of training teachers to understand gender issues rather than leaving change strategies to be determined by conventional and misinformed staff room wisdom.
- The value of academics and practitioners working alongside each other.
- The continued need to consider how different dimensions of equality interact with each other in relation to educational achievement.

In the late 1990s schools need support in developing more sophisticated approaches to meeting the learning needs of different groups of children and young people, at different stages of their schooling. Central to school development plans need to be sensitive and informed whole-school strategies for helping boys and girls from different social and ethnic backgrounds to build their identities, maximize their learning and prepare for their adult lives. While some strategies will be relevant to all pupils, others will need to be targeted at times towards particular groups who have a shared experience of barriers to learning and achievement. The 1985 Schools Council project report included the following statement in its recommendations and conclusions:

> At a time of social and economic insecurity, we suggest that schools should lead the way, by enlightening pupils (and parents) about changes in employment patterns and family structures and in trying to anticipate the knowledge and skills appropriate for the first decade of the twenty-first century.
>
> (Millman and Weiner 1985: 73)

Clearly, we still have a long way to go! Girls, as well as boys, need our continued understanding, insight and commitment to their futures.

A personal postscript

I believe that the Schools Council sex equality projects successfully helped to bring about change because they used strategies that reached 'both hearts and minds'. At this time, the enormous energy that participating teachers brought to their jobs was born of personal, professional and sometimes political commitment to change on behalf of the young people with whom they were working. This collective energy and commitment proved to be a powerful learning experience for those of us involved in educational change at this time. New professional relationships were established and strong friendships formed with both women and men who supported these changes. I am pleased to have had the opportunity to contribute to this book alongside many others with whom I worked at this time and I would like to thank Gaby Weiner for her helpful comments on this chapter.

Sadly, in the intervening years, three significant women colleagues and friends have died from breast cancer: Val Mason, the Coventry teacher who took up the first sex discrimination case, Pat Goodman, who was secretary to the Schools Council project, and Lynda Carr, principal education officer of the EOC, who provided such widespread support and inspiration for these changes.

References

EOC (1982) *Do You Provide Equal Opportunities? A Guide to Good Practice in the Provision of Equal Opportunities in Education.* Manchester: EOC.

Millman, V. and Weiner, G. (1985) *Sex Differentiation in Schooling: Is There Really a Problem?* York: Longman for Schools Council.

Myers, K. (1987) *Genderwatch: Self-Assessment Schedules for Use in Schools.* London: Schools Curriculum Development Council.

Myers, K. (1992) *Genderwatch! After the Education Reform Act.* Cambridge: Cambridge University Press.

Weiner, G., Arnot, M. and David, M. (1997) Is the future female? Female success, male disadvantage, and changing gender patterns in education, in A.H. Halsey, H. Lauder, P. Brown and A. Stuart-Wells (eds) *Education: Culture, Economy, and Society.* Oxford: Oxford University Press.

Chapter nine

Has the mountain moved?
The Girls Into Science and
Technology Project 1979–83

Barbara Smail

Introduction

In May 1979, I opened the newspaper one morning to find a job advertised. The university and the then polytechnic in Manchester were starting a joint project about 'Why so few girls study science'. They wanted a project officer.

As a chemistry undergraduate at Manchester University in the early 1960s I had been one of only three young women in a class of forty-five. By 1979, I was married with two school-age children and teaching chemistry in a former girls-only secondary modern school which had become a girls-only comprehensive in 1977. Chemistry and physics were new opportunities for the girls in my classes, as the only science taught in the school until 1975 was biology. They were enthusiastic about science. I had been one of the growing number of women with children entering the workforce in the mid-1970s. Surely, I thought, the world has changed in the last twenty years. Intrigued, I applied for and got the job, unaware of the extent of the task I was preparing to tackle.

The Girls Into Science and Technology (GIST) Project was a four-year action research project which not only investigated the reasons for girls' underachievement in science and technology but also encouraged teachers to develop strategies for change in their own schools. In this chapter I want to reflect upon my personal experience of the project. I also want to ask if the situation of young women in school science has changed since 1979 and, if it has, what this might tell us about the process of educational change.

The Girls Into Science and Technology Project

The project followed a cohort of children who entered ten coeducational comprehensive schools in Greater Manchester in September 1980 until they made their option choice at the end of their third year. Two of the schools, where attitude testing took place but where the team made no attempt to influence the teachers or their pupils, acted as controls.

The story of the GIST Project and its research findings have been reported widely in a series of academic papers and two popular books (Whyte 1986; Kelly 1987). There were two important aspects to the research:

- to explore the processes by which children's attitudes to science, engineering and technology changed during the early years of secondary school
- to investigate, by working with teachers, how the gendered nature of subject choice could be affected by changes in teachers' attitudes and behaviour.

This second facet of the research proved far more problematic and interesting than the first.

Intervention strategies

In all the action schools, the project team provided six hours of workshops with science, craft, design and technology and pastoral staff in each school. At the end of the workshops, all the schools agreed to the administration of the research questionnaires with their new intake. They were also offered help with implementing the following interventions:

- programme of visits by women working in scientific and technical jobs
- working with the teachers to modify and develop curriculum materials linked to girls' interests including women's contributions to science
- lunchtime science and technology clubs for girls
- observation and feedback to teachers of teacher–pupil and pupil–pupil interactions in the laboratory or workshop to identify and prevent ways in which girls are discouraged
- review of options booklets and options systems to remove in-built gender bias
- parents' evenings to alert them to the implications of choice
- class discussion about the difficulties of making non-traditional career and subject choices.

At the beginning of the project, in all the action schools, the teachers were interested only in the programme of visits. However, after the results from the first round of pupil questionnaires had been reported to them, they became noticeably more enthusiastic and, by the end of the project, all the other intervention strategies had been tried in some, but not all, of the action schools.

Children's attitudes: research results

The results on children's attitudes to science (Kelly and Smail 1984) can be summarized as follows. At 11 years of age, the boys in the 1980 cohort were much keener than the girls to learn about physical science. The girls were more enthusiastic about nature study and both sexes were interested in learning about human biology. By the third year of secondary school, the girls' and the boys' interest in all branches of science had declined, except for human biology. Opinions about science and scientists which were positive at 11 became less favourable by age 13. On entry to secondary school, attitudes to science were virtually unrelated to ability, but by age 13, there was a clear trend for more able pupils to exhibit greater interest in learning about science. At option choice at 13 plus, girls who expressed liking for science as a subject tended to be interested in physical science. Physical science interest at option choice at 13 plus was closely associated with physical science interest on entry.

By 13 plus, girls and boys were aiming for vastly different occupations. They rated 'usefulness for getting a job' as the most important criterion when choosing subjects. The boys saw physics and technical subjects as useful for the technical jobs to which they aspired, for example as electricians, or car mechanics, or those in engineering and computing. They also rated these subjects highly with regard to interest and enjoyment and were more likely to estimate their performance accurately. The girls saw physics and technical subjects as less useful for a career, less enjoyable and interesting, and they underestimated how well they performed. At the time of subject choice, the careers that the girls in the GIST cohort most expected to enter were hairdresser (17 per cent), nursery nurse (15 per cent), typist/secretary (14 per cent), nurse (11 per cent) and teacher (9 per cent).

Throughout the project the boys were much more gender stereotyped than the girls and drew clearer distinctions between activities which they thought suitable for women and men. The boys were more likely to agree with statements which implied that women do not need to know about science or that the study of science and technology is for men only. These attitudes were reflected in their behaviour in the laboratory and workshop, where boys tended to monopolize the equipment and taunt girls who made mistakes.

Teachers and their attitudes

At the time, GIST attracted international attention from groups across Europe, North America and Australia who were engaged in similar projects and an international forum for researchers in the field, Gender and Science and Technology (GASAT), met for the first time in 1981 and has continued to meet regularly ever since. As a result of the work, the EOC, which had funded the GIST Project together with the Social Science Research Council, launched a national campaign Women into Science and Engineering (WISE) in 1984. Despite these positive outcomes in the wider community, at the end of the GIST Project, we, the project team, were disappointed in the impact it seemed to have had on the teachers in the action schools. Throughout the project, we firmly believed that all the staff, both men and women, were equally capable of implementing equal opportunities strategies. Unfortunately, the male–female ratio of the science and crafts staff in the schools reinforced the notion that some subjects were male preserves. Of the eight science departments in the action schools, only one was headed by a woman. All the heads of physics and chemistry were male, but six of the heads of biology were female. Staff for technical crafts were exclusively male.

Writing in 1985, I reported the results of an external evaluation of teachers' attitudes as follows:

> It was hoped that the evaluation would reveal teachers' perceptions of the project's effect on their attitudes and behaviour. Even though the GIST teachers could talk at length about the project and its aims, the evaluators found that most were reluctant to admit that the project had changed them personally. The evaluators report that the teachers viewed the project 'as interventionist in the lives of pupils rather than the lives of teachers'. They also 'seem almost grudging to concede' that there have been even marginal changes in their classroom behaviour.

These comments illustrate a difficulty in the way the teacher–researcher relationship was established. Throughout the project, we treated teachers as collaborators in traditional research focusing on children's attitudes and behaviours. We found that teachers, particularly science teachers, were not convinced by evidence, anecdotal or otherwise, from schools in London or abroad. They demanded 'hard facts' based on research with *their* pupils. As women researchers, with an overtly feminist philosophy, we were allowed access to schools at the discretion of local authorities and headteachers primarily to investigate the phenomenon of girls' opting out of physical science and technical subjects at 13 plus. There was an explicit understanding that any changes proposed would be discussed at all levels within the school and that no action would be taken without the substantial support of the staff. In 1979, thinking about equal opportunities was so new in schools, that without the collaborative research stance and the staff veto on action, we would have had difficulty in recruiting any schools to take part.

As we were unable to directly focus on the key issue of teachers' attitudes, we hoped that teachers would realize, as they became interested in the research, that they must change themselves before they could change their pupils. However, even with this strong unemotional emphasis on research, the issue of the differential socialization of girls and boys in school released powerful feelings in teachers. Many became decidedly less interested in taking action to increase the number of girls opting for physics and technical subjects when they realized the logical implications for themselves of the changes needed. Not only would they have to treat girls more equally in the classroom, but also this strategy could have repercussions in other relationships. For example, if a male teacher accepted that girls can use a power drill competently and safely, then logically, his wife or daughter could take over some of the household tasks through which he defines his masculinity and dominance in the home.

During informal discussions, many teachers gave illustrations from their own families to justify a traditional division of responsibilities, showing that they were aware that this was the issue. Changes of attitude which affect family relationships do not happen quickly, nor can they be forced. The GIST schools where most progress was made were those where the school ethos had already incorporated ideas of provision of genuine equal opportunities. Even in these schools, some teachers showed signs of feeling very threatened by the project and its aims. There were occasions when, after a majority of the science department had agreed to take part, one teacher, almost always male, found that he was far too busy to attend any of the teacher workshops. In one case, a physicist, who had been rounded up by his colleagues, arrived carrying a piece of equipment with which he continued to tinker throughout the discussion – a visible indication of his priorities!

Explicit support for the project from senior management and the LEA was a factor in enabling teachers to innovate, but even where such institutional backing was available, individual teachers differed markedly in their attitudes. Older teachers, both men and women, who had raised families with a traditional breadwinning father and stay-at-home mother, were the ones who often found the GIST ideas difficult to assimilate, perhaps because they saw the ideas as an attack on their own lifestyles.

At that time even a common curriculum for boys and girls was an issue. One school where hostility to ideas of a similar curriculum for girls and boys was expressed openly to the evaluators, segregated the sexes for crafts at the beginning of the project. By the end of the project they had not only abandoned this practice but also joined with another project school in the same LEA to organize a three-day work experience course for girls at a local engineering firm. The reasons for this change were complex and difficult to disentangle. This inner-city school had a head who was sympathetic to the project's aims and a very effective woman head of science. The project team spent a lot of time in discussion with the technical crafts and home economics department staff and the head of the technical crafts department became convinced that there was a future for young women in local engineering companies, who were having difficulty recruiting high calibre apprentices. The other school involved in the joint course was perceived as one of the best in the LEA, where innovative schemes were being implemented. The more traditional school, therefore, gained kudos by association.

Even though changes at a structural level could be carried through by the headteacher, staff in the school sometimes subverted these attempts to provide more equal opportunities by their behaviour in the classroom. For example, in the same inner-city mixed school mentioned above, the needle-work teachers did not want to teach boys. By maintaining the curriculum which they had previously found successful with girls-only groups, they could ensure that, after a brief compulsory 'taster' course, the boys would opt out of the subject because they did not find the projects met their needs. Similarly, in other schools, teachers of physics, chemistry and technical subjects could provide hidden and overt curricula which ignored girls' interests and resulted in male domination of these classes after option choice.

Across all the schools, there was a marked tendency for teachers to embrace interventions by the project team directly with the pupils but to be reluctant to embark on major changes to their own teaching and learning strategies. Schools which were already thinking about equal opportunities opted for classroom observation studies with feedback to teachers of teacher–pupil and pupil–pupil interactions by sex or discussions with staff and pupils about the limiting effects of sex-role stereotypes on careers advice linked to option choices. The more conservative schools would allow the project team only to organize interventions such as visits by women scientists, but were, initially, unwilling to go further.

In the early days of the project, we realized that masculinity and femininity were constructed across the whole curriculum in schools and that change would not come about just by changing what happened in science lessons. The values transmitted through other subject areas also had an effect.

Lessons from GIST about educational change

In the GIST *Final Report* (Kelly *et al*. 1984) we assessed our success using Morrish's (1976) model of the time and difficulty involved in bringing about educational change. Morrish suggested that the easiest step (I) is to advance the state of knowledge about a situation. It is hard (II) to change individual attitudes and more difficult still (III) to alter individual behaviour. The final stage in curriculum reform is the changing of institutional behaviour (IV). GIST claimed considerable success at step I, some changes, particularly of pupils' rather then teachers' attitudes at step II, limited effect in pupil's option choice behaviour (III) and very little effect on institutional ethos.

This verdict was disappointing to those who looked for dramatic changes in the number of women scientists and engineers as a result of the project's work. On average, about 4 per cent more of the year group of girls chose physics in the GIST cohort than in previous years and there were slight increases in numbers of girls taking technical crafts, but changes in option choice behaviour were small.

However, consistent differences between children's attitudes in the action and control schools emerged by the end of the project. They are, perhaps, a truer reflection of the project's success than option choices, being less influenced by structural restraints such as the nature of the option system and the size of the teaching group. As mentioned earlier in this chapter, when the project started, both boys' and girls' attitudes to science deteriorated between 11 and 13. By the end of GIST, positive attitudes to science at age 11 deteriorated less by age 13 plus in the action schools than in the control schools.

In addition, dramatic differences were found between action and control schools on measures of gender stereotyping. For example, girls in action schools were much more likely to mention a job with some scientific or technical content as their expected occupation. They were also more likely to want to be employed while they had young children and less likely to want a husband cleverer than themselves. It appears that we were more successful changing girls' attitudes than those of boys or teachers.

The time of action was limited by the research design, which focused on a specific cohort. This group was followed for three years, from entry to secondary school to option choice. Towards the end of the project's life, teachers of personal and social education, careers and pastoral tutors in the GIST schools became involved. The project team organized class discussion about the difficulties of making non-traditional career and subject choices, and evenings with parents about the stereotyping of option choices. The involvement of these larger groups in the ideas of the project could have initiated a shift in school ethos. However, it was only in schools with an established policy about equal opportunities that the teachers were willing to conduct these sessions themselves. In six of the eight action schools, these sessions were run by members of the project team and were met with some scepticism by the staff.

Ideally, much more time would have been devoted to in-service training throughout the project. But most of schools did not perceive the need to improve their practice in these respects nor were they willing to allocate more time to the project's aims.

Policy changes since GIST

Of course, since the late 1980s with the National Curriculum, both girls and boys have had much less freedom of choice concerning the subjects they choose to study. Nowadays, there is much less subject choice at 13 plus. One of the GIST findings, which provided a strong argument for those who wished to see a national core curriculum, was that pupils at age 13 plus in mixed schools seemed to be using subject choice as a means of asserting their gender identity. It was thought that deferring choice to 16 plus, when students had matured beyond the early stages of adolescence, would mean that more boys would opt for traditionally 'feminine' subjects like French, English and biology and more girls would opt for science and maths. Findings that girls' and boys' attitudes to science were so different on entry to secondary school gave a strong boost to the move for primary science as an element in the National Curriculum.

Looking back now, I believe that the most important outcome of the GIST Project was the way it raised the issue of the low number of women in science in education and government circles, so that it became a legitimate topic for discussion rather than a taken-for-granted feature of the education system and the workforce. While the actual experiment we were engaged in school had limited and mixed success, the national and international attention it attracted eventually brought many other institutions and agencies into the debate, which led to some major reforms.

Where are we now?

While GIST focused attention on girls' needs and the way in which they were not being met by the science and technology taught in schools, later researchers, particularly in the USA and Australia, have broadened the perspective to consider the interaction of race/ethnicity, class and gender on access to science education (Clewell and Ginorio 1996). In the early 1980s in the UK even collecting individual data about school students, broken down by race/ethnicity and class, was technically difficult and seen as problematic. Although during this period some LEAs appointed equal opportunity advisers with this broad brief, the resistance they met to their work was enormous.

There is a growing awareness worldwide that access to knowledge about science, engineering and technology is important for all citizens and is necessary, as we enter the twenty-first century, for decision making in a democratic society. Science education is not just about training future scientists and engineers, it is part of a broad general education for everyone.

So, has the imposition of a National Curriculum in the UK achieved our goal? Now that girls and boys study the same curriculum to GCSE level, will more young women go on to study science at A level and beyond? Can change be imposed upon schools from above or do the attitudes and values of the teachers still play a role in determining the subtle ethos of the education provided? Does exposing everyone to the same curriculum achieve equity or do we sometimes have to treat students differently to achieve similar outcomes?

Table 9.1   Ratio of %male:%female in examination entries in A level subjects in England, Northern Ireland and Wales and in Higher examinations in Scotland

	England, Wales and Northern Ireland			Scottish figures for comparison[c]	
	1981[a] M:F	1991[b] M:F	1996[b] M:F	1991 M:F	1996 M:F
Biology	43:57	36:64	39:61	30:70	29:71
Chemistry	67:33	57:43	54:46	53:47	52:48
Mathematics	74:26	65:35	64:36	52:48	51:49
Physics	81:19	76:24	76:24	69:21	69:21

Notes
a Based on DES (1982) *Statistics of School Leavers CSE and GCE 1981*. London: DES.
b Based on figures produced centrally for the GCE A level boards by the Associated Examining Board. Data for all syllabuses/modes within the same subject category were combined for each board (human biology, social biology and so on are aggregated within biology). Data from AS examinations are not included.
c Based on data in booklets published annually by the Scottish Examination Board.

Patterns in A level choice 1981–96

Table 9.1 shows the number of males for each female studying science subject at A level in 1981, 1991 and 1996 and at Higher level in Scotland (1991 and 1996).

Table 9.1 illustrates that the situation is a complex one. While there has been considerable improvement in the gender balance between girls and boys studying chemistry and to some extent maths, physics remains highly gendered in England, Wales and Northern Ireland. There were more than three times as many boys as girls entering in 1996. The overall numbers entering for A level physics fell dramatically from 52,300 in 1981 to only 33,033 in 1996. Even taking into account the falling numbers of students in the age cohorts from 1981 to 1995, these figures make depressing reading. Biology, with a rising number of entries over the period (from 41,800 in 1981 to 52,053 in 1996 despite the falling cohort numbers), has attracted more girls than boys, so that it is even more a girls' subject in 1996 than it was in 1981!

Comparison with Scotland shows similar trends, but the gendering of physics appears to be less extreme, perhaps, because more students (as a proportion of the year cohort) choose to study physics as one of five subjects for Scottish Highers than choose to study it as one of three subjects for A level. Fewer students in Scotland study biology for Highers and a greater proportion of them are girls than in England, Wales and Northern

Ireland. The near gender-neutral position of maths and chemistry in both educational systems and the shift in the numbers of girls and boys entering since the early 1980s suggest that these subjects may be seen by students as useful for entry to higher education and the job market. It could also be that the way in which they are approached up to GCSE level has changed so that both girls and boys feel confident in choosing them for further study.

The continuing polarization of physics as the masculine science and biology as the feminine one requires further scrutiny. Teachers' attitudes have a role to play and the nature of advice given to students entering A level and Higher courses, but we also need to look at the wider picture of the job market and the requirements for entry to degree courses, before we can be sure that changing teachers' practice will make any difference. Today's 16-year-olds have many sources of information at their fingertips and are influenced by press and media images as much as by their teachers.

Indeed, a strand of debate is emerging which points to the nature of physics and physicists as the place where change is most urgently needed (Wertheim 1995). Questioning how one might write about physics for the truly uninitiated, Wertheim points to the fact that most writing about physics focuses on answers rather than questions. She also draws some interesting parallels between physics and religion and points to the 'priestly' culture of physics as the factor which distinguishes physics from the other sciences and preserves the barrier to women's entry.

It seems to me that a number of questions are raised by the figures in Table 9.1 with respect to the complex nature of educational change. We need to investigate why there have been changes in the gender balance for chemistry and not for physics and biology. If we look back to the late 1970s, have the teaching methods, textbooks and teachers changed for the better in chemistry in a way which is not matched in biology and physics? Have they incorporated the ideas about the importance of showing the social usefulness of the science, which has been shown to attract and interest girls? Or is it simply that starting from a higher base of girls studying chemistry at A level it was easier to recruit more? Or are the HE courses, such as nursing, which have traditionally attracted more women than men, now demanding chemistry as an entry requirement? There is a need for research into the effects of the changes that have been made in schools since 1989 to find out if they are leading us in the right direction.

Another model for change

In the USA and Australia, where there has been a great deal of research on equity education since 1989, a staged model for curriculum change has been proposed (Kreinberg and Lewis 1996):

Stage 1 the absence of women is not noticed
Stage 2 the absence is noted and a search for the missing women begins
Stage 3 questioning why there are so few women in science
Stage 4 studying woman's experience in science
Stage 5 challenging the paradigm of what science is
Stage 6 reconstructing a gender-free curriculum

The model can apply to the development of thinking in an individual teacher, a department, a school or college or university, or at the societal level.

Since the late 1970s in the UK, the curriculum in science education has moved from a situation where the absence of women in science classrooms, textbooks, on HE courses and in research laboratories was seen as unproblematic, through stages 2 and 3 of making women more visible in science through visiting women scientist programmes as in GIST and adding photographs of girls and women and stories of women scientists to textbooks. As a result of studying the experience of girls in GIST classrooms (stage 4), I proposed (Smail 1984) the notion of girl-friendly science, which was approached from its human and social applications rather than as a detached framework of rules. In Australia, the McClintock Collective employed a wide range of teaching strategies, which provided active learning contexts, organized the classroom as cooperative groups and started from and valued students' experience in planning the curriculum. Approaches like these have been used in the UK and incorporated into materials such as those produced by the Science and Technology in Society (SATIS) project (Association for Science Education (ASE) 1990). I suggest that in schools in the UK we are now at the same point in the staged model as Kreinberg and Lewis (1996) place their projects, hovering between stages 5 and 6.

The questions they are left with in attempting to construct a gender-free curriculum are challenging:

> How can we value the diversity of female and male cognitive styles? How can we work constructively, when our power and professional status are invested in traditional science structures? How can we include other classes and cultures that science also has excluded? What sort of science and science practices do we want to promote in developing countries? How do we make sure that the practices, ethical questions and future dilemmas of science are explored with students?
>
> (Kreinberg and Lewis 1996)

In conclusion

I am conscious that, in writing this chapter, I have posed more questions than I have answered. At the end of the GIST Project, I felt that we understood the problem very well, but that constructive change was difficult and slow.

We had also realized the enormous implications of the sort of changes we were demanding, for the whole structure, not only of science education, but of education and science as well and felt powerless to tackle them. As Kreinberg and Lewis (1996) conclude, 'Equity education is political education.'

The world has moved on and perhaps now things are possible which seemed impossible in 1983. If they or we in the UK are to be successful in moving to stage 6 of the model, we must work in a way which rethinks schooling, challenging many of our most fundamental assumptions to provide an education which will develop not only the scientists, engineers and technologists for the twenty-first century, but also the informed public who will sanction their work. A review of research reported to GASAT conferences to date was published by the Development Unit on Women in Science, Engineering and Technology (SET) of the Office of Science and Technology (Department of Trade and Industry (DTI) 1997). It concludes:

> In recent years, girls have made considerable advances in their academic achievement in the UK, to the point that debates have focused upon 'underachieving boys' rather than the difficulties faced by girls. While this is a proper concern, it needs to be recognised that the world of science, engineering and technology is still, in the main, a masculine domain.
>
> (DTI 1997: 26)

Time for another intervention project ... ?

Acknowledgement

I am grateful to Dr Jon Osborne at King's College, London, for the 1991 and 1996 exam entry figures.

References

ASE (1990) *Science and Technology in Society (SATIS)*, edited by A. Hunt. Hatfield, Herts: Association for Science Education.

Clewell, B.C. and Ginorio, A.B. (1996) Examining women's progress in the sciences from the perspective of diversity, in C. Davis, A.B. Ginorio, C.J. Hollinshead, B.B. Lazarus and P.M. Rayman *The Equity Equation*. San Francisco, CA: Jossey-Bass.

DTI (1997) *Breaking the Mould: An Assessment of Successful Strategies for Attracting Girls into Science, Engineering and Technology*. London: Development Unit on Women in SET, Department of Trade and Industry.

Kelly, A. (ed.) (1987) *Science for Girls?* Milton Keynes: Open University Press.

Kelly, A. and Smail, B. (1984) Sex differences in science and technology among 11 year old school children: I cognitive, II affective, *Research in Science and Technological Education* 2: 61–76 and 87–106.

Kelly, A., Whyte, J. and Smail, B. (1984) *GIST: The Final Report*. Manchester: Department of Sociology, University of Manchester.

Kreinberg, N. and Lewis, S. (1996) The politics and practice of equity: experiences from both sides of the Pacific, in L.H. Parker, L.J. Rennie and B.J. Fraser (eds) *Gender, Science and Mathematics: Shortening the Shadow*. Dordrecht and London: Kluwer.

Morrish, I. (1976) *Aspects of Educational Change*. London: Allen and Unwin.

Smail, B. (1984) *Girl-Friendly Science: Avoiding Sex Bias in the Curriculum*. York: Longman for Schools Council.

Wertheim, M. (1997) *Pythagoras' Trousers: God, Physics and the Gender Wars*. London: Fourth Estate.

Whyte, J. (1986) *Girls into Science and Technology*. London: Routledge and Kegan Paul.

Chapter ten

Working with boys at Hackney Downs School 1980–4

Frances Magee

Context: the school

Hackney Downs was an all-boys' comprehensive school in the Inner London Education Authority. It had a long and distinguished history in providing for its local, working-class community, opting at the earliest opportunity to go comprehensive and to abolish caning. Among its many initiatives in teaching and learning was a curriculum course dedicated to extending the range of curriculum content and experience at that time offered to boys and to changing the attitudes and behaviours of pupils to themselves as learners and citizens.

The course came to be called Skills for Living and was put into the formal curriculum in 1982. This was preceded by several years of development work within the school. The course was timetabled for all the first form (Year 7) and, after two more years of development work, was extended to all the second form (Year 8). During that time I was a deputy head with responsibility for the curriculum.

How the course came about

Within the school, the origin of the concept came from the school women's group and was taken forward by a mixed staff working party, including Chris Baxter, Kay Coussens, Mike Davis, Jon Duveen, Sue Hughes, Jo Rex, Vicky Sholund, Jeremy Stone, Helen Turner and Claire Widgery. These people also pioneered the teaching of the course. Unfortunately it was not possible for all of us to get together again to write this chapter: I acknowledge that what follows is my personal recollection and others would have much more to add. When I left the school in 1985, I left all the archive material relating to the course and its development. Two summers ago I cleared my home shelves for another life change and most of my historical 'boys stuff' was severely weeded out to face the new order in education. But what follows is how I remember our work at Hackney Downs. In the first instance, it is possibly true to say that there was no clear aim until the concerns raised in the women's group – about ourselves in a male environment, harassment, aggression, bullying, peer group pressure among the boys, teaching and learning styles, the negative manifestations of race, sex and class issues – were moved into a curriculum development framework. With hindsight it is obvious that the current discourse about raising achievement was, at that time, much more implicit. The emphasis at that time was on relationships, behaviour, culture, ethos, attitudes and values. It is interesting to note the return of these matters in the raising achievement portfolio. The Ofsted/ EOC (1996) publication, *The Gender Divide*, on performance differences between boys and girls, highlights factors affecting pupil achievement which include attitudes to learning and to self, dealing with harassment, the narrowing of experience in single-sex groupings, peer group pressure, the role of language in learning. Skills for Living was a pre-National Curriculum and Assessment agenda.

Although some of our impetus for creating the course was also premised on improving behaviour and relationships, I do not believe there was ever an issue about exclusions. The school was an orderly community, although a number of us believed that some of the order was based on traditional male values of competition, strength and power and a conventional, authoritarian approach to 'discipline'. In many aspects, the school was liberal and progressive, but pastoral care was unstructured and tended to respond to individual problems rather than the creation of a culture and ethos in which such problems might be minimized. There certainly was a social inclusion agenda of its time; we were very conscious that we were a school in a working-class, ethnically diverse community and took great pains to be inclusive and to address discrimination.

The curriculum

The rationale for the course was twofold. Its aims were first to extend the curriculum and experience opportunities in an all-boys' school and to combat sexism. The curriculum extension aspects included food work, childcare studies and domestic crafts. The intention was to give the boys experiences, understanding and skills in these areas, to prepare them for domestic responsibility, competence and autonomy. We also hoped they would come to take these areas of activity seriously and review the inferior status that many males attribute to them because they have been women's work. This proved to be a naïve objective, or maybe just one which cannot be measured at the time. Working in these areas alone was insufficient to give us any evidence of transformed attitudes to women's work. Neither did these 11-year-olds broadly imagine a world in which they would ever have to be responsible, autonomous or even competent for their own sakes. They enjoyed the work. They accepted it and respected it as part of the regular curriculum. But it became increasingly evident that we were more effective in reaching our aims when we planned lessons that were structured to be collaborative, when the emphasis of the work was on the quality of pupil interaction. Feedback from pupils indicated that we were successful in this. They commented positively on their individual and group organization in the work. They reflected back positive attitudes about the benefits of helping each other. They had good opportunities for creativity and for social caring. But it was not home economics or child development even as defined in the curriculum orthodoxies of the 1980s! We drew on the curriculum content of such courses, but arranged it in a modular format. Our success criteria were less about skills than about understandings of their social contexts.

The second aim of Skills for Living was specifically and explicitly anti-sexist. We had devoted much thinking and researching time to trying to understand what this meant for the education of boys. Most of us were much clearer about what it meant for women. For working with boys, we focused on helping boys to develop a repertoire of expression and ways of relating which included intimacy, trust, cooperation, mutual supportiveness, taking responsibility for their own and each other's emotional well-being. Among other things, we were deliberately selecting pedagogies that developed speaking and listening skills. We also chose to have teaching programmes and materials that included the examination of male and female stereotypical roles, attitudes and values. This examination was intended to raise awareness of the existence of stereotyping, its negative and restricting effects on both males and females, and to explore positive alternatives.

In 1982 the Schools Council's Sex Differentiation Project with the ILEA ran a conference on Equal Opportunities: What's In It for Boys? Hackney Downs staff participated, contributing to workshops and to the post-conference pack of materials for teachers. This post-conference pack included a statement that summed up for us our view at the time. It is in grown-ups' language but it captures our stance. What's in it for boys is the opportunity to

• acquire a more accurate and honest view of themselves
• recognize and understand the causes of bias evident in images of society and history
• contribute positively to a more just society.

How?

1 By learning that sex-role stereotyping limits behaviours.
2 By learning in particular to (a) question and challenge those traditional masculine values which are destructive; and (b) accept and promote those constructive values which have traditionally been seen as feminine.
3 By learning to see that those routine practices and relationships which have seemed normal, DO oppress women, (a) helping them to understand the causes and effects of those practices; (b) giving them the opportunity and the means to reject such practices and to create positive alternatives.

(Carter *et al*. 1983)

The process of getting the course going

It took us several years to move from major concerns of sexism and sexual harassment to a curriculum innovation. The process began in the late 1970s with the autonomous women's group in the school, about twenty of us including support staff. The benefits of this were unplanned. It gave us a cross-curricular, interdisciplinary forum for wide-ranging discussion. We had no formal place in the school consultative structure. We shared our understandings and experiences and found a collective strength to identify the things that puzzled us and the things we would like to change. We reflected on the kind of text and images that our pupils came across in the media and in our own lessons. The Humanities faculty was still running a programme entitled 'Man the hunter, farmer, town dweller'. Other curriculum areas were reinforcing traditional male roles and values. Women's experience and contribution to history, society, the economy and to culture was invisible. It was roughly two years later that a part-time art teacher and the media resources technician proposed the idea of a curriculum innovation. Only then did it move into the formal structure of the school by the establishment of a working party.

The process of bringing about the change to the formal school curriculum included informing and consulting all the staff at the school. Three full staff meetings were held in the year. The first opened up the issues, raised awareness and clarified the terms of the idea. Members of the women's group led this, making presentations and fielding the discussion. A point, which must not be underestimated, is that parts of the process like this brought women staff into new positions of public prominence and gave them leadership roles. Neither must the warmth and strength of the mutual support we provided for each other be underestimated, particularly to those stepping out anxiously for the first time. It is an aspect of professional development that deserves more recognition.

The second staff meeting presented the draft outline of the course. Practical implications were discussed. The general principles were more readily agreed than the implementation. Implementation meant change and change meant challenge. The challenges were to the existing order of curriculum time, staffing and resources. With the support of the school leadership, the working party was given the go ahead to define a separate, additional course to commence in September 1982. From then on the working party met every week! A third full staff meeting in autumn 1981 completed the consultation on a whole-school policy on sex equity and anti-sexism, which finally put Skills for Living into a clear policy context, which previously had been missing.

Funding

We knew what we had to do but we needed help – and time. We applied for funding to the EOC, which funded a post for a researcher/developer, Carol Ross. I learned a bit more about the law and about how certain bodies worked. It helped the media response to know that the EOC was supporting the initiative. What we did not know when we started was where we could turn to outside for financial resources to take the initiative forward. Our first approach to the EOC resulted in an iterative correspondence between us, the EOC and officers in the local authority. What we learned then was that the EOC would not fund anything that a local authority ought to fund.

Sorting out, or at least coming to a common agreement about, what a local authority ought to provide in those days was not transparent in the area in which we were working. Both the ILEA and the EOC, in principle, wished to be positive about the initiative. Testing the Sex Discrimination Act for equal treatment, access and entitlement in an all-boys' school turned the focus on to the provision of the home economics element of the course. The outcome was to locate that responsibility with the local authority. The ILEA funded the cost of creating a specialist teaching space and pump-priming funding for a teacher, Sue Askew, to coordinate the work. The ILEA inspectorate and advisory team supported us and created the local conditions for sharing and developing ideas and good practice across the authority. The basis of school funding was also far from transparent to us then. I have a strong memory of a top-level meeting between our school governors and very senior members of the ILEA, which was in effect checking out if the LEA money would be well invested in this unusual project. No doubt in members' minds there was also a concern about setting a precedent for all the other all-boys' schools in London. Now I think about that; then I did not. I do recall overhearing a member and an officer as they left the meeting, saying to each other, 'So you think it will last?' The members' decision came back in the affirmative, and the capital programme began.

This part of the action has its ironies. It was a big hurdle and probably a necessary one, but our anti-sexist initiative was anchored in the curriculum access field and the values and attitudes field took a back seat in negotiations for funding. Home economics and childcare for boys was not comparable to the curriculum access arguments for girls into maths, science and technology. Those are about access to learning and experience which have high status and lead to futures with prospects in the world of paid work. Home economics and childcare provision for boys was our vehicle for leading a values and attitudes shift in the curriculum, for which legislation is only partly effective. It was a way to influence these, but not guaranteed to secure them. These days I see similar issues arising in values and citizenship education and look with interest to see how they find their vehicles.

What happened

What we did then could not have been done now in a single school in the current and recent context of the National Curriculum and Ofsted inspection. We devised a programme, piloted lessons, evaluated them using pupils as well as each other, researched resources and made materials. We gave up parts of our subject teaching time and our non-teaching time. We documented and circulated the evaluations. We treated it as a serious curriculum development project, giving it rigour and imagination. We assembled evidence to show that it was a sound educational idea that would benefit the pupils. These days I look at the massive investment in, say, the national literacy and numeracy strategies and compare the resources for development, evaluation and staff training with what we had then. No staff training days. No Standards Fund. We gave massively of our evenings and weekends to the project. One palpable outcome was the sense of ownership and commitment that it generated to all who worked on it, and that included contributions of varying scale.

We learned a thing or two about communication and consultation. The involvement and positive support by pupils, parents, governors, the headteacher, John Kemp, and the majority of staff was a significant feature. The involvement of pupils and parents in the planning and the evaluation of the pilot course were one of the most powerful strategies for securing success. The care with which we recorded the work, the photographs and displays helped us communicate widely about what was going on. The enthusiasm of the pupils spread around the whole school and older pupils were asking to join in. Parents wrote to our governors supporting the course and influenced resourcing decisions. They also built up the grapevine in the community so that we could be confident that a significant number of families knew about the course, its rationale and its implementation and gave it their support. We made presentations at several parent–teacher association (PTA) meetings and genuinely sought parents' views. At a time when the national media were giving a hard time to many equal opportunities initiatives, Skills for Living received a gentle press: 'Baby care – a job for the boys. An all-boys' has added a fourth R to its syllabus. Rearing babies has joined reading, writing and arithmetic' (*Daily Express*, 11 January 1983). By that time, of course, we had well worked-out ways of describing the course. In those days we did not seek out media coverage for a single school. These days we would be looking for a press office to assist a sensible spin: it seems an essential part of marketing for recruitment.

There was some interest in the educational press. In January 1983 the magazine of the Advisory Centre for Education published a four-page article about Skills for Living. Later on there were approaches from television programme makers, with whom we collaborated. One programme showed a class using role play, in which pupils improvised responses to bullying and then reflecting on the issues and alternatives. Being filmed was a special experience for the pupils and added weight to the seriousness of our subject. They and their parents were proud of it. It was a powerful tool for making anti-sexist education acceptable. We were fortunate in that the programme maker was sympathetic to the cause, which we are well aware is not always the case. The school received a number of congratulatory letters. Only one gave me cause for concern, which was one enthusing about the beauty of the boys and asking for an address of one of them!

The impact of the work

The central government agenda is clearer now and the strategy of earmarking funding for specific ends is well established. And boys are back in the frame, both in the literacy strategy and in the social exclusion agenda. Then, there was very little to refer to and we were conscious that if we had been in a mixed school or an all-girls' school we would probably have been dedicating our efforts to the girls. At the time, our concern with literacy started with modes of communication. The majority of boys, in a class or a group, seemed to depend on rather rigid, stylized and competitive ways of relating to each other. The customary tough talking and the practice of 'running down' often barred personal and intimate communication. 'Running down' we saw as a manifestation of bullying, where being good at deriding others was a sign of power and status in the group. The discourse was competitive and destructive of trust and supportiveness. We knew from first-hand experience that most boys often behaved differently in a one-to-one situation and probably with their families. We also knew that many of them were engaged in a full range of domestic responsibility, including shopping, cooking, cleaning and childcare at home. This did not stop them denying the normality of such activity in a male life. One of our strategies was to set about creating ways in the classroom to legitimize those experiences and to open up different channels of communication. We developed careful discussion strategies, which would draw out the 'expert' in the boys. So we asked, 'Do any of you know a baby of 1 year? What toys does it like to play with?' Boys were eager to give their first-hand knowledge and thoughts when asked this way. If asked, 'What toys do 1-year-old babies like to play with?', they would be reluctant to participate. We deemed this to be because the question came like so many other classroom questions, one where they expect the teacher to judge if they are right or wrong or to judge if what they said was valuable. Using the development of talking and listening as our first base, we then used the discursiveness, trust and interest generated to lead into writing and reading. As the Skills for Living teaching team was cross-curricular, the lessons which we the staff learned about managing class talk and reading and writing we could all take back to our other curriculum commitments. Our emphasis on developing group work, discussion and using role play not only broadened the communications repertoire of the boys, but also provided the environment in which awareness of sexism and the exploration of alternatives were managed educationally rather than didactically.

We also worked a lot with images and pictures. One of our main threads in deconstructing sex-role stereotyping was to challenge images of masculinity and femininity. Carol Ross was invaluable with her artistic skills, creating pictures of situations which would promote discussion and role play. We tried a media studies module in the pilot course and found it did not work: it was too abstract. Instead we incorporated media awareness throughout the course, using clips and images, references to television and advertising, to provide illustration or stimulation as appropriate. In approaching stereotyping we were cautious that in no way did we reinforce it. We approached it from the standpoint that stereotyping limits us. Men and boys do not have to be hard, unemotional, always rational, independent, mechanically and technically skilled. Women and girls do not have to be dependent, emotional, irrational, caring, soft and good at domestic skills. Nowadays for both boys and girls there is a wider range of role model (and warning model) than we had then. However, today young people are even more the target of aggressive marketing and they have wider access to representations of life and society, some of which require deconstructing far beyond gender roles.

Which brings me to sex education. Skills for Living began an approach to sexuality and relationships in the curriculum, which had previously been cornered into the plumbing facts about human bodies in the science curriculum. Sue Askew and Carol Ross developed a twofold approach: the biological, what your body does and how you feel about it; and relationships, what your feelings are regarding other people. The boys were very anxious about getting biological information, as most teachers of sex education know. Our emphasis was also on reassurance about differences being normal. Self-esteem and self-image are also related to how we each understand and deal with stereotypical images of masculinity and femininity. We were also strong on ensuring that we were talking about people not just bodies. Hence the emphasis on relationships. For the 11- and 12-year-olds we chose to focus more on friendship and intimacy rather than sexual relationships. We believed that this was in any case the basis of better future relationships, sexual and non-sexual. There was a great deal of work on what we called 'empathy', putting yourself in someone else's shoes, taking responsibility for your effect on others, dealing with feelings, especially those which are tender and promote caring. We also created live situations in which the boys took care of others. They took responsibility for shy visitors, welcoming a newcomer, providing nourishment and comfort.

Sue and Carol wrote a report for the EOC on Skills for Living which included numerous examples of lesson plans and materials. If it were still available I am sure that many teachers today would find valuable material for their personal, social and health education (PSHE) programmes. They also reported on issues that I have not covered here, which included the experiences of men and women teachers in a team-teaching situation and the gender issues raised for them. Briefly they are around what boys expected of each and how delicately the men and women teachers negotiated their roles between them in the classroom. These days partnership teaching is more of a rarity, although there are classroom assistants, special needs assistants, Section 11 language staff and other adults in our classrooms. I suspect that some of the issues about how those adults work together and the messages received by pupils about sex roles and power relationships are still current.

Lessons learned

A learning point for us in the context of managing the change, was to understand how organizations work, formally and informally. That is, how you can get them to work for you. I did not understand then how local authorities worked, how the bits joined together (if they did) and who to go to to start to get things to happen. A number of the recent Ofsted inspection reports on LEAs comment on continuing obscurity of some LEA organization and recommend LEAs publish a 'where to go and who to go to' directory for their communities. I have seen some drafts from LEAs responding to this recommendation and am trying one for my own. It will be a good test if they light the way to how to make equal opportunities more effective! On the other hand we are now into a regime of challenge funding and bidding, where the skills of bid writing, project management and the leverage of external funding against mainstream budget match are high on the agenda. All this is very different from the early 1980s.

The informal ways of making things happen was then, and still is, through networking. I was a novice at it but have come to appreciate that it is an important part of any change process. Friends and contacts are useful sounding boards for trying out ideas, learning about what is going on elsewhere, learning about how others are using the systems, for making other contacts. Street knowledge and market intelligence of this sort was limited in the Skills for Living working party. The ILEA equal opportunities (gender) team and the Schools Council sex differentiation projects were our mainstays. Where are their equivalents now?

Finally, a major item in 1999 is that of monitoring and evaluating outcomes. The raising achievement agenda focuses strongly on measurable outcomes for pupils. We are enjoined to raise the measurable success of boys' literacy levels and to reduce the number of them excluded. Our Education Development Plans will set out how we are going to achieve this and the Standards Fund is there to resource our plans.

Skills for Living would now be deemed to be short on monitoring and evaluation. We did not have a tool for measuring outcomes; neither did we have that concept so clearly as we have it now. What would we have used if we had? Would it have gone back to the home economics and childcare curriculum knowledge, understanding and skills? Where would values and attitudes and behaviours come in? We did do evaluation. What lessons 'worked' and why. Our documentation, if it still exists, is probably good material for someone's PhD. Classroom action research was our limit. Our evaluation was of the process of course development, including satisfaction surveys of pupils, parents and staff. These surveys gathered feelings and impressions. The evidence from pupils was that they enjoyed and valued the course. With hindsight it is possible to say that their discourse indicated that there were increased levels of awareness both of sexism and of positive alternatives. One of my recurring longings is to come across some of those pupils now, twenty years later, and find out whether they can attribute any impact of Skills for Living on them, their lives and relationships. One thing I do know for sure, though, is that for the staff involved in the initiative, what we tried and what we learned has a great deal to bring to the tasks of today.

References

Carter, A., Edwardson, S., Eke, R., et al. (1983) Equal Opportunities: What's In It for Boys? A Pack of Materials for Teachers. London: Schools Council and ILEA.
Ofsted/EOC (1996) The Gender Divide: Performance Differences between Boys and Girls at School. London: HMSO.

Chapter eleven

Teachers, femocrats and academics: activism in London in the 1980s

Diana Leonard

Introduction

This chapter seeks to record and celebrate the commitment to progressive and innovative education of many women and men in the 1980s, at a time when there was intense central government conservatism and reaction. It looks at three projects in which I was involved as a feminist working in higher education in London: the Women's Education Group, the Local Education Authorities' Consortium for Equal Opportunities; and, more briefly, a link between them: the Centre for Research and Education on Gender (CREG) at the Institute of Education, London. In all three, teachers in schools, feminists employed in a community agency and in local education authorities, and teachers and researchers in universities worked together in different ways at different times. Teachers and non-governmental workers took the lead in WedG; femocrats in LEAC; and academics in CREG.[1]

In each case I shall first give a brief outline of the history of the project and then look at some of the main problems encountered and what was achieved, ending with an assessment of the (continuing) difficulties and advantages of working across the schools–LEA–HE divide. It is, I think, a local history from which we can learn broader lessons.

This is written, of course, with all the provisos one must make when giving accounts of events in which one was a supposedly central character – 'the meta question of what and how we remember, both individually and collectively, and the process of turning memory into history' (Liz Jacka, quoted in Bashford 1998: 52). These are my recollections, supplemented by archival material and conversations with a few key actors. A full account would need far more work than I had time for, though I think it is important that it should be done. In particular, I would have liked to interview more of the people involved, and those who have taken up post in these localities subsequently, to help in assessing the (intended and unintended) influences we had for good or ill, and to investigate the opposition we encountered more fully. I would also have liked to analyse more closely the texts (magazines, reports, teaching programmes and materials) which remain, though this account does give a context for reading them and some sense of the excitement at the time and the material circumstances in which they were produced.

But whatever its shortcomings, this chapter fulfils a duty to remember, since feminism is in danger of forgetting its recent history, and memories of anti-sexist and gender work done in the past are certainly very short in many London boroughs. This is partly because the work we did was trashed and networks broken up, as I shall show, and partly because of high staff turnover. But it means that current initiatives to improve boys' achievement are not crediting the contribution of feminist work of the 1980s to the improvement of girls' – and boys' – academic performance (see also Arnot *et al.* 1996) and may be unwittingly undoing improvements to pedagogic and management practices.

Women's Education Group 1980–8

WedG grew out of a meeting [in 1980] of grassroots teachers, youth workers, career [guidance] workers and lecturers who felt the need to make contact with others committed to equal opportunities and positive action for girls. We wanted to create a network of teachers and other workers to exchange experiences, ideas and to provide each other with support and encouragement. Many of us felt isolated in our work situations and when we publicised our existence as a group the response was overwhelming. Over 400 London teachers have attended our meetings and we have made contact with others outside London.
(Beecham 1981: 1)

That is to say, the original group resulted from a professional and friend-ship network between school teachers, several of whom had been doing Masters degrees; the academics teaching these courses and involved with initial teacher training and in-service education; advisory teachers who had been holding workshops on gender issues in teachers' centres; LEA inspectors and advisers; local Labour Party council members; those working in the Schools Council (Weiner 1994: 18) and the EOC; and research students and visiting academics from abroad. We held regular seminars at the Institute of Education, which is part of the University of London and has a building in the centre of the city, but the field was constructed as much extramurally as academically. It drew on the passion and excitement of the women's movement, and the experience of community organizing many of us had acquired in the 1970s. We constituted the group's presence by producing a newsletter, which was circulated to everyone who put their address on a mailing list.[2] After the first year, we held a conference on Equal Opportunities across the Curriculum. This was attended by more than 700 students, teachers and interested individuals, of whom 150 were from outside the ILEA catchment area (WedG 1981).[3]

> Following the conference, some WedG members went ahead with trying to raise funding for a more established support/information network to maintain contact around Britain. Ie 'to provide a resource centre and . . . an anti-sexist educational magazine and newsletter'. Open meetings were held throughout 1982 to discuss how best to achieve these goals. We decided to apply to several funding bodies to support these projects. Finally, in January 1983 the GLC Women's Committee and the Inner London Education Authority approved joint funding.
>
> (Editorial collective GEN 1, 1983: 2)

Thus they caught the rising tide of the ILEA's Race, Sex and Class initiative (ILEA 1982, 1983; see also Frances Morrell, Chapter 5) and the new urban left's local government women's initiatives (see Boddy and Fudge 1984; Lansley *et al.* 1989; Halford 1992). The ILEA provided two rooms in its Tape and Drama Centre in Princeton Street, central London, and, together with the GLC, funding for the wages of three workers, the purchase of resources, and to run a newsletter/magazine.

The funders required a formal constitution, which recorded that: 'The name of the organisation is [the] Women's Education Group (WedG) to run a centre called the Women's Education Resource Centre (WERC) and to produce a magazine called *GEN*' (minutes 21 January 1984). The 'workers', who had obtained the funding, established and staffed the resources centre and, in collaboration with volunteers, made up the WedG collective. The collective planned weekly meetings – talks, the showing of videos, workshops, a day festival, and exhibitions at outside galleries, such as the Cockpit. A separate section of the collective planned a newsletter and the magazine *GEN*, an anti-sexist education journal. An attendance allowance was available for childcare for those who came to meetings.

Despite resistance from the ILEA, the centre, or more specifically the workers' office, soon became a service for women only. However, the fact that both its hours and collections were geared around the needs of school teachers and youth workers, and to a lesser extent further education teachers and parents, certainly reflected the populist interests of the politicians who provided funding as well as those of the employees:

The Women's Education Resource Centre is open to all women interested or involved in education. It is a library of non-sexist children's books, reference books and periodicals covering a wide range of topics, many [solely] devoted to anti-sexist, anti-racist education. These together with research on sex differentiation, examples of anti-sexist school policies, curriculum developments, conference reports and teaching materials make-up the resources housed in WERC.

We also maintain a contact network and the centre can be used by women for meetings. All women are welcome to drop in. Holborn is the nearest tube station and there is a car park off Sandland Street.

opening hours   11.00–6.00 Mon and Wed
11.00–8.00 Tues and Thurs
11.00–5.00 Fridays

(In school holidays we are open to 6.00 Mon–Thurs and to 5.00 on Fri)
(note on back page of *GEN* 3, summer 1984)

GEN soon combined with the newsletter, and ran for 13 issues (including several double issues), produced at somewhat irregular intervals, from autumn 1983 to February 1988. It was available on subscription, or free to ILEA teachers, with its print run increasing from 2000 to 6000. Funding allowed it to be quite glossy and well designed from the start.[4]

GEN tried to cover national initiatives and events as well as those in London and, from issue 5 (spring 1985), it consciously increased the amount of material it included on non-western countries. Collective members said they regretted it being initally an all-white collective, and sought new, black members and articles on racism and on issues affecting black women. But they were none the less fiercely attacked in a black women's issue edited by 'front-line activists, Women-Warriors from Five Continents and at least one ocean with a global perspective and so for the first time truly relevant to an extremely broad cross-section of people' (*GEN* 6, Oct–Dec 1985: 1).

New workers had by then been appointed, and each was encouraged to concentrate on a specific topic. These included self-defence for girls and for women teachers, which was controversial (an article on it in *GEN* 3, summer 1984, was defended in the editorial in *GEN* 4, 1984) and a black women's creativity project (for writing and the visual arts, see supplement to *GEN* 7/8, March 1986). There were also special issues on young women (*GEN* 9, 1986) and on challenging heterosexism (*GEN* 10/11, March 1987), with a final slim double issue when the end was in sight because the GLC had been abolished in 1986 and ILEA was under threat, on the centre's 'continuing . . . work with refugees' (*GEN* 12/13, February 1988). This last edition makes no mention of education.

GEN covered a very wide range of topics, and included a lot of reprints from fringe and local publications. It could, however, make uncomfortable reading. Disagreements were freely aired and there were a number of sharp personal attacks and self-righteously critical, even hectoring, articles, when legitimate anger should have been directed to issues rather than to individuals. The journal also did not hesitate to criticize its funders' actions and their publications. But from my personal point of view, what was sad about it was that the editors did not include articles on higher education: neither general discussions of what was happening to women students and staff, nor women's studies, nor specific discussions of teacher training and in-service education and training (INSET) (except in *GEN* 10/11 on heterosexism) – even though important changes with major gender implications were being put in place, and even though the ILEA was responsible for polytechnics as well as schools and further education. After issue 2, it did not even include events and courses in HE in its listings or resources section.

This was certainly partly because a number of us who had connections to HE had 'gently disentangled themselves' from WedG to work elsewhere (editorial, *GEN* 4, 1984: 2). Personally, after having been seconded to the Open University to head the team in Milton Keynes producing its first Women's Studies course (1980–3), my involvement on return to teaching in London was mainly with continuing the work within the Institute of Education which had started with WedG. Moreover, since there was considerable staff turnover in WERC from 1985 onwards, although at first I kept in close touch even when I could not manage to get to meetings, as the staff members I knew moved on, I stopped dropping in. But it was also a reaction to WedG's view that the real EO work was being done in the schools – which I did not and do not agree with – and its 'anti-elitism', maintained despite the fact that an increasing proportion of the population and especially of women were then going to university. I do, however, understand teachers' reaction to the arrogance of higher education and the use of theory as mystification, and to the teacher blaming present in much 1960s educational research.

Centre for Research and Education on Gender 1985 to the present

With the departure of WedG from the Institute of Education, getting sexism addressed in our educational research and teacher education had been left hanging. An informal group (coordinated by Janet Maw, Lynne Chisholm and myself) of women at the institute continued the work, holding seminars, producing booklets on who was interested in women's and gender issues in the institution, and coordinating teaching on gender in initial teacher training and in-service courses. But the group had no official existence or resources and we were unable to go down the route followed by the universities of Kent and Lancaster and gather individuals together around a women's studies course because of the prior existence in the institute of a Masters degree in human rights. While this had some illustrious feminist alumni, it did not fulfil a networking role and it precluded others from teaching in its area.

However, we persevered – and the story deserves to be told in full elsewhere. Here suffice it to say that although during 1982–5 we tried to establish a unit to parallel the Centre for Multicultural Education which had been established in the institute in 1979, gender was not of as much concern to the senior management of the institute as race, and we had instead slowly and laboriously to network and push proposals through committees, eventually being allowed to set up a working party to consider, and then to develop a proposal for a Centre for Research and Education on Gender, provided it was at 'no cost' to the institute.[5]

We then had to seek funding externally – unsuccessfully from the ILEA and the GLC, but we did get a small ESRC grant to build a database on current research on gender and women which enabled a one-day-a-week researcher/administrator (Margaret Littlewood) to be employed; she continued for the following two years (1987 and 1988) when we ran self-funding international summers schools. We also worked with teacher researchers from various LEAs on one-day-a-week secondments to develop equal opportunities initiatives in primary and secondary schools, and ran INSET courses in LEA centres, which gave anti-sexist teaching some credibility within our institution.[6]

Eventually, in 1990, ten years after the first WedG meetings and after some very difficult negotiations, we were able to start a women's studies and education Masters course, and in 1993 to make an appointment (Debbie Epstein) in this area: up to then all such work had been done on top of people's other commitments. We have since successfully competed for ESRC-funded research projects within CREG and become a major centre for feminist research in education in the 1990s.

The 'virtual' centre was, however, used through the 1980s as a base for topics considered too hot to handle in teachers' centres, such as for lesbian and gay issues (see *GEN* issue 10/11: 23–4) and a day course on the Harassment of Women and Girls: Sex and Power in School.[7] It was also a central, neutral ground between LEAs in which to base a network and support group, and in April 1986 CREG organized 'the first ever conference for advisory teachers, advisors and inspectors with responsibilities for equal opportunities and those working in the field of pre- and in-service training for teachers, whose work involves them with issues of gender' (*Times Educational Supplement* 7 January 1986). Moreover, resources and individuals came to us in extremis, for example when the ILEA was finally disbanded in 1990 and teachers' centres premises were 'recycled', many of the WedG resources came to rest, and continued to be used by teachers, within the Institute of Education. Hence CREG was an obvious base for a major cross-LEA initiative in the late 1980s.

London Boroughs' Consortium Equal Opportunities (Gender) Project, later the Local Education Authorities' Consortium for Equal Opportunities 1987–90

LEAC had its origins in a 1985–6 SCDC/EOC pilot project in the London Borough of Merton, where Kate Myers worked with eight schools to promote EO work (Myers 1991; see also Kate Myers' Chapter 7). One outcome was *Genderwatch*, a set of self-evaluation schedules for schools (Myers 1987, revised in 1992); and another, when she was appointed as Equal Opportunities Organizer by Ealing LEA, was a collaboration with Jenny Hall (of SCDC) to gather together a group of seven outer London LEAs committed 'to change the image of [EO] work' (Myers 1991: 5; see also Myers' Chapter 7).[8] They deliberately involved both Labour and Tory-led councils to stress that EO was not political but 'simply good educational practice'.

It was proposed that each LEA make a £4000 contribution towards the salary of a central coordinator, to be based in the Institute of Education, who would be the centre of a support network for the one or more equal opportunities advisory teachers (ATs) and the EO inspector or adviser in each LEA. Schools which volunteered to participate could use 'quality' in-service education organized centrally by the coordinator, and the LEAs would provide a supply teacher to cover for the times when the head and/or the school-based EO coordinator (a class teacher who had one afternoon a week free to organize anti-sexist work) were attending INSET or promoting EO work in their school.

The institute appointed the coordinator, Lina Patel (who sadly died in 1997), and provided an office, seminar rooms and conference venues, and the support of a member of its teaching staff. The SCDC initially provided support for the meetings of a steering/advisory group consisting of all the LEA inspectors/advisers, representatives of the ATs and from the institute, and the coordinator.[9] Some of the funds were used to pay for an evaluation by two external consultants (Julie Janes and Penny Lloyd).

The LEAC coordinator and the ATs then organized a programme of conferences and INSET, with occasional specialist input from the Institute of Education, and meetings for ATs, and for officers and advisers, to share and discuss their problems and successes in implementing EO initiatives. The LEAC produced annual reports, including accounts of the LEAs, the ways in which the coordinator and ATs were working together, and reports on the work being done in individual LEAs and schools;[10] reports from the evaluators (Lloyd and Janes 1988; Janes and Lloyd 1989) and a policy documents on the timing of in-service sessions to best suit women, as some LEAs were moving to twilight and weekend sessions with no supply cover to release teachers during school hours (French *et al.* 1990).

The participating LEAs changed in the second year and again in the third, with an increasing geographical spread out to the shire counties and an increased political and ideological range in the member authorities.[11] There was also an increasing disparity in the numbers of ATs in the LEAs, such that, in the final year, one authority had four experienced people, and another only one: a part-timer with no EO experience. Also some schools had coordinators with regular EO time allotted, while others had no time, or not even a named coordinator at all. Several EO-committed officers and ATs left and were (or were not) replaced. The first coordinator moved (autumn 1988) to a more permanent post, and her place was taken and developed by a successor (Mary Packer).

Moreover, after a year the SCDC was transformed into the National Curriculum Council, and those of its employees who were retained were moved to York, including the officer and administrator who had supported the Merton/Genderwatch project and then LEAC. The institute therefore had to take over the coordination of the advisory group (which later became a steering committee, with the chair and administrative support rotating among the LEAs); it also provided the administration for a smaller management group – as recommended by the evaluators – to provide day-to-day support for the coordinator. Finally, the institute had to take over billing and extracting money from the LEAs.

By 1990, central government cutbacks in LEA financing; sensitivities in Haringey around gender and sexuality (following the Positive Images initiative, 1986–8: see Cooper 1989, 1994); and a change of political party in local government in Ealing (in May 1990: see Myers 1991) – two key LEAs for LEAC – meant it was no longer possible to get enough authorities to commit themselves in advance.[12] So, despite the plans for 1990–1 being well developed early, and better presented, and the consortium having finally formally sorted out its aims to everyone's satisfaction, it came to an end.

Despite my efforts to get the Institute of Education to give the coordinator a two-year rolling contract, on the basis that we did have four boroughs signed up to continue in June 1990 and could certainly continue to raise more than her salary each year from INSET work, she was given only a one-year fixed term continuation, and the organized programme of gender INSET ceased. So she spent most of 1990–1 contributing to mainstream institute Postgraduate Certificate in Education (PGCE) and Curriculum Studies teaching and to Women into Management short courses, and then she moved to another job.

Problems faced by WedG

The group from the earlier WedG, who wrote the proposals and got financial support from ILEA and GLC, suffered early and continuing pangs of guilt. They were worried about 'taking money from more worthy causes' and about the journal being elitist and 'ivory tower'. This was exacerbated by a public contestation of their having got the money and taken the jobs without advertising them, which led to an open meeting held at the London women's movement centre, A Woman's Place. One special line of attack was the fact that all three were white.

The EO policies which were part of local Labour Party municipal projects in the early 1980s involved having separate and equal committees and units for each set of social inequalities. The establishment of these units was important as an indicator that social differences other than those related to social class were now considered important and were going to be tackled; but having separate race, women's and lesbian and gay units did not allow for the interaction of the various sets of power relations, nor for the fluidity whereby which status is most salient varies with context. It did, however, feed into a politics where power relations were reduced to questions of personal identity and minority status essentialism – where people had to accepted as what they identified themselves as being, and where they had a right to be heard on the basis of experiences they were assumed automatically to have had as a member of a particular group – as a black, working-class lesbian, for instance.

Certainly at the time of the establishment of WedG/WERC/GEN in 1983, feminism was changing from stressing women's differences from men, to an increased stress on differences among women; and from a politics based on group membership and individuals' involvement in oppositional practices, to identity politics. Subsequent appointments to WedG were therefore primarily (race) identity based, with feminist and school and community activist experience coming second. The politics of the group thus moved from gender-based oppositional separatism to a stress on the diversity of women and identity affirmation strategies, including the promotion of cultural and artistic endeavours: from 'sisterly' support to guarded coalitions.

But although these changes made important interventions and allowed some individual, previously silenced, voices to be heard, they prevented other political issues being debated openly. Since the management structure established for WedG was egalitarian,[13] with open consultation, it was possible for identity politics to be used to allow intolerance of others, and to cover personal antagonisms and ambitions, with little resistance. Because the editors of the journal (from issues 1 to 4) felt privileged, highly visible and responsible, they narrowed their audience down to the 'grassroots' and stressed political correctness; this well-intentioned practice allowed some authors to adopt a self-righteous and critical, rather than a generous and encouraging tone, which discouraged risk-taking theoretical discussions and writing from potential contributors who want to avoid personal attacks.

Problems faced by LEAC

LEAC also spent a considerable time defining its management structure, but it was a much larger and much more unwieldy being. The first coordinator was committed to a 'cooperative' style of working, but her appointment late in the academic year – and her taking school holidays – meant a slow start, made slower by consultation, and there was not the large inaugural conference at the start of the school year in September, with a programme planned for the term presented in a well-produced booklet, which those concerned with visibility wanted. It was also what headteachers needed, because they had to fit time out from school for INSET into their staff diaries.

Issues of management also lead to pressure from feminist ATs and the coordinator to reduce the hierarchy they saw embedded in ATs being only represented (by one of their number) on the management committee. They wanted to be involved in the discussions about LEAC as a whole and to agree the aims, policies and practices before starting. This sat ill with their line managers' views on their time commitments, and it was difficult to agree on aims anyway because of the very different commitments to EO of the LEAs involved – whatever the common commitments of the officers who had pressed to get the LEA into the consortium in the first place.[14]

The differential commitment of LEAs involved both political differences around the desirability of EO work, and a very differential provision of resources for such work – the two being, of course, interconnected. So, in the first year of LEAC, one of the Conservative authorities had virtually to hide its involvement, the inspector in charge was not able to come to the steering group and only a dozen schools were involved; while at the other extreme, Ealing, with a newly urban-left Labour controlled council, had a full-time, specially appointed EO expert, with three (later four) full-time ATs, and 40 volunteer schools.[15] But even in some Labour districts, ATs were rather unsupported. Some initially did not have even a desk and a phone; some could work with cross-departmental women's units and race units in their boroughs but others were isolated within Education; and the amount of time devoted to EO, and the knowledge of gender issues, of the officers they were working to and who represented them on the LEAC management committee, also varied considerably.

Moreover, as the political pressure on some LEAs forced them to withdraw in the third year, and the consortium was desperate for new members, it had to accept any LEA that came, so its members became geographically wider and wider spread (Kent, Bucks and Surrey). Hence the distance that teachers had to travel in to INSET, or the coordinator and ATs to travel out, was considerable. LEAC also had to accept that some of the ATs being put forward had no feminist background knowledge.

Hence what LEAs could put in and wanted to take out of the consortium became increasingly diverse. All wanted (and had to show their chief education officer and finance committee that they were getting) their money's worth out of the centre, but none was keen or able to release much time to help a neighbouring LEA. There were complaints that some ATs spent too much of their time at the institute, helping the coordinator or other ATS, or improving their own expertise (prior to moving on to another job). While all the LEAs were keen for LEAC to produce some publications, most did not want their staff to take time out from working with schools to do the writing, and many were nervous of writing anyway. Moreover ways of tackling issues which might be politically contentious had to be tailored to the sensibilities of the more conservative authorities.

It was thus difficult to know even what INSET to provide – the very *raison d'être* of the consortium. Which phase or topics to prioritize? Assuming what levels of prior knowledge and experience? How frequently to run meetings? If coordinators came in regularly, when did they have time to follow up ideas in their schools? If they did not come often, did they feel isolated and discouraged? Some authorities released most of the school-based coordinators each Thursday afternoon, and if they all came into the institute, they 'swamped' those from other LEAs. There were complaints that there was not enough information in the programme to allow schools to know which sessions to choose to attend; that sessions were not written up fully for those who could not attend; that there was not systematic needs identification; and that the evaluation of the sessions was poor – not analysed and written up systematically, or that events were evaluated, not the programme as a whole. Which is not to say that most people did not get a lot out of the sharing of ideas which took place, but rather that no one could be fully satisfied.[16] All of which was compounded by the impossibility of long-term planning. We were never certain until late summer who would be involved the following year, or if the programme would continue at all. Basic sessions had to be constantly repeated; contentious issues continually put on the back burner. And the poor conditions of employment in a low status (even if interesting and personally compelling) field encouraged many to pass through rather than commit themselves to the project.

The basic problem was of course underfunding. The consortium always needed a few more member LEAs, or a few more thousand pounds from each, to be really viable. Consequently, although the coordinator had a good office and salary, and plenty of teaching rooms were available, there was no money for secretarial support (till spring 1989) and no computer. (I got one on loan.) Each coordinator therefore had to do a lot of routine administration and preparation at the expense of other activities focused more closely on the promotion of EO in education; and needed desktop publication and marketing skills they did not necessarily have. The consortium therefore never achieved the national profile it merited, and it did not fully develop possible links with other institutions (for example, work with the TVEI, the National Curriculum Council (NCC), school governor training and the EOC, *inter alia*, were all mentioned in meetings, but not followed up).

The short-termism and shortage of funding in LEAC also undoubtedly contributed to the uncertainties about my own role. LEAC was centred at the institute because of the existence of CREG and to get 'cost-effective, guaranteed quality INSET'. But there was little income for my teaching time and no money to buy in other institute expertise, and it was not possible to recruit a second institute representative.[17] Instead of using higher education as a teaching and research base, LEAC used it as a geographical centre and as an editorial base for publications; as the evaluators noted, LEAC expected me to be the line manager for the coordinator – though I thought I had volunteered to work with her. This grew more marked when the NCC severed not only administrative but also financial links, and the institute was left in charge of chasing money and supporting the evaluators and servicing the meetings of the advisory committee and the management group.

Achievements

To evaluate properly what the two projects did, none the less, manage to achieve, unfortunately needs more than the resources available for this chapter. One of the problems of EO work in the UK (compare Australia and the USA) has been the lack of evaluation or the restricted evaluation that was undertaken (or possible) given the resources available and the fact that the projects were cut off in mid-career.

WedG certainly provided resources and support for teachers; it allowed the exchange of ideas; it gave individuals a sense of being part of a strong movement; and it helped raise the visibility of gender in education through its talks, videos, exhibitions and its journal. It could be very outspoken and produced material on race and sexuality and violence against girls and women, and critiques some of ILEA's own publications (such as the Hargreaves and Fish Reports), which ILEA itself could or did not. Most importantly it helped develop 'mothers' (as opposed to parents) and black women and lesbians (as mothers and teachers) as communities in which to campaign and as constituencies (or as we might now say 'stakeholders') to be consulted.

LEAC had far more resources, but was much more bounded, not only by the managerial problems outlined above, but also because radical approaches were organized out and liberal pluralism prevailed. This was partly a result of the policy-making processes proceeding by consensus and voluntary involvement. But it was also because (and here I refer to general discussions on the fall of the urban left which are developed in the next section) the dominant ideology of education in the 1980s suggested that articulating alternative, counterintuitive forms of knowledge and explicitly advocating the contestation and transformation of social meanings was transgressive of Education's proper role and remit. This was rarely challenged even by progressives working in LEAs.[18]

Where it was challenged and views which were commonplace in feminism were put forward – for example critiques of the family, or saying that homosexuality was acceptable and lesbianism a mode of resisting male dominance, or that sexist and racists should change their behaviour at work or be dismissed – it aroused phenomenal opposition and LEAs allowing such discussions were represented as fascist.

What we did manage to achieve was getting these institutions up and running. WedG and LEAC clearly worked 'because people willed them to' (Janes and Lloyd 1989: 1) and because committed women and some men worked hard to make EO part of their jobs as educators, and then put in many extra hours voluntarily to make change happen. That both these projects ended was not because they were not used or wanted; nor was it because of political differences among feminists (which are so often blamed for the fragmentation and decline of the women's liberation movement). Rather the answer to whatever happened to these particular equal opportunities projects was that they were attacked, indirectly or directly, by Conservative central government and ridiculed by the tabloid press as part of more general moves against left-wing local government and 'progressive' education. And they were not supported by the national Labour Party because of its distancing itself from 'loony leftism' from 1987 onwards, in its overriding concern with electability.

They none the less produced changes in individual teachers careers, in the patterns of girls' achievement, and a lasting effect on the culture or at least the rhetoric of education.[19] There is much less attention to improving the position of women and girls in education now than there was in the late 1980s; 'political' people concerned about the subordination of women no longer use the language of EO, and the renewed concern with boys' underachievement is certainly partly a backlash; but there is undoubtedly much more concern with gender in education, and a very changed situation, than there was in the late 1970s. Two-thirds of the schools surveyed for the EOC in 1995 had instituted EO policies since 1988 (Arnot et al. 1996), Ofsted inspections look at EO issues; and government agencies have gender working parties. EO now has become quite managerialist – transformed but embedded in institutional language. But schools I visit hold on to (at least) two discourses on gender – the managerial *and* the socially transformative one, and continue to work creatively even with the National Curriculum.

The attack on left-wing local government

The history of Tory moves against left-wing local authorities in the 1980s when the government saw their potential for undermining Thatcherite reforms, and its use of projects around anti-racism and lesbian and gay equality, and to a lesser extent around gender, to castigate the socialist municipal project, has been told elsewhere (see Gyford *et al.* 1989; Leach 1989; Mather 1989). Here I shall just note how the government and media represented the improved funding for community projects addressing women's issues in the 1980s as reprehensibly luxurious provision, and the establishment of local council women's units to develop and implement women-friendly policies as a 'Kremlin-like' abuse of power. Supporters of such initiatives were thereby put on the defensive – which certainly did not encourage innovative thinking and indeed made many severely censor themselves. Labour councillors concerned with electability, and local government employees/femocrats concerned with accountability, held back. Added to this, central government intervened legally to diminish local government powers and imposed major budgetary cuts. Thus many previously local responsibilities were moved to newly established central bodies; the new urban left largely disappeared with the remodelling of local government during 1987–93.

As regards education, left-wing councils' activities were tied to and dismissed as further examples of the problems with 'progressive' teaching. Encouraging girls to take science was acceptable, but discussion of sexist violence and sexual abuse in schools was another example of misguided modern teaching, while 'promoting' 'positive images' of homosexuality was beyond the pale. Some chief education officers, including Haringey's, were sent bullying letters by the DES to remind them of the limits of LEA discretion, which raised education service anxieties (Cooper 1994: 119). There were media panics and arguments for the 'banning' of certain books (notably *Jenny Lives with Eric and Martin*: Bösche 1983) and, conversely, attacks on the supposed banning of 'classics' like Barbie dolls (see Sue Adler's Chapter 13). Central government and the media presented education which confirmed the gender status quo as 'not political', while purposive efforts to change relations between men and women (in radical directions) (by local government) were constructed as inappropriate or 'brainwashing' of children (who were presented as empty vessels accepting everything that teachers said).

That is to say, in the attack on the left's local government project, and on left-wing LEAs, it was not only what was being said that was objected to, but also (indeed mainly) the purposive nature of the intervention which was rubbished as being 'ideological'. All of which ended with councils defensive about policies, and willing to allow only incremental change and nothing that could be seen as radical reform. To this were added cuts in central funding, which affected LEA equal opportunities work because the numbers of advisers and advisory teachers fell drastically. (Many were Scale 2 teachers on short-term contracts who could be returned to the classroom.) Anti-sexist and anti-racist initiatives were additionally disrupted by the brutally swift introduction of major educational change in a series of Education Acts, including the Education Reform Act 1988 (which among other things introduced a National Curriculum and national standard attainment testing). This required LEAs to concentrate their resources on implementing the new (supposedly gender-neutral, 'non-political' and non-ideological) requirements of the new legislation. Finally the ILEA itself was broken up in 1990, in part at least because of the socialist majority among its elected members and its record of commitment to equality of opportunity (see Frances Morrell, Chapter 5).

For WedG and LEAC this meant that, whether or not we would have been able to resist ideological pressures and ridicule, all the structures we were using were continually being remodelled, cut back or disbanded, with less and less money available and more and more conservative, centralized control – and consequent insecurity of jobs and resources and time wasted chasing funds. It became impossible to make sensible forward plans; finally each institution broke down, confirming earlier radical feminist concerns about becoming dependent on the state.

Operating across the educational sector

To a certain extent we managed to counter some of these restrictions by operating creatively across the school–voluntary sector–LEA–HE divide, as well as across our political differences. Of course each sector had its own specific immediate priorities, whether these were raising awareness in youth clubs, or changing the pedagogy and curriculum content to improve the experience of girls in classrooms, or developing actions in minority communities, or finding practicable and not too contentious projects with swift and visible results in local politics, or trying to research and theorize ongoing changes in academe. Not surprisingly, we did not manage to overcome all the hierarchical relationships and tensions which exist between the groups: between primary and secondary and tertiary education, and between teachers and LEA inspectors and HMI; nor the requirement for femocrats to appear confident and authoritative (not to exposing their uncertainties) and to engage in a certain amount of competitive power dressing!

But ILEA and LEAC did manage to use the extra-governmental WedG and CREG to construct meanings and strategies outside the boundaries placed on local government itself, as noted above: WedG as a source of critiques of ILEA in-house documents and a constructor of specific campaigning constituencies; CREG as a location for discussing dangerous topics. (It is no accident that the photos of individuals in the *GEN* issue on homosexuality are all of workers in lesbian and gay units, in WedG and in the Institute of Education. School teachers and education inspectors could not and cannot afford such visibility.) *GEN* published articles on topics which LEAC could never have tackled, while LEAC got an assurance of academic credibility from the university and its INSET could include 'the latest feminist thinking' without committing LEAs to such ideas.

The institute itself unquestionably benefited for several years from the contacts made through WedG and especially through LEAC. It helped us to develop ideas and also to recruit to our MA in women's studies and education, which began in 1990–1, and to PhD studies. I sorely miss having this extensive contact with schools and LEAs, especially since it has not been possible for many HE teachers and researchers to contribute to initial teacher education since the mid-1980s because we do not have recent school classroom teaching experience (see Wormald 1985; Leonard 1989).

Conversely, work done in HE and particularly in women's studies (often by teachers in their dissertations) was an important intellectual base for EO work and politics, and the powerful innovative and oppositional discourses developed by HE have been missing from grassroots school and adult education work on women and gender of late. One of the enduring legacies of the Thatcher and Major years was the splitting of feminist networks and the informal cross-sectoral, as well as the institutional support, that they built.

CREG has survived and even strengthened, however, and far from being a small esoteric activity remote from the real world of schools and LEAs, it can now provide the continuity and memories lost in the fluctuations and short-termism of LEAs: archives, libraries – and a location for DfEE researchers to phone and ask 'Do you know anything about what ILEA did in the 1980s?' (January 1999).

Which returns me to the issue of memory with which I started. Feminists active in the 1980s grew up with just a caricature of what was achieved by the first wave of western feminism. Today, although we have to some extent recovered our long-term history, we have lost the recent past; this matters for the future, for without this knowledge we are condemned to repetition, to rediscovering and saying again from the start what was said in 1900 and 1968 and 1988, rather than updating and moving on. When I talk about the events described in this chapter, people say they had no idea how hard we had to struggle then. They thought being a feminist was just difficult nowadays because of shortage of money and time and interpersonal and inter-institutional competitiveness.

Certainly the modes of resistance have changed. But the important point is that the things women achieved in the 1970s and 1980s have either now been made to seem inevitable: in the course of things, or misattributed (such as girls' achievement as due to the National Curriculum), or if they did not survive the trashing, completely forgotten. Our successes then were the result of a strong social movement, and this movement was at the time, and has also subsequently been covered in mud. Women are still unwilling to affiliate fully with it and use the classic phrase 'I'm not a feminist, but . . .'. We therefore owe it to each other to reflect upon, and to declare repeatedly and in detail, what feminism has actually managed to achieve, and how.

Notes

1 'Femocrats' is an Australian neologism which was produced to refer to official or state feminists, namely women who are employed within state bureaucratic positions to work on advancing the position of women in the wider society through the development of equal opportunity and anti-discrimination strategies of change (Yeatman 1990: 65). They are distinguished from women career public servants in that a femocrat is 'a feminist in an official capacity, that is, someone for whom their feminism is considered a qualification for which they are selected to do the job they are performing' (Eisenstein 1987, quoted in Yeatman 1990: 65). This would therefore include those employed as women's officers in political parties and trade unions, women's units in councils, law centres, Oxfam and economic development agencies, but not those working in voluntary agencies if they do not have full-time, professional or career-level positions (Yeatman 1990: 66). See also Halford (1988, 1992) and Watson (1992).

2 The newsletters were first produced by Dale Spender and Renate Klein; an early survey of those on the mailing list was analysed by Maureen Dyer (then on a study visit from Australia).

3 The conference planning group consisted of Geraldine Locise (ILEA Careers), Sheridan Welsh (ILEA FE), Gaby Weiner (Schools Council), Cathy Moorhouse (ILEA Learning Materials Service), Yvonne Beecham (ILEA teacher), Diana Leonard (Institute of Education), Ruth Van Dyke (London School of Economics), Kate Myers (ILEA teacher), Liz Wynton (CASSOE) and Margherita Rendel (Institute of Education). The conference was sponsored by the ILEA, the Schools Council and the Institute of Education, London.

4 This was unlike the Manchester produced Women and Education, which started with a Women and Education conference in 1974 and was typewritten and roneoed. The CASSOE newsletter was produced more regularly than GEN and was very thorough in its coverage of events, but it also consisted of simple roneoed sheets.

5 'No cost' meant no staffing, though we have always had an office/resources centre and have been able informally to use other fixed resources, even if we have had to cover variable costs.

6 For example, Valerie Wakerdine collaborated with the ILEA inspector, Carol Adams, to run short, research-based courses (Adams and Walkerdine 1986) and Janet Holland and I developed ten session 'twilight' INSET courses in Ealing (1987 and 1988), Waltham Forest (1988) and Merton (1989).

7 The day course was held in May 1985 with funding from ILEA; the ILEA adviser, Hilary Bourdillon, and two teachers, Carol Jones and Margaret Sandra, organized it with me, and the Isledon Teachers' Centre did the administration.

8 'Key people involved in the SCDC/EOC's equal opportunities project were now working in Merton, Hounslow and Ealing and were prepared to develop strategies that were tested in the project. The SCDC agreed to trawl other London boroughs to see if any of them would be interested in joining an Equal Opportunities Consortium. Enfield, Haringey, Redbridge and Waltham Forest became part of the group' (Myers 1991: 5).

9 Participants in 1987–8:
Ealing Hilary Claire, Kate Myers, Sybil Naidu, Kathleen Pepper, Diane Reay
Enfield Alan Mutter, Kath Terrell
Haringey Bob Crossman, Jean French, Sheila Miles
Hounslow Sue Holmes, Mary Linnington, Bunny Veglio Merton, Iain Porteus, Sue Taylor
Redbridge Simon Black, Maureen Dainty
Waltham Forest Christine Archer, Roy Blackwell, Joan McKenna
SCDC Gillian Baderman, John Blakemore, Jenny Hall
Institute of Education Diana Leonard, Lina Patel

10 The first annual report, for 1987–8, was well produced, with photos and cartoons, largely thanks to one of the Ealing advisory teachers, Hilary Claire, and the LEAC secretary, Helen Lai, but it did not appear till 1989. Later ones were more modest.

11 In 1988–9: Ealing, Enfield, Haringey, Hounslow and Merton continued; Barnet, Hillingdon and Kent joined; Redbridge and Waltham Forest left.
Participants (Ealing, Haringey and Hounslow unchanged):
Barnet Jay Myers, Anne Bulloch, Jenny Collinson
Enfield Jane Hobday replaced Kath Terrell during the year
Hillingdon Dick Ewan
Kent Maggie Gregory, Barbara Brown, Gillian Watson
Merton Rosalyn George, Mary Linnington
Institute of Education Mary Packer replaced Lina Patel
Evaluators Julie Janes, Penny Lloyd
NCC Gillian Baderman
HMI Margaret Caistor
In 1989–90: Ealing, Enfield, Haringey, Hounslow, Kent, Merton and Hillingdon (partial membership) continued; Bucks and Surrey joined; Barnet left.
Participants (Merton, Institute of Education and HMI representatives unchanged):
Buckinghamshire Pam Davies, Christine Alger
Ealing Hilary Soper replaced Diane Reay
Enfield Alan Mutter, Jane Hobday
Haringey Jean French, Lesley Hagan
Hillingdon (associate) Paul Saundercock
Hounslow Iain Porteus, Sue Harrison
Kent Annie Carruthers replaced Barbara Brown
Surrey Penny Gaunt, Geoff Taylor, Pauline Williams
TVEI Judith Black/ Heather Flint

12 To contributing not only to the central, institute costs but also to guarantee the salary of an EO advisory teacher, plus a portion of the time of an adviser/inspector, plus the costs of supply teachers, plus travel expenses.

13 Initially through the debates over the problem of men, which continued through many sets of minutes, and then through lengthy discussions of the collective's policies and working methods (see editorial, *GEN* 2, spring 1984).

14 Here again identity politics and race – expressed in a stated concern about whether *Genderwatch!* was a proper basis for the consortium's work – was also a cover for other things, including a personal antagonism between an AT and its author.

15 In 1987–8 the numbers of schools participating were: Ealing 40, Enfield 8, Haringey 15, Hounslow 23, Merton 41 (including second wave, after the earlier SCDC project), Redbridge 12, Waltham Forest 20.

16 The annual report for 1989–90 records the following topics (with the numbers attending). Day conferences: Education Reform Act (59); men's (9) and women's (33) groups; equal opportunities issues (54); International Women's Day (36); further education, cross-curriculum (47); sexuality (31). Half-day sessions: pastoral care, assessment and testing (54); working with others (32); sexuality (26); school-based awareness-raising skills – two sessions (30 + 19); evaluation and monitoring (34); planning for 1990–1 (10); working with men and boys (22); harassment (25); science (none given) geography in the humanities (16).

INSET series for ATs series of visits from members of the EOC, HMI and DfE.

17 The institute took 10 per cent of the total income in the first year and 20 per cent in the second and third, to cover the costs of office, rooms, on-costs for the coordinator and supposedly £3000 for my time.

18 See the very interesting and detailed work of Davina Cooper (1994) on the effects on lesbian and gay activism of engagement in local government in Haringey in the same period.

19 A friend started her first teaching job in Ealing in May 1990 on the day the council leadership changed hands. She described to me how at the first staff meeting the head 'quite matter of factly' offered day release to anyone who wanted to go to a lesbian teachers' group, and how all the parents were invited to the launch of the new school policy on EO. The teachers were outraged on hearing that the equality units staff had been locked out of their offices by the Tory councillors. These experiences were formative and stayed with her through her entire teaching career.

References

Adams, C. and Walkerdine, V. (1986) *Investigating Gender in the Primary School: Activity-Based Inset Materials for Primary Teachers*. London: ILEA.

Arnot, M., David, M. and Weiner, G. (1996) *Educational Reforms and Gender Equality in Schools*, Research Discussion Series no. 17. Manchester: Equal Opportunities Commission.

Bashford, A. (1998) The return of the repressed: feminism in the quad, *Australian Feminist Studies*, 13(27): 47–53.

Beecham, Y. (1981) The herstory of WedG, in WedG (ed.) *Equal Opportunities across the Curriculum*. Institute of Education, London: Schools Council.

Boddy, M. and Fudge, C. (eds) (1984) *Local Socialism?* London: Macmillan.

Bösche, S. (1983) *Jenny Lives with Eric and Martin*. London: Gay Men's Press.

Cooper, D. (1989) Positive images in Haringey: a struggle for identity, in C. Jones and P. Mahony (eds) *Learning our Lines: Sexuality and Social Control in Education*. London: Women's Press.

Cooper, D. (1994) *Sexing the City: Lesbian and Gay Politics within the Activist State*. London: Rivers Oram.

Eisenstein, H. (1987) Women, the State and your complexion: towards an analysis of femocracy. Paper presented at SAANZ Annual conference, 14 July, University of New South Wales.

French, J., Harrison, S. and Packer, M. (1990) *Equal Opportunities and INSET*. London: Local Education Authorities Equal Opportunities Consortium.

Gyford, J., Leach, S. and Game, C. (1989) *The Changing Politics of Local Government*. London: Unwin Hyman.

Halford, S. (1988) Women's initiatives in local government . . . where do they come from and where are they going?, *Policy and Politics*, 16: 251–9.

Halford, S. (1992) Feminist change in a patriarchal organization: the experience of women's initiatives in local government and implications for feminist perspectives on state institutions, in M. Savage and A. Witz (eds) *Gender and Bureaucracy*. Oxford: Basil Blackwell and *The Sociological Review*.

ILEA (1982) *Sex Differences in Educational Achievement*. London: ILEA.

ILEA (1983) *Race, Sex and Class 1: Achievement in Schools*. London: ILEA.

Janes, J. and Lloyd, P. (1989) Local Authorities' Equal Opportunities Consortium evaluation: Final Report. Mimeo, Julie Janes and Penny Lloyd.

Lansley, S., Goss, S. and Wolmar, C. (1989) *Councils in Conflict: The Rise and Fall of the Municipal Left*. London: Macmillan.

Leach, S. (1989) Strengthening local democracy, in J. Stewart and G. Stoker (eds) *The Future of Local Democracy*. London: Macmillan.

Leonard, D. (1989) Gender and initial teaching training, in H. De Lyon & F.W. Migniuolo (eds) *Women Teachers: Issues and Experiences*. Milton Keynes: Open University Press.

Leonard, D. and Littlewood, M. (1988) The database of the Centre for Research and Education on Gender, Institute of Education, in R. Pankhurst and S. Graves (eds) *Information for Women's Studies in Universities and Polytechnics: Proceedings of a Seminar held at Sheffield Polytechnic*, 24 June 1987. Sheffield: Sheffield City Polytechnic.

Lloyd, P. and Janes, J. (1988) London Boroughs' Consortium Equal Opportunities Development Project evaluation: Final Report July 1988. Mimeo, London.

Mather, G. (1989) Thatcherism and local government, in J. Stewart and G. Stoker (eds) *The Future of Local Government*. London: Macmillan.

Myers, K. (1987) *Genderwatch! Self-Assessment Schedules for Use in Schools*. London: Schools Curriculum Development Council.

Myers, K. (1991) Perspective 3: Equal Opportunities?, in E.C. Team (ed.) *Curriculum and Learning*. Milton Keynes: The Open University. Reprinted in this book, in Chapter 7.

Myers, K. (1992) *Genderwatch! After the Education Reform Act*. Cambridge: Cambridge University Press.

Watson, S. (1992) Femocratic feminisms, in M. Savage and A. Witz (eds) *Gender and Bureaucracy*. Oxford: Basil Blackwell and *The Sociological Review*.

WedG (ed.) (1981) *Equal Opportunities across the Curriculum.* Institute of Education, London: Schools Council.

Weiner, G. (1994) *Feminisms in Education: An Introduction.* Buckingham: Open University Press.

Wormald, E. (1985) Teacher training and gender blindness: review symposium on teacher education and teaching quality, *British Journal of Sociology of Education,* 6(1): 112–16.

Yeatman, A. (1990) *Bureaucrats, Technocrats, Femocrats: Essays on the Contemporary Australian State.* Sydney: Allen & Unwin.

Part IV

Whatever happened to . . .

Chapter twelve

A Black perspective

Marina Foster

Retrospect – one

Invisibility

In 1983, the EOC consulted nationally on the issue of gender equality. Women's organizations, educational institutions and individuals were invited to submit evidence, data, research, recommendations and ideas. On the surface, this was an open-ended process, limited only by time constraints. Most people who were involved in or concerned with women's issues were aware of the process through their networks and publications or because they had been approached by the EOC.

It was fortuitous therefore that I became aware of this process while talking to an officer of the EOC about an allied educational issue. I discovered that the educational institution in which I was employed was in the process of responding. On the insistence of the officer in question I proceeded to write an individual response, having been excluded from the institutional response. The resulting paper was later edited and included in a collection entitled *Just a Bunch of Girls* (Weiner 1985).

This account speaks volumes about the legitimacy or otherwise afforded to the black voice historically within institutions involved in matters of equality. It is thus very appropriate to pose the question: whatever happened to equal opportunities? Given the levels of awareness, the positions of ethnic minority respondents of the time and the opportunities 'given' to them to make their voice heard on the question of their perceptions about equality of opportunity, accounts such as this, of which there are a few, strengthens in retrospect the disquiet and dissatisfaction expressed by many at the time.

My paper was entitled 'Sexism, racism, a curriculum for all?' It raised many issues, threw down many challenges and confronted practices that were not enabling in the pursuit of gender equality. When reviewing progress in the intervening period, can we say with any assurance that the gauntlet thrown down then as it were, has been picked up in any convincing way? The rhetorical title was well chosen by the editor of the day. Challenging the 'isms' of race and sex has proved to be not merely a matter of curriculum change. These introductory paragraphs highlight the inherent contradictions and the fickleness of the power relations which claim to campaign for equality while denying to some a voice. They demonstrate in one small way that the institutional mechanisms which reproduce inequalities are as robust as the social contexts in which they are rooted.

Retrospect – two

The data or lack of them

Reviewing the progress of ethnic minority pupils since the late 1970s is problematic, since there was no centralized and systematic ethnic or gender monitoring during this period. At least no national data exist which are accessible to researchers or to the public from which clear trends can be extrapolated. Nevertheless the research that exists on the achievement of ethnic minority pupils indicates that there are significant differences in the educational achievement of different ethnic groups after eleven years of compulsory schooling which are likely to have serious effects on their educational and employment chances (Gillborn and Gipps 1996). The differences are further compounded by economic and social class membership and by gender. These findings have to be viewed against a background of nationwide improvement in the performance in the school population as a whole.

African Caribbean pupils have not shared equally in the improving rates of educational achievement. In many LEAs, their average achievements are significantly lower than that of other ethnic groups. Of particular concern, is the achievement of African Caribbean boys and concern about them has gained national interest. As a consequence, the plight of girls from the same ethnic group within the education system has been rendered almost invisible.

Gillborn and Gipps (1996) draw attention to the difficulty of using multilevel modeling, a statistical method which tries to separate out all the different factors that might possibly affect pupils' performance, a difficulty also encountered by another team, Arnot *et al.* (1996) in their research into *Educational Reforms and Gender Equality in Schools*. Arnot *et al.*'s publication, a major national study published by the EOC, contributes to the debate on equal opportunities outcomes. Other major sources from which we are able to infer outcomes and consequences are the 1991 Census and Labour Force Surveys. One has to be aware of course that the labour force at any one time does not consist exclusively nor wholly of those who have gone through the whole compulsory education system.

The research carried out by Arnot *et al.* (1996) on gender reforms in education received responses from 38 per cent of primary school and 26 per cent of secondary schools and from 44 per cent of the 112 LEAs contacted. This research attempted to establish a national profile on equal opportunities. However, it took place during a period in education when other major national agendas were having to be addressed by schools, like the National Curriculum, standardized assessment tests, the publication of examination results, performance standards, the setting up of the School Curriculum and Assessment Authority and Ofsted. Confronted with the plethora of educational reform, it is not surprising that the researchers found that schools did not keep systematic records, making it difficult for many to respond to their survey. This takes us back to the issues of gender equality in education, issues of central and national concern and legitimacy in the pursuit of improving schooling. We need to address the question 'Improving schooling for whom?' What were the competing power relations of the time which characterized the context in which Arnot *et al.* were conducting their research?

One major factor which did emerge from their study was 'the continuing dominance of white male cultures in school and LEA hierarchies' (Arnot *et al.* 1996: 133). In the secondary schools surveyed, more than 75 per cent of headteachers were male (Arnot *et al.* 1996: 133). In primary schools, over 50 per cent of headteachers were male. In the case of chairs of governing bodies of both primary and secondary schools and City Technology Colleges, 75 per cent were male. From their case studies a picture emerged of tight financial control on staff costs for equal opportunities initiatives and the lack of black staff. In some institutions, all the academic staff were white, all or most of the cleaners were black, the majority of the catering staff (who were employed on outside contract) were black, although catering managers were sometimes white (Arnot *et al.* 1996: 135).

Outcomes

Both the Gillborn and Gipps (1996) and the Arnot *et al.* (1996) studies see the introduction of the GCSE as a positive reform which has benefited girls' educational performance. The incorporation of new subjects into the curriculum and the opening up of science subjects to all pupils delivered benefits for girls. Another public benefit derived from the introduction of GCSE is that it opened up data collection to public scrutiny and made it possible to compare standards of achievement nationally by gender and (when authorities collected appropriate information) locally by ethnicity. Unfortunately analysing examination results by ethnicity was not used universally, hence the necessity of now using sampling techniques in order to scrutinize outcomes and examine trends.

Since the publication of the Swann Report *Education for All*, the final report of the Committee of Inquiry into the Education of Children from Ethnic Minority Groups (1985), discourse about the differences in the educational achievements and school experiences of ethnic minority pupils has run concurrently with debates about equal opportunities.

Some may argue that many of the reforms introduced in education since 1989 were directed to improving pupil performance, achievement and standards, while other reforms were intended to bring about wider changes in the organization and management or administration of schools. We are currently entering yet another wave of reforms to achieve similar objectives. With reference to the 1990s, though, one would be quite justified in asking who benefited.

According to Arnot *et al.* (1996), the consequences of the reforms are a mixed bag, some of which were positive. Among the gains from the reforms since the mid-1980s are:

- Female students have improved their performance markedly in relation to exam entry for GCSE, mathematics and particularly in science.
- The ten-year period (1985/6–1995/6) has seen a considerable rise in the achievement of compulsory and post-compulsory qualifications, particularly by young women.
- At A level, pronounced gender differences in subject choices and entry qualifications emerge with female students failing to close the traditional gap, favouring male students in mathematics and science.
- Female students have improved their performance in almost all other subjects, often when they are in the minority.

(Arnot *et al.* 1996: 42–6)

It is important to look at these gains within the context of this chapter, and to note that while they are gains to be celebrated, this report gives no insights into the outcomes of this period for ethnic minority pupils in general nor for black girls in particular. So once again one has to go back to a point made right at the beginning about the power relations that prevail and the legitimacy within the pursuit of equality of opportunity of the relative position of black girls.

The pathologizing of black families

Brah and Minhas (1985) put forward an analysis which still holds good and is powerfully demonstrated in what has just been discussed. They argue that to understand the position of Asian girls (and I would argue by extension, all ethnic minority pupils in our education system), one has to

identify why and in what ways race, gender and class inequalities are produced and reproduced. Consider also how the discourse on race and gender
is constructed within the field of research into equal opportunities.

We have entered into an era in which, as Horace Lashley in a lecture on
Race Inequality in Research and Society (1996) pointed out, pathological
models underpin and pervade most research on black people. At this same
conference Avtar Brah again drew attention to the way in which research
constructs discourse and the manner in which this discourse is positioned
within a culture of racism.

Account has to be taken, therefore, in reviewing research that sets out
to explore the differential outcomes of compulsory schooling for different
groups, of the underlying features which implicitly informs such research,
mainly the pathologizing of black families, rather than the structural
inequalities which characterizes the settings within which schooling takes
place and the ideological constructs of ethnic minority communities which
are prevalent in the social settings in which schools are located. To match
these differential outcomes are the underlying differential constructs. In
the case of Asian families, it is the generalized notion of generational and
cultural conflict as if these families are fused and fixed in time. In the
case of black families, it is the general view of deviance and poor deficit
family structures. In the case of African Caribbean boys, studies characterizing descriptors of their behaviour and attitudes to schooling have
become almost common currency in the discourse around schooling, achievement and behaviour, uncommon in the description of any other group in
society.

In another study, *Education for Some*, a report on the educational and
vocational experiences of 15- to 18-year-old members of minority groups
by Eggleston *et al.* (1986), the reviewers comment on the low profile the
researchers maintained during the duration of the study:

> It demonstrates beyond a peradventure that racist attitudes and prac-
> tices are currently doing much to hinder the education of African-
> Caribbean pupils. It also shows that many of those pupils are coming
> to see academic qualifications as an essential defence against the dis-
> crimination they fear they will meet in the labour market.
>
> (*Times Educational Supplement* 25 October 1985)

That was in 1985. Twelve years later Unison's Equal Opportunities and
Policy Research Department wrote: 'Black women have been invisible to
researchers and policy makers when examining patterns of employment.
The effect of this invisibility is that women of different ethnic origins
who experience multiple discrimination are ignored in social policy and
bargaining' (Unison (EO/PRD) (1997)). Here I would add as well patterns
in education.

Table 12.1   GCSE exam results 1988, 1992, 1994

	Five A–C passes	*Five A–G passes*
1988	30%	NA
1992	38.3%	82.2%
1994	43.3%	86.5%

Girls' and boys' achievement within ethnic minority groups

In their review of the Youth Cohort Study (YCS) of 1985 carried out by Drew and Gray in 1990, Gillborn and Gipps (1996: 16) identify social class and gender as important variables in considering GCSE achievement. They tabulate the average exam scores by social class, ethnic origin and gender for the 1985 cohort. African Caribbean and Asian males from professional and intermediate economic backgrounds outperform girls in their social class, whereas white girls from these economic backgrounds scored approximately two average points higher than boys.

The situation is different for pupils from manual backgrounds. Asian males have the highest average exam scores, next are white males lower by two average points and last of all black girls lower by five average exam points relative to the highest scores.

Gillborn and Gipps draw attention to the fact that the 1985 YCS is a nationally representative sample and they go on to state: 'Social class is strongly associated with achievement regardless of gender and ethnic background: whatever the pupils gender or ethnic origin, those from the higher social class backgrounds do better on average' (Gillborn and Gipps 1996: 16–17).

By the 1990s, however, the situation has changed for pupils in state maintained schools as demonstrated in the 1990 Youth Cohort Study. This indicated that girls improved at a faster rate than boys, but YCS does not focus on ethnicity (Gillborn and Gipps 1996: 18). To establish trends and the links between the component factors, Gillborn and Gipps analysed data from several metropolitan LEAs in the most exhaustive research document of recent times.

They demonstrated that overall levels of GCSE achievements have improved in recent years. The proportion of pupils gaining five or more higher grade (A–C) passes in state schools has risen (Table 12.1). Their data, taken from DfEE returns and the Youth Cohort sample study, show these improvements over time (Gillborn and Gipps 1996: 18).

As discussed above, no centralized data existed for analysing the relative improvement of different ethnic groups, so Gillborn and Gipps (1996) examined information provided by LEAs. Since 1990, DES and then the DfE have expected all LEA-maintained and grant-maintained schools to collect information on the ethnic background of their pupils. Local authorities, however, are under no obligation to analyse examination results by ethnicity. This presents a dilemma because until there is a centralization of ethnic monitoring, any research analysis is likely to be partial at best, haphazard at the very worst. Similarly, the analysis of gender patterns over time and the impact of educational reforms and equal opportunity initiatives also have their limitations. Lack of data which constitutes a wide enough representative sample, the lack of availability of any such data in some areas, the inconsistencies in the nature of the data, which has made comparability difficult, have all placed constraints on research analysis.

Despite these limitations, there are some important findings from existing research. While Gillborn and Gipps point out the dangers of basing conclusions solely on data from one LEA in which examination scores were analysed by ethnicity and gender, two notable trends are indicated. One is that, 'on average, black pupils have not shared equally in the increasing rates of educational achievement and . . . Caribbean boys scored 3 points lower on average' (Gillborn and Gipps 1996: 29).

When gender is taken into account, the pattern changes significantly. Girls achieve more highly on average than boys and this holds true for African, Caribbean and white girls, although white girls still outperform the rest. Thus, it is an oversimplification to speak of 'black underachievement'. It is also misleading to imply that all black girls are performing well. Gillborn and Gipps (1996: 29) highlight the fact that despite differences in methods and definitions 'the relatively lower exam achievements of Caribbean pupils, especially boys, is a common feature in most of the academic and LEA research publications'.

The next set of data is taken from the archives of a shire county just outside London, abolished in March 1998 by local government reform. These data show similar trends to those discussed by Gillborn and Gipps and although average examination points scored are higher, and the percentage of pupils in all ethnic groups attaining five A–Cs GCSE passes are greater than those in metropolitan authorities, what they continue to demonstrate is the differential achievement of boys and girls and of different ethnic groups (Table 12.2).

Table 12.2 shows white girls outperforming all groups except Chinese girls and while black African and Caribbean girls perform better than boys, there are significant differences between the performance of black girls from various ethnic communities relative to each other and to white girls.

Table 12.3 takes another snapshot of data from this authority and looks at variations over two consecutive years.

Comparison of Table 12.3 with data taken from DfE sources and Gillborn and Gipps (1996) data above shows that the performance of pupils in this LEA is well above national averages for most ethnic groups except boys and girls from African Caribbean and Pakistani communities.

Table 12.2   Average examination points scored: Year 11 GCSE candidates by ethnic group and gender 1995

	Boys	Girls
White	38.3	42.2
Black African	31.0	36.4
Black Caribbean	24.2	30.0
Black Other	39.2	32.4
African Caribbean	28.3	32.0
Indian	37.5	38.8
Pakistani	27.0	32.4
Bangladeshi	31.6	31.0
Chinese	37.8	52.3
Other	41.9	42.6
Not known	30.6	38.1
All candidates	36.6	40.9

Source: Berkshire County Council (1996)

Table 12.3   Changes in performance of ethnic groups by gender and ethnicity 1993/4–1994/5

Proportion of pupils gaining five or more GCSE Grade A–C by ethnicity and gender

	1993/4 (%)	1994/5 (%)
Female		
White	56.1	57
African Caribbean	17.4	31
Indian	42.2	52
Pakistani/Bangladeshi	26.7	37
Chinese/Other	59.3	67
Male		
White	46.0	50
African Caribbean	7.4	25
Indian	42.2	50
Pakistani/Bangladeshi	25.9	27.6
Chinese/Other	56.4	57.1

Source: Berkshire County Council (1996)

Equal opportunities is OK, OK?

Equal opportunities as a principle has become widely accepted as an object-ive to regulate relations at work or in school. That is until any one chal-lenges inequality or tries to invoke the principle as many have learnt to their cost. Whether this is at a common-sense level of a primary age pupil appealing for 'fairness', or at the judicial level of women police officers or female army and naval officers having to go right up to the level of the Appeal Court in order *to prove* that they have been unfairly treated or discriminated against. It would appear then that equality of opportunity is an entitlement but not a right in the sight of the law. While this dichotomy continues between rights and entitlement, the principle is not secured for anyone.

One can range backwards or forwards over time into accounts of schooling and training and find a set of responses when the issue of equality is raised of 'We treat all children the same in this school', or variations on this theme. Then how do we account for the differentiation in the achievement of pupils within the same institutions by race and by gender which is now beginning to emerge from Key Stage 1 through to GCSE.

Exclusions

The ultimate sanction against school pupils who do not conform to a pattern of behaviours and expectations is exclusion (Wright 1986: 166). The exclusion of pupils from school is a central issue which has emerged in research about equal opportunities and in the period under review, one that has 'given cause for concern' among ethnic minority communities since the late 1970s. In her literature review for the CRE, Osler (1997b) lists the first official figures released by the DfE in a press notice in 1992.

In 1995–6 a total 11,084 pupils were permanently excluded from schools of which 1600 were girls (DfEE press notice, November 1997). The total number represents 0.13 per cent of the total school population of 8 million who will not have the opportunity of completing their schooling in their original school. A significant factor that emerged is the race and gender specific nature of these data. African Caribbean boys are four to six times more likely to be excluded than white pupils and this fact has most rightly sparked off national concern. Osler (1997a: 26–38) in her review of racial justice and policy frameworks over the same period draws attention to the increasing number of national surveys into rising levels of exclusion. She puts forward the view that educational research agendas are now beginning to recognize links between factors such as race, ethnicity, gender, sexuality and social background. Similarly, policy development also increasingly recognizes the links and their impact on equalizing opportunities (Osler 1997a: 27). Gillborn and Gipps state: 'black pupils experience school in ways that were significantly more conflictual and less positive than their peers regardless of ability and gender: the patterns were true for black pupils of both sexes and included some whom teachers described as having excellent academic potential' (Gillborn and Gipps 1996: 55).

One of their major findings is important in any evaluative review of research into equal opportunities in the past two decades, mainly that 'qualitative approaches reveal a considerable gulf between the daily reality experienced by many black pupils and the stated goals of equal opportunities' (Gillborn and Gipps 1996: 55).

The plight of African Caribbean boys has sparked off a national crisis. There is much less discourse about the exclusion of African Caribbean girls. There are two significant factors that have been overlooked. First, in any one academic year, 1600 girls may not be statistically significant against the total school population but as a percentage of the total number of African Caribbean pupils represented in the school population this is hugely significant to African Caribbean communities. Second, black girls inhabit the same domains of learning and discrimination that undermine, stereotype and exclude black boys. More often than not they are in the very classrooms in which their male counterparts face harassment, discrimination and exclusion, and they are not immune to these processes. To state the same point differently, this is as much an institutional issue as it is a gender issue, not two separate issues. But some girls survive and succeed, because while it may be a matter of honour for African Caribbean boys to defend their self-esteem and themselves from constant public humiliation and harassment, girls have other strategies for survival.

Prospect

At the start of the new millennium, what prospects are there for black boys and girls in future British society? However simple or complex one considers the relationship to be between racism, sexism and social class inequalities, what vision do we have of schools and society in the future? The UK stands in the millstream of social reconstruction in Europe, all be it reluctantly so. While the discourse in the UK replicates itself and searches for the causes of disadvantage within a reconstruction of itself in its imperial and historical past, one needs to ask what does it require on behalf of its ethnic minority settlers to be accepted unreservedly as British? What hoops or hurdles do our children need to jump through to be the beneficiaries of policies aimed at delivering better standards of academic achievement and equality of opportunity?

Who is and who is not British in the discourse of post-colonial Britain and in the differential inclusion and exclusion of social change?

What have we as women learnt from our efforts in this passing century from our struggle for universal suffrage, comprehensive education and against anti-nuclear pollution? What vision are we able to construct from struggles against fascism in Europe, apartheid and ethnic cleansing, against sexism and discrimination on the grounds of social class that can help to carry us forward into the era of the new technologies into the new millennium?

How can we work to create a more just society, where the entitlements, of those who endure discrimination as a constant feature in their daily lives, are delivered as rights rather than daily struggles?

References

Arnot, M., David, M. and Weiner, G. (1996) *Educational Reforms and Gender Equality in Schools*, Research Discussion Series no. 17. Manchester: Equal Opportunities Commission.

Berkshire County Council (1986) *Equal Opportunities Code of Practice*. Reading: Berkshire Education Department, County Archives.

Berkshire County Council (1990) *Monitoring and Evaluation*. Reading: Berkshire Education Department, County Archives.

Berkshire County Council (1996) *Statistical Information Bulletins* (February). Reading: Berkshire Education Department, County Archives.

Brah, A. and Minhas, R. (1985) Structural racism or cultural difference: schooling for Asian girls, in G. Weiner (ed.) *Just a Bunch of Girls*. Milton Keynes: Open University Press.

Committee of Inquiry into the Education of Children from Ethnic Minority Groups (1985) *Education for AU* (Swann Report). London: HMSO.

DfEE (1997) Permanent exclusions from schools in 1995/96. Press notice, London: DfEE.

DfEE (1998) Exclusion in schools in England (1996–97). Press notice, London: DfEE.

Drew, D. and Gray, J. (1990) The fifth year examination of Black young people in England and Wales, *Educational Research*, 32(3): 107–17.

Eggleston, J., Dunn, D., Anjali, M. and Wright, C. (1986) *Education for Some: Educational and Vocational Experiences of 15–18 Year Old Young People of Minority Ethnic Groups*. Stoke-on-Trent: Trentham Books.

Gillborn, D. (1990) *Race, Ethnicity and Education*. London: Unwin Hyman.

Gillborn, D. and Gipps, C. (1996) *Recent Research on the Achievement of Ethnic Minority Pupils Office for Standards in Education*. Institute of Education, London: HMSO.

Howson, J. (1998) Bulk of cast-outs are boys, *Times Educational Supplement*, 18 December.

Lashley, H. (1996) Race inequality in research and society. Unpublished lecture, 18 October, University of Reading.

Osler, A. (1997a) *The Education and Careers of Black Teachers: Changing Identities, Changing Lives*. Buckingham: Open University Press.

Osler, A. (1997b) *Exclusion from School and Racial Equality*. London: Commission for Racial Equality.

Owen, D. (1996) *Towards 2001: Ethnic Minorities and the Census*. Warwick: National Equality Minority Data Archive, Centre for Research in Ethnic Relations (CLER), University of Warwick.

Unison (EO/PRD) (1997) *Black Women's Employment and Pay*. London: Unison Equal Opportunities and Policy and Research Dept.

Unison email http://wwwunison.org.uk/

Weiner, G. (ed.) (1985) *Just a Bunch of Girls: Feminist Approaches to Schooling.* Milton Keynes: Open University Press.

Wright, C. (1986) School processes – an ethnographic study, in J. Eggleston, D. Dunn, M. Anjali and C. Wright (eds) *Education for Some: Educational and Vocational Experiences of 15–18 Year Old Young People of Minority Ethnic Groups.* Stoke-on-Trent: Trentham Books.

Chapter thirteen

When Ms Muffet fought back: a view of work on children's books since the 1970s

Sue Adler

Introduction

Once upon a time, educators looked at the learning experiences of girls and young women from a wide spectrum of feminist and reformist perspectives. Before (and after) that time boys' achievements and underachievements dominated the conferences, journals and minds of many who taught and thought about learning. But for a period within second wave feminism, there was action and academic research, and lively debate, on women, girls and gender equality in education. This included examinations of children's books and other learning resources, and of reading as a gendered activity.

Since the mid-1970s, there has been a shift from exposing sexism in children's books using mainly quantitative research to more complex investigations of subtle as well as overt messages. There has been a change from looking at sexist stereotyping as confirmed or confronted by individual books to examination of the complex relationships between children as readers and texts. This chapter is a personal and partial account of that time of opposition to prevalent sexist stereotypes (as exemplified by prim, frightened Little Miss Muffet) and of explorations into gender and children's reading. Throughout, I have drawn on my experiences as a librarian in the ILEA and have included a section on that authority.

Books

Analyses

Early researchers had to make obvious the biases that were so prevalent that they were 'normal'; they had to prove and make visible the existence of

sexism and racism in children's books. Their research findings raised consciousness – not only of teachers and librarians (who sometimes worked
with children to pass on critical sensitivity) but also of parents, authors,
illustrators and publishers. Their methods for detecting and revealing sexism
were based on enumerating male and female characters and male and female
activities. The results – whether of picture books (Children's Rights Workshop 1976), science books (Walford 1980a, 1980b, 1981), maths books
(Northam 1982), dictionaries (Schram 1979) or reading schemes (Lobban
1974, 1977; Burgess 1981; Stones 1981) – were basically the same: girls
and women were under- and misrepresented.

There was widespread agreement that children's early reading experiences
in school had an impact on their future lives and that even the simplest
texts reflect and form cultural values and were more than mere tools for
teaching reading.

> Current knowledge suggests that children's books and particularly their
> first readers do influence children's attitudes. They do this by present-
> ing models . . . for the children to identify with and emulate [and] present
> an official view of the real world and 'proper' attitudes.
>
> (Lobban 1974: 57)

In the UK much of the work on sexism in children's books was done from
the mid-1970s to the early 1980s. (In the USA, this happened a decade
earlier.) British publications include Bob Dixon's (1977) *Catching Them
Young*, with volume 1 on sex, race and class in children's fiction, and
one chapter devoted to sexism. Dixon criticized reading schemes and early
readers for their stereotypes of sex roles. He provided a critique of Alcott's
Little Women, Spyri's *Heidi*, Noel Streatfield's novels and two genres of
so-called 'girls' fiction' – school stories and horse stories – and he also
described some non-sexist books of the time, noting that jobs and games
must lose their labels of being for one sex rather than the other. On
socialization and the fiction read by girls he asked 'Why, if it's "natural"
for girls to be like that, is so much time and effort spent on forcing
them? What's natural doesn't have to be taught, surely?' (Dixon 1977: 32).
Dixon also commented briefly on male aggression, sexual harassment and
oppression.

Glenys Lobban analysed six of the reading schemes (*Janet and John,
Happy Venture Readers, Ladybird Key Words Reading Scheme, Nippers,
Breakthrough to Literacy* and *Ready to Read*) used in most British schools.
She found that sex roles were rigidly divided with males outnumbering
females by two to one and that male characters were shown in a far wider
range of activities. Almost all female roles were domestic. All the schemes
she analysed showed males as 'superior in everything except the ability to
cook, dust, clean and smell flowers' (Lobban 1977: 105). She argued the
need for both qualitative and quantitive change and noted 'certainly girls

learn to read in spite of the male bias in readers but at what price to their self attitudes?' (Lobban 1974: 60).

In her widely read and influential *Pour Out the Cocoa, Janet*, Rosemary Stones (1983) provided an analysis of sexism in children's reading and gave guidance on selection. The pamphet was a joint venture between the Schools Council and EOC and is still useful. (It is out of print but should be in academic libraries.) In 1981, Stones reviewed some of the 'radically revised reading schemes' that appeared in the 1970s. Criticisms of schemes on the grounds that they were sexist and ignored the realities of Britain's multicultural society had led some publishers to respond with new titles but Stones was sceptical about the value of 'tinkering' with dreary material. Her comment on the *Ladybird Key Words Reading Scheme* was:

> While it is good to see a publisher respond to feedback from teachers and take on board new perspectives on sex role representation and presentation of the multi-ethnic society that is Britain today, the revisions of the Ladybird reading scheme nevertheless begs the more fundamental question – are Jane and Peter's doings worth revising at all, considering the intrinsic dullness of the scheme?
>
> (Stones 1981: 4)

Stones also challenged the idea that there had been any great improvement in gender terms. Analysing Longman's *Breakthrough to Literacy* she found that only 2 of the originally 69 titles stood out as sensitively told, amusing, non-sexist stories. Of the new titles published in 1980, 16 showed equal distribution of male and female central characters and a number of read-able non-sexist stories but 'no serious thinking about sex role presentation'. There was, she pointed out, some effort to represent multi-ethnic society with 4 of the 16 new titles featuring black central characters and 3 showing black characters in illustrations.

Celia Burgess (1981) analysed all 80 books of *Breakthrough to Literacy* page by page. Her video, *Breakthrough to Sexism*, was produced while she worked at the ILEA Centre for Urban Educational Studies (CUES) and a written version appeared in *Teaching London Kids*. Using the criteria set out in the EOC booklet *Ending Sex Stereotyping in Schools* (Hannon 1981) she exposed the sexism permeating the scheme, tabulating her findings in three sections: Housework/Servicing of Family; Child Care; Games and Sport. 'The results staggered and upset me' (Burgess 1981: 6). 'Is this what we have to offer our girls? Be a mother, be a housewife, and if you don't like it, get dreaming or go mad' (Burgess 1980: 8). Burgess observed that the scheme's illustrations, rather than its text, were sexist.

Publishers

Sometimes sexism and racism can be seen as parallel issues. While this approach can be useful for assessing books and the two oppressions were considered together in some criteria/guidelines, in publishing there are major differences between the two 'isms'. Women dominate children's mainstream publishing – white women, that is. They are also the majority of authors and illustrators of children's books. Few black women and men work in mainstream children's publishing, very few at senior editorial level. While the presence of (white) women should not be taken to imply that anti-sexism and feminism are considerations in all publishing houses, the absence of black people has implications for anti-racist perceptions. Significant small publishing houses in the UK were established in the 1980s to produce books for black children, teachers and parents as well as a growing white 'multi culturally aware' market. Of these, Mantra Publications and Tamarind Ltd. continue to exist and to produce high quality books for today's children. Feminist presses produced an increasing amount for a booming adult market, and while the Women's Press and Virago Press contributed to teenagers' reading with their 'LiveWire' and 'Upstarts' lists, only Sheba Feminist Publications (now defunct) produced books for young children.

There *were* contributions from some mainstream publishers. While ana-lyses had focused on problems with books, the lists pointed out positive aspects. Penguin Books was one of the publishers that commissioned lists drawing attention to equality issues in their existing titles, recognized that multiculturalism and non-sexism were topical and worthy of their marketing enterprises. Rosemary Stones, who reviewed for *Children's Book Bulletin* (which she co-edited) and *Spare Rib*, was, again, a pioneer. She was the author of the first editions in the late 1970s of *A Multi-Ethnic Book List for Children of all Ages* and *Ms Muffet Fights Back: A Penguin Non-Sexist Booklist*. (I later compiled four new editions of both lists.) A few of the books were written to challenge racism or sexism; many more could be used to initiate discussion with children, or simply to present a range of images and stories. The lists' introductions and annotations were, to me, the most important parts as this was where ideologies and interpretations were revealed, however gently. The free lists were made available to schools and, through book shops, the general public, thus taking the issues to a wide audience.

Making books

Concerned by the blatant sexism in reading schemes, some teachers' strat-egy was to draw children's attention to bias and, as the 1980s were a time when some funding was available, were occasionally able to produce their own resources. For example, Mara Chrystie made an alphabet book with her class of 4–7-year-olds in a school in East London. The result, entitled *Anna to Zoulla*, was a part of a project looking at 'how girls and boys, women and men, are portrayed in books and magazines'. Mara and her pupils decided that they 'wanted to make a book which showed girls and boys who were adventurous, friendly and co-operative' (Chrystie 1983, quoted on the back cover of *Anna to Zoulla*). The book, now out of print but available in some schools and libraries, has stood the test of time. It still interests and delights children and can be used to stimulate discussion.

Not all materials published outside of the profession were that successful. Sheffield Women and Education Group was given a grant of £4500 from the EOC to produce a series of non-sexist, non-racist books for early readers. The resulting books were worthy but bland, stilted text and their clumsy layout prevented them being serious alternatives to mainstream publications, demonstrating that good stories need more than good intentions.

Promoting books: the story of Letterbox Library, a children's book club

In 1982, two London women turned their frustration at the lack of availability of good resources for their daughters to positive action, and decided that they would start a book club supplying non-sexist and multicultural books. They spent 18 months on research, forming an advisory group of teachers, parents and librarians, and getting advice from the GLC together with some funding – a loan of £9000 from the Greater London Enterprise Board and a grant of £1000. Letterbox Library's first catalogue was sent to *Spare Rib* subscribers, members of The Women's Press Bookclub and to a network of equal opportunities teachers. It immediately attracted 400 members.

'You'll never find enough books to meet your criteria', Letterbox Library was told by one mainstream publisher at its onset. Not so. With imports as well as British publications, selection is quite difficult to make from a wealth of 'positive' titles. Today, Letterbox Library employs eleven part-time workers in its London office, has ten regional contacts and an annual turnover of £400,000. It remains a cooperative. The survival of this organization is perhaps surprising. It is not that the books sold by Letterbox Library are no longer needed but that the commercial and educational climate has changed. 'Letterbox Library is a business driven by values. That's out of sync with the times', said Gillian Harris, one of the founders, in conversation with me (November 1998). However, the organization has continually adapted. For example, in 1998 it compiled an imaginative list to support the National Literacy Strategy. Its quarterly catalogue includes a newsletter, and all equality and green issues are covered. Letterbox Library gives schools and individuals all over the UK (and beyond) the opportunity to purchase 'alternative' and unusual books as well as the 'best' – in terms of equality criteria – of mainstream publications.

Letterbox Library has also held conferences, including one on feminism and children's books. (Very little has been written on feminism and children's books: see Goodall 1982; Paul 1987; Adler 1993a). This conference attracted around 100 women and included an inspiring keynote speech by Valerie Walkerdine. But some of the black women present asserted that the conference portrayed a white, middle-class feminism and did not acknowledge black perspectives. The day was a reminder of the divisions between black and white women and dangers of creating hierarchies of oppressions. Needless to say, the debate on feminism in children's books did not go much further, nor did the racial conflict get resolved in any productive way.

Readers

Although research into children's literature frequently assumes a male reader, using the false generic 'he', where studies have considered the sex of the child, they have consistently found this to be the main determinant in reading choice and skills. Whitehead *et al.* (1977) in a survey of children's reading reported that at all ages girls read more than boys, and that there were fewer non-book readers among the girls than among the boys. In 1964, gender issues were part of Helen Huus's research into post-war reading issues in the USA (quoted in Huck *et al.* 1989). She found that there were few differences of choice before the age of 9, but from 10 to 13 there are 'notable differences' with girls reading more that boys; boys having a wider interest range and reading a wider variety of materials; girls showing an early interest in adult romantic fiction; boys preferring adventure stories. Both sexes enjoyed mysteries. Boys seldom read 'girls' books' but girls were shown to be happy with 'boys' books'. Huck *et al.* (1989) note that all Huus's statements, apart from the first, still hold true. They comment that the differences in interest start far earlier, even in the kindergarten, with young girls preferring fiction and boys information texts.

Davey's (1980) report into the reading patterns of girls who later became engineering technicians showed that those girls read far more non-fiction than their female peers. They also selected fiction genres more usually read by boys. One would expect 'rebel' readers to later become 'rebel' workers – reading differently because of their attitudes and expectations. Books themselves did not inspire the girls as, at that time, there were very few showing role models for girls in science and engineering.

Recent research confirms that girls get off to a better start than boys in reading and this continues into Key Stages 2 and 3 (Arnot *et al.* 1998). Barrs and Pidgeon (1993) in their introduction to *Reading the Difference* note the difference in achievement, with girls' superior ability widely acknowledged. They comment on the paradox characterizing this: despite the apparent obstacles faced by girls in primary classrooms, including sexist stereotypes in the books, they do better than boys. As well as differences in reading skills, ability and choice, girls and boys also interpret texts differently (Barrs and Pidgeon 1993). Sarland (1991), looking at out-of-school reading, provided insights into how boys and girls take different things from the same text. B. Davies (1989) documented two pre-school children's responses to Munsch's (1982) story *The Paper Bag Princess*. Anika saw the story as being about relationships and love; Sebastian read it as an adventure. Neither children appreciated the anti-sexist message. 'Impeccable anti-sexist tales – to our adult eyes – can be created to challenge sex-stereotypes. It's not so easy to convince the children! But what is clear is that those two children have experienced the same book, enjoyed it – and interpreted it quite differently' (Adler 1993b: 85).

However, while much research on literacy skills focused and continues to focus on fiction, data may be distorted. Elaine Millard (1997) found that boys and their teachers may not regard their out-of-school reading (newspapers, comics, magazines) as literacy. 'Boys, therefore, experience a dissonance between the literacy they practised skilfully at home and that demanded from them by teachers' (Millard 1997: 13). Boys' abilities here are largely ignored and issues of girls' non-fictional reading and ICT skills, too, are not prevalent topics in the literacy debates. Some of today's books require high-level skills in interpreting visual images, with some text which may be in speech bubbles or unconventional typography. If boys' skills here are more developed than girls', should we not be working with girls so that they do not fall behind in what will become *the* important literacy?

An LEA's contribution

The ILEA, as one of the UK's biggest LEAs, was a significant leader in many activities, including its equal opportunities initiatives, and its influence has been noted elsewhere in this book (see Frances Morrell's Chapter 5). Work on gender and resources was done throughout the ILEA and in particular by the English Centre and the History and Social Science Teachers Centre. As well as producing materials specifically on gender – such as *The English Curriculum: Gender* (1985) and *Herstudies: A Resources List* (Adams and Hargreave 1983) respectively – equality issues were deeply embedded in all their work. In the provision and promotion of quality learning resources, the ILEA's librarians and media resources officers had real impact in schools, teachers' centres and colleges, and their status as educational professionals helped emphasize the importance of learning resources.

The Centre for Urban Educational Studies had a key role in multicultural education in the 1970s and 1980s. It provided courses for teachers on issues of 'race', culture and language. In the 1970s, the CUES library promoted children's books for the multicultural society and provided a forum and stimulus for debate on issues of ethnic, religious and cultural diversity in children's books. Commenting on the CUES Library Exhibition in 1975

Resources for Education in a Multicultural Society, Gillian Klein, who set up and developed the library, noted that visiting teachers realized that the resources they had in school were not appropriate or relevant to their pupils and, responding to their needs, she organized INSET and offered guidance on publications. 'Looking back, the mid-1970s mark a stage at which there was debate and remarkably little complacency and when no backlash seemed yet to have begun' (Klein 1997: 62). But the backlash was not far off.

The year 1980 was something of a watershed. Following the debates, the ILEA/CUES published selection criteria *Assessing Children's Books for a Multi-ethnic Society* (Jones and Klein 1980). Tabloid press and journals reacted swiftly. The ILEA faced claims in the *Daily Telegraph* and some tabloids of banning and censoring children's reading. In a series of articles entitled 'Race, sex and class in children's books' in the *New Statesman* (November–December 1980), antagonists asserted that issues of social conscience (the forerunner of political correctness?) would 'cripple' (*sic*) creativity in children's literature (for example Walsh 1980). Social relevance and responsibility was argued by protagonists (Leeson 1980).

CUES was the ILEA's centre for multi-ethnic education and its library was, therefore, the ILEA's multicultural resource centre. Throughout Britain, multicultural resources centres were set up by LEAs in the 1970s, initially to support English as a Second Language teaching and later broadening their scope to provide, and advise on, resources reflecting society and its diversity of religions, languages and customs. Increasing, diversities were viewed as strengths and negative attitudes were countered. There were around 20 such centres in the 1980s; in 1999 the London Borough of Barnet had one of the few to remain.

In the early 1980s, when I was the librarian at CUES, we continued to seek out multicultural and anti-racist material to use in classrooms. Gender issues featured on CUES courses and expanded the library collection to include anti-sexist material. While we sought out books showing women working outside the home in paid employment and men doing domestic chores in the home and looking after children, we also looked for books that overtly challenged the status quo. Conferences included sessions on book assessment and criteria. Discussions were lively and there was a wry standing joke that if we applied all the criteria on quality and equality we would agree on four and a half books. More seriously, the limitations of rigidly applying checklists were acknowledged.

I left CUES to take up the post of ILEA's Equal Opportunities (Gender) librarian in 1984 and for the next six years was a femocrat (see Diana Leonard's Chapter 11). The post was assisted by a full-time library assistant, Allison Pollard, who was transferred from another post just before my appointment; fortunately we found it easy to work together and to support each other. Our brief was to establish and develop a specialist collection covering the entire curriculum with resources in all formats from mainstream and minority publishers, LEAs and other organizations, and to work with other individuals and groups on equality matters. The collection was housed in the ILEA's Centre for Learning Resources in south London. It was used by teachers, librarians and media resources officers and attracted national, and occasionally international, enquiries and visitors. Gender equality was not afforded the status of dedicated resource centres, but I do not know of any other LEA who invested in both staff and materials to promote gender equality in this way.

A sad tale of two ILEA resource lists

Not long after I started the Equal Opportunities (Gender) job, Carol Adams, then inspector for equal opportunities, arranged for me and Annie Cornbleet, a teacher seconded to the Learning Resources Branch, to collaborate on a resources guide. I knew Annie from her work in the Developing Anti-Sexist Innovations (DASI) project. Our publication *Anti-Sexist Resources Guide* (Adler and Cornbleet 1984) listed groups and organizations and learning materials. We were aware of how quickly resource guides go out of date and the *Guide* was produced ring-bound with space for notes. It was favourably reviewed in feminist journals; predictably it raised the hackles of *Daily Telegraph* journalist Peter Simple. It sold well but after just two years, it was withdrawn by the ILEA, with unsold copies pulped and copies in the Education Library discarded. Reasons given were that the Guide was inadequate, particularly as the information had become out of date. It was also stated that the Guide's appropriateness had to be considered in the light of the ILEA's guidelines on selection and use of learning resources in the teaching of controversial issues in schools.

The Relationships and Sexuality Project was set up in 1984 to 'work on resources and to enable teachers to develop strategies and approaches for use in courses dealing with sex-role stereotyping and personal relationships, including sexual orientation' (ILEA 1984a: 1). The project's list *Positive Images: A Resources Guide for Teaching about Homosexuality, Including Lesbian and Gay Literature for Use in the Library and Classroom* (ILEA 1986) was the result of two years' work by teachers and librarians. Just before its launch, it was withdrawn and reprinted. A lot of the fuss centred around Bösche's (1983) *Jenny Lives with Eric and Martin*, a Danish book about a gay father and his child. (The book was included in the *Anti-Sexist Resources Guide*, too.) This little book attracted attention in the press and television following an article in the *Times Educational Supplement* (23 May 1986) and objections were raised by a few ILEA primary schools. The book became famous overnight, the 'offensive' picture of Jenny breakfasting with the men in bed being splashed across the tabloids. The annotation in the April 1986 version of *Positive Images* reads: 'At the time of printing this book is under review by the ILEA Inspectorate as to its suitability for use in schools'. In the final version (September 1986) *Jenny* disappeared and a note (stapled to the contents page) drew attention to the Education Act 1986 which required heads, teachers and librarians to 'take such steps as are reasonably practicable to secure that where sex education is given to any registered pupils at the school it is given in such a manner as to encourage those pupils to have due regard to moral considerations and the value of family life.'

Members of the ILEA Librarians Anti-sexist Group and individual librarians defended *Jenny* because, despite reservations about its production and quality of the translation, we welcomed the unique opportunity it gave to discuss homosexuality and homophobia with children. Advice from the education officer and chief inspector was that the book was not considered suitable for general use in schools. A year later, with Section 28 of the Local Government Act 1987, schools were forbidden from intentionally promoting homosexuality and teaching about 'pretended family relationship'.

What were sound equality practices in 1984 became 'controversial issues'. The ILEA was fighting for its survival with Margaret Thatcher determined to see off the ILEA, despite support from parents in London. The Labour Party was seeking re-election and was cautious of perceived alignment with 'radical' left-wing educationalists. The ILEA's reaction to attack from outside was to become defensive, including in one of the areas that attracted hostile media attention – children's books. The backlash faced by feminists and anti-racists came, therefore, from the right wing, as expected. It also came (unexpectedly) from some former friends, colleagues and comrades.

Changes – changes?

The work of Davies (1981), Stones and others has had most impact on non-fiction publications. Some of today's quality information books include girls and boys from many ethnic groups, and very occasionally meet other equality criteria. Count the girls, count the boys in the illustrations of new books from major publishers such as Dorling Kindersley, Wayland, Franklin Watts, and you will see more or less equal numbers and more or less equal roles. It is not unusual to see that the child at the computer is a black girl, while the child shown making a fruit salad is a white boy. The result is a kind of androgynous globalization in images – which is welcome but not enough. Work on sexism in children's books was, I believe, limited by an underlying assumption that sexism is perpetuated almost by accident; that it is not spawned by misogyny and homophobia; that it could be overcome by redressing balance. Walkerdine (1984), in considering the analyses of liberalism and liberal feminism, points out that while those researchers and critics raise the issue of content, they tend to minimize the importance of the text itself as productive of meanings. Thus they assume that by widening

and 'correcting' texts, children will be shown other views and that these resulting views will change stereotyped thinking. This approach, argues Walkerdine
(1984), assumes a rationalist reader and does not deal with the complexity
of the problem.

While critical of aspects of quantitative research, I do think that there
is still a place for it and that teachers should 'audit' resources, remaining
aware that the struggle for equality – even in surface representation – is not
over. One example, *Biography and Children* (Marcella *et al.* 1993), considers 204 biographies, lists a selection of representative monographs and
draws attention to particularly significant series. Of the 166 titles listed,
just one-third have female subjects yet the compilers complained that it
sometimes seems that too great an effort is made to include women as some
are not well known. One-third seems to be 'too much' attention to women
– recalling Dale Spender's observation that teachers giving girls around
35 per cent of their time seemed, to them and boy pupils, to be over-
compensating (Spender 1982: 56–7). Another example shows how sex bias
exists even in the representation of animals – three books in a series for
very young children identify twelve animals as male, only two (one a cow)
as female (Hess 1998).

Fiction still shows a huge divide between 'girls' books' and 'boys' books'.
Leisure reading (discussion of which is outside the scope of this chapter)
is almost totally divided on gender lines, the BBC's series *Girl Talk* being
one example of magazines and books exclusively for girls, and with an
old-fashioned view of femininity. Titles by Roald Dahl and, for young
children, *Thomas the Tank Engine*, remain best-sellers, their sexism rarely
challenged or even noticed. In education, current concerns on literacy focus
almost entirely on boys. I work in a schools' library service and observe
teachers' efforts to encourage boys into fictional reading. Our library fiction
stock now consciously caters for reluctant young male readers, trying to
entice them with stories featuring sport and computers, and seeking out
books with cool covers. The pedagogy of the National Literacy Strategy,
which makes reading seem active and breaks activities into short periods of
time, may well suit boys. I do not, however, see anything in the courses and
lists promoting boys' fictional reading that confronts the resistance to read
anything that could be construed as 'girls' books'. Rather, the spin on
reading is that it can be a 'laddish' activity.

Reading covers a myriad of activities requiring a range of skills. I believe
that failure to give equal access to all literacies (see Kress 1996) will continue to deny some girls and boys, some of the time, the opportunities to
which they are entitled in an educational system espousing relevance to the
needs of the new millennium. In this chapter, I have tried to tell part of the
'story' but there is no ending – happy or otherwise. There is, however, an
acknowledgement of the work of the past, and a hope that there are women
and men who will continue to explore the subject in the future.

References

Adams, C. and Hargreave, D. (1983) *Herstudies: A Resources List for Teachers of History and Social Sciences*. London: Schools Council.

Adler, S. (1993a) Aprons and attitudes: a consideration of feminism in children's books, in H. Claire, J. Maybin and J. Swann (eds) *Equality Matters: Case Studies from the Primary School*. Clevedon: Multilingual Matters.

Adler, S. (1993b) Great adventures and everyday events, in M. Barrs and S. Pidgeon (eds) *Reading the Difference*. London: Centre for Language in Primary Education.

Adler, S. and Cornbleet, A. (1984) *Antisexist Resources Guide*. London: ILEA.

Alloway, N. and Gilbert, P. (1997) Boys and literacy: lessons from Australia, *Gender and Education*, 9(1): 49–58.

Arnot, M., Gray, J., James, M., Ruddock, J. with Duveen, D. (1998) *Recent Research on Gender and Educational Performance*, Ofsted Reviews of Research. London: The Stationery Office.

Barrs, M. and Pidgeon, S. (eds) (1993) *Reading the Difference: Gender and Reading in the Primary School*. London: Centre for Language in Primary Education.

Bösche, S. (1983) *Jenny Lives with Eric and Martin*. London: Gay Men's Press.

Burgess, C. (1981) Breakthrough to sexism, *Teaching London Kids*, 17: 6–8.

Children's Rights Workshop (1976) *Sexism in Children's Books: Facts, Figures and Guidelines*. London: Writers & Readers.

Chrystie, M. (1983) *Anna to Zoulla: An A.B.C. Colouring Book By Infants at a Hackney School*. London: Centerprise.

Davies, B. (1989) *Frogs and Snails and Feminist Tales: Preschool Children and Gender*. London: Allen & Unwin.

Davies, J. (ed.) (1981) *Sex Stereotyping in School and Children's Books*. London: Publishers' Association.

Davey, A. (1980) *Ballet Shoes or Building Sites: The Role of Books, Reading and Libraries in the Encouragement of Girls to Take Up Careers in Engineering*. Birmingham: Birmingham Library School Co-operative.

Dixon, B. (1977) *Catching Them Young 1: Sex, Race and Class in Children's Fiction*. London: Pluto.

The English Centre (ILEA) (1985) *The English Curriculum: Gender*. London: ILEA.

Goodall, P. (1982) Children's books: a feminist view, *Schooling and Culture*, 10: 47–59.

Hannon, V. (1981) *Ending Sex Stereotyping in Schools*. Manchester: Equal Opportunities Commission.

Hess, P. (1998) *Farmyard Animals; Polar Animals; Rainforest Animals* (Animal World series). Berkshire: Zero to Ten and London: De Agostini.

Huck, C.S., Hepler, S. and Hickman, J. (1989) *Children's Literature in the Elementary School*, 5th edn. New York: Harcourt Brace.

ILEA (1984) Relationships and Sexuality Project (leaflet, autumn). London: ILEA.

ILEA (1986) *Positive Images: A Resources Guide for Teaching about Homosexuality, Including Lesbian and Gay Literature for Use in the Library and Classroom*. London: ILEA.

Jones, C. and Klein, G. (1980) *Assessing Children's Books for a Multi-ethnic Society: Practical Guidelines for Primary and Secondary Schools*. London: ILEA.

Klein, G. (1985) *Reading into Racism: Bias in Children's Literature and Learning Materials.* London: Routledge and Kegan Paul.

Klein, G. (1997) The development of multicultural and antiracist books for use in schools 1973–1993. DPhil thesis, University of Central England in Birmingham.

Kress, G. (1996) Literacies or literacies, *Basic Skills,* Part one, spring: 14–18; Part two, June/July: 8–11.

Leeson, R. (1980) Race, sex and class in children's books: what were we arguing about?, *New Statesman,* 5 December: 28–9.

Lobban, G. (1974) Presentation of sex-roles in British Reading Schemes, *Forum,* 16(2): 57–60.

Lobban, G. (1977) Sexist bias in reading schemes: paper presented to Children's Book Circle, 18/3/1974, in M. Hoyle (ed.) *The Politics of Literacy.* London: Writers and Readers.

Marcella, R., Hannabuss, S., Farmer, J. and Allard, M. (1993) *Biography and Children: A Study of Biography for Children and Childhood in Biography.* London: Library Association.

Millard, E. (1997) *Differently Literate: Boys, Girls and the Schooling of Literacy.* London: Falmer.

Mosley, F. (1985) *Everybody Counts! Looking for Bias and Insensitivity in Primary Mathematics Materials.* London: ILEA.

Munsch, R.N. (1982) *The Paper Bag Princess.* Leamington Spa: Scholastic.

Northam, J. (1982) Girls and boys in primary school maths books, *Education 3–13,* 10(1): 11–14.

Paul, L. (1987) Enigma variation: what feminist theory knows about children's literature, *Signal,* 54: 186–202.

Sarland, C. (1991) *Young People Reading: Culture and Response.* Buckingham: Open University Press.

Schram, B.A. (1979) D is for dictionary, S is for stereotyping, in J. Stinton (ed.) *Racism and Sexism in Children's Books.* London: Writers and Readers.

Spender, D. (1982) *Invisible Women: The Schooling Scandal.* London: Writers and Readers.

Stones, R. (1981) Radically revised reading schemes?, *Children's Book Bulletin,* 6: 3–6.

Stones, R. (1983) *Pour Out the Cocoa, Janet: Sexism in Children's Books.* London: Longman for Schools Council.

Walford, G. (1980a) The masculine face of science, *Education 3–13,* 8(1): 51–3.

Walford, G. (1980b) Sex bias in physics textbooks, *The School Science Review,* 62: 220–7.

Walford, G. (1981) Do chemistry text books present a sex-biased image?, *Education in Chemistry,* 18(1): 18–19.

Walkerdine, V. (1984) Some day my prince will come: young girls and the preparation for adolescent sexuality, in A. McRobbie and N. Mica (eds) *Gender and Generation.* London: Macmillan.

Walsh, J. Paton (1980) Race, sex and class in children's books: the devil and the deep blue sea, *New Statesman,* 28 November: 28–30.

Whitehead, F., Capey, A.C., Maddren, W. and Wellings, A. (1977) *Children and their Books.* London: Macmillan.

Part V

Conclusion

Chapter fourteen

Lessons learned?

Kate Myers

Introduction

This book is a celebration of the workers and the work they were involved in which addressed issues of inequality in schooling following the implementation of the Sex Discrimination Act in 1975. As always, much of what we now take for granted is due to pioneers who went before. Newfangled ideas that work are adopted and adapted until they become the norm and their, perhaps controversial, origins long forgotten.

There are, no doubt, still people who would write 'Fathers generally become the willing providers – ever heard of the birds and the bees? . . . Why not pack up your troubles and prejudices. Get married – raise a traditional family and be happy', as some well-wisher did to the Schools Councils Sex Differentiation Project (quoted in Val Millman's Chapter 8). But I suspect there are fewer of them.

What seems to have happened since the SDA was implemented is that the interests of relatively small numbers (and predominantly feminists) in girls' aspirations, subject choices and examination outcomes have been replaced by a more widespread concern about boys' underachievement. In this chapter I discuss some of the issues raised by contributors earlier in the book; argue why we should still be concerned about girls; and suggest how we may address these concerns at the beginning of a new millennium.

National initiatives

Successive governments have for a range of reasons made some attempts to tackle gender equality issues including as Paddy Orr discusses in Chapter 2, the need to raise standards, increase cost-effectiveness and respond to the demands of a changing and often unpredictable labour market. There are of course also issues of social justice.

> Social justice concerns about the relations between the sexes should be as high a priority as improving male and female school performance. Judging from the types of innovative projects currently found in schools in the United Kingdom, concerns about social justice in the name of both sexes need to have considerably more political support from the UK national government and European agencies.
>
> (Arnot *et al.* 1998b: 28)

However, as Paddy Orr also points out, up to now none of these reasons have got equal opportunities very high on any government's agenda. Unfortunately, the Equal Opportunities Commission, established by a Labour government under the Sex Discrimination Act in 1975 has never been fully staffed, as Anne Madden makes clear in Chapter 3. Nevertheless it has had some impact using the law, though sometimes this has been in spite of the UK government rather than because of it. In the 1980s when there was strong leadership in the EOCs education section, through a variety of strategies (such as sponsoring projects, publicity campaigns, publications and fostering networks) the organization had considerable influence with teachers. In 1990, education work was downgraded and the number of people working in this section drastically reduced. It appears that the rationale for this move was that the implementation of the National Curriculum would drastically reduce the need for the EOC to be proactive in education. Sadly this has not been the case.

During this period, some of the teacher unions were very supportive of equal opportunities issues with regard to both teachers' careers and pupils' experience of schooling. 'In the main, the work of teacher unions in relation to equal opportunities has been viewed as reasonably helpful and positive' (Arnot *et al.* 1996: 126). Ruth Blunt in Chapter 4 describes the initiatives of one of them. Activists in the NUT ensured that the union's policy had three themes: a commitment to achieving equality for teachers, equality for pupils and equal representation within the union.

Local education authorities

During the 1980s several LEAs were proactive in promoting equal opportunities. Some of them are highlighted in this book. Policies adopted by the ILEA pre-empted much of what we now take for granted, particularly the emphasis in the current discourse about raising achievement. Frances Morrell (Chapter 5) suggests that ILEA's three-pronged initiative – race, sex and class – was least successful in the last aspect and that arguably this, the biggest single obstacle to achievement in school, remains unresolved. She explains that the ILEA's initiative focusing on equality was heavily influenced by research findings and, she argues, paved the way for the Blair government's education agenda. However, having a mission is not the same as implementing one. As she and many of the contributors discuss, working through, with and sometimes against bureaucracies meant challenging the status quo. The status quo can invariably rally considerable defences to maintain itself. As enthusiasm for these initiatives was not shared by everyone, it is not surprising that issues of change management (regardless of content) are dealt with in several chapters.

Brent was another LEA that had a high profile during the period covered by this book. Hazel Taylor (Chapter 6) charts the context and the issues that she and her colleagues faced while trying to implement an anti-sexist agenda. She and several other authors discuss how most of these initiatives attempted to work *with* teachers rather than impose change on them. Influenced by change writers such as Fullan (1987a, 1987b), work was started with the committed and enthusiastic few, success established and then others were invited to join. Several of the contributors acknowledge the importance of allowing teachers to take ownership of the change. Initiatives implemented in this manner may take longer, with the final results not always resembling the original plan. But change introduced this way is less likely to be scorned and covertly hijacked. Hazel Taylor's five-year strategic plan in Chapter 6 and the school-based equal opportunities development plans that I described in Chapter 7 are both forerunners of current development planning. Brent was frequently in the media spotlight and often publicly criticized for its approach, but action research projects resulting in publications, in-service training, collecting and using data – the mainstay of Brent's anti-sexist work – seem hardly controversial in the late 1990s.

Seeped in now what seems like common sense but is actually derived from the research on school effectiveness and school improvement, it seems amazing that I attempted any school-based change (as I did for the SCDC/EOC project in Merton) without involving headteachers. This omission was remedied in the work with Ealing schools described in Chapter 7. A lot was learned from early intervention initiatives and much of the philosophy underlying the work in Ealing, like that in Brent described by Hazel Taylor, has resonance with current school improvement strategies and what we now know about change:

- change takes time
- a school's capacity for change will vary
- change is complex
- change needs to be well led and managed
- teachers need to be the main agents of change
- the pupils need to be the main focus for change

(MacGilchrist *et al.* 1997: 9)

Race and gender

One issue that Hazel Taylor raises in Chapter 6, the attempt to fuse anti-sexist work with anti-racist work, is referred to in other chapters too. Many of the workers and most of the leaders in the anti-sexist/gender equality camp were middle-class, white women. Most anti-racist work in high-profile authorities such as ILEA, Brent and Ealing was led by black men and women. Some of the anti-sexist work, especially early on, was insensitive to issues of race and a white, middle-class perspective was presented as the norm. Many black workers saw gender as at the very least irrelevant and some anti-racist work and workers ignored the issue. There was a view that gender was a distraction from the real issues and that any work in this area meant that scarce resources had to be shared. A few did not actually believe in sex equality. In some cases this context made it difficult to forge alliances and resulted in very painful encounters between black and white workers.

This issue has not yet been resolved and no doubt this book will be criticized for focusing on gender. I still feel that it is a proper activity to be engaged in as long as issues of race and class are an important part of the analysis. For example, the scandal of the number of exclusions among African Caribbean boys discussed in Marina Foster's Chapter 12 needs to be addressed as a gender as well as a race issue.

Marina Foster picks up issues that thread through many of the preceding chapters about the situation for black girls and boys. Recent moves towards monitoring and accountability have resulted in test and examination results being disaggregated by gender and so it is now relatively easy to compare the performance of boys and girls. However, these data are still not collected in a systematic way nationally with regard to ethnicity so it is much more difficult to ascertain how particular groups of girls and boys are doing (Gillborn and Gipps 1996). The data that do exist are not encouraging and it is evident that although some girls are doing well (as far as examinations are concerned) this does not apply to all girls. Furthermore (as mentioned above), some boys are being badly served by the education system as demonstrated by the high proportion of African Caribbean boys being excluded. Collecting the data is the first step. The second is to join forces to do something about it. Perhaps this is one area where the EOC and the CRE could work together by sponsoring and coordinating examples of good practice.

Projects

Projects can be an effective way of promoting change (Myers 1998) and several early and influential ones are described in the third part in this book. Under the auspices of the Schools Council's Sex Differentiation Project, a range of initiatives developed. As Val Millman explains (Chapter 8) most of them were enthusiastically teacher-led (in their spare time) but supported, encouraged and coordinated by the project staff.

Barbara Smail writing about the Girls Into Science and Technology Project (Chapter 9) is another contributor who emphasizes the importance of teachers owning the change proposed. In the early 1980s there was still resistance (particularly from some male science and CDT teachers) to the idea that girls could and should be taking physical sciences and traditionally male crafts in school. Her description of what happened in the GIST Project is a textbook account of what happens when people feel threatened by change and why these issues were tackled successfully in some schools but not others. The importance of support from the senior management team and dealing with equality as a whole-school issue rather than a 'bolt-on' will be of no surprise to readers familiar with recent change and school improvement literature.

In line with that literature too, the projects described in this book were successful when

- change met a perceived need
- there was a combination of top-down and bottom-up support
- those implementing the change were given support and had opportunities to network with others in similar circumstances
- adequate resources were forthcoming.

Boys and men

Current discussions about equal opportunities generally focus on boys' under-achievement. The Skills for Living course for pupils at Hackney Downs School for Boys in the early 1980s was one of the first attempts to show that equal opportunities and anti-sexism had something to do with boys and men (see Frances Magee in Chapter 10).

Equal opportunities was (and is) not just about achievement and employment (important as both these are). For me, the fundamental issue is the expectations that men and women have of each other and how they behave towards each other. To coin a contemporary phrase – how they 'walk the talk'. There have been changes in the way that men relate to their partners and children and although real men may not eat quiche, they are now more likely to be present at the birth of their children and they are less likely to think that it is acceptable to beat their wives. Sadly, many young men seem to be finding it difficult to come to terms with what masculinity means in our times. The loss of many traditional jobs and the notion that many young women are not financially dependent on them (indeed may be able to survive and flourish without them) has left a considerable number of young men rootless and confused. It *appears* that there is an increase in 'laddish' behaviour often condoned by the media as amusing (as exemplified in the BBC Television programme *Men Behaving Badly*). The way that this materializes in schools is well documented by Mac An Ghaill (1994). This area is one of increasing concern for many teachers. In a study published in 1998 ascertaining the number and type of equality projects prevalent in schools and local authorities the authors wrote:

> the most significant finding was the current primacy of *'improving boys' achievement'* projects. Out of 96 named school or LEA projects, 40 were targeted on boys only, 35 projects focused on both sexes, although often boys' under-achievement was mentioned as a particular issue to be tackled, and only three projects were specifically targeted at girls.
>
> (Arnot *et al.* 1998b: 18)

Unlike the Skills for Living initiative, most of these projects focus on achievement in examinations, not personal and social education. It is of course important to focus on achievement but achievement is more than attainment. Schools should be encouraging achievement in a range of areas including personal and social education (Hargreaves 1984). This may be an area that is of particular importance to boys, who often do not have the networks or opportunities to work through these issues outside of school.

Literacy is a high-profile issue with the Blair government. There is some concern about boys' reading (or lack of it) and some attempt to encourage men to read to their sons and act as positive role models. However, the effort seems to be solely directed at changing texts and reading habits to suit boys' laddish preferences as if these preferences are given and non-negotiable. There seems to be little attempt to encourage boys to change their habits and preferences in order to enjoy what are now considered 'girls' books'. Sue Adler's Chapter 13 charts the work in this area from the mid-1970s when researchers started analysing books to see in what proportion men and women were visible and how they were portrayed. At the same time other researchers were looking at how young readers reacted to text and the differences between girls and boys. During the 1980s, various ILEA teachers' centres including the Centre for Urban Educational Studies were at the forefront of researching and disseminating this work. Like some of the other contributors, Sue Adler describes what happened when some of the work of grassroots enthusiasts was profiled and rubbished by the media, in this case in the context of an education authority fighting for its existence.

Networks

The importance of networks is a theme that runs throughout this book and one lesson we need to learn from previous initiatives, is that there is only so much individual teachers can do. The majority of the teachers working on the projects cited by Arnot *et al.* (1998b) are working in isolation. As Frances Magee asks in Chapter 10, where are the equivalent of the ILEA equal opportunities team or the Schools Council's Sex Differentiation Project to help and support teachers working on these initiatives now? Teachers working together on whole-school interventions are more powerful than isolated teachers. Schools with LEA and/or higher education support, networking with each other to reflect on experiences and share good practice, are in an even stronger position to make positive changes. (Though it is always important to remember that while schools can make a difference they cannot be held responsible for all society's ills. They do not operate in isolation and there is only so much within their sphere of control and influence.)

Higher education through research and networking has an important role in fostering change in school. The establishment of the Centre for Research and Education on Gender at the Institute of Education in the early 1980s, described by Diana Leonard in Chapter 11, was and is an important resource for researchers and practitioners. As well as making a major contribution to research, a small group of feminist academics, played a significant role in supporting isolated teachers by fostering networks. Diana Leonard describes how the Women's Education Group involving practitioners and researchers came together at the institute. For some time its activities (publications, courses and conferences) were a source of strength for many teachers. Later the overt separatist and anti-sexist stance taken by some of those involved brought WedG into confrontation with the ILEA, which was then funding the group.

Shortly after the SCDC/EOC's Equal Opportunities in Education Project came to an end in 1986, the SCDC was disbanded. The Institute of Education agreed to build on this work by hosting the LEAC Project on Equal Opportunities. Diana Leonard describes the rise and fall of this initiative. Issues of management structures, hierarchies, funding, local politics, internal politics and planning are only too familiar today for those involved in short-term projects.

Education reforms

There have been positive changes in girls' achievement since the period described in this book. It would be naïve to attribute these changes solely to the initiatives described. However, I do believe they made some contribution to the current situation and discourse. As successful projects do, they also had a major impact on those involved with them, advisers, teachers and students, many of whom carried on this 'effect' into future work. These initiatives were not operating on their own, however, and other 'reforms' were also having an impact on the situation – some of them positive. The Technical and Vocational Initiative introduced in 1984 was the first major national initiative (coordinated by the Manpower Services Commission) where equal opportunities was a criteria for funding. It 'was reported to have had a positive (or even a very positive) effect on equal opportunities by 87 per cent of secondary schools; similarly 72 per cent saw positive effects of GCSE' (Arnot *et al.* 1996: xvi).

The Education Reform Act 1988 can be seen as a mixed blessing with regard to encouraging and enhancing equal opportunities. A common compulsory curriculum meant reduced choice and less opportunity for young people to choose courses traditionally associated with their gender rather than their aptitudes. The recent reduction of the common core has again brought the issue of subject choice back on to the agenda; even when students are following the same course, the issue of choosing which level to enter for examinations is a cause for concern, as discussed in Chapter 1 (Elwood 1995). Furthermore it is not enough just to ensure a compulsory curriculum. The content of the curriculum is also important, that is *how* and *how often* women and men, and people from different social backgrounds and cultural heritages, are portrayed. The pedagogy adopted is also relevent. Recent research on the brain and on preferred learning styles of girls and boys must have implications for teaching styles.

The new inspection system administered by Ofsted started well, with equal opportunities being a significant part of the original framework for inspection. Although as Paddy Orr discusses in Chapter 2, the previous inspection system had the potential for incorporating equality issues, it was not in the systematic or overt way that Ofsted offered. Unfortunately, a significant number of the freelance Ofsted inspectors appear not to understand the issues. Consequently, the potential of this reform has not been realized. The majority of reports do not deal with equality in any meaningful way and the issue is rarely included in key points for action.

The publication of league tables combined with open enrolment has brought to the public arena the contrasting achievement of girls and boys in SATs and GCSE. The advent of grant-maintained schools and open competition for the same pupils have put considerable pressure on headteachers, in some areas, fighting for their school's survival. In this 'market economy' girls have become a valuable (if not valued) resource. This 'market' may have had an impact on the rising number of boys excluded from school. Unfortunately, competition does not encourage cooperation for example in the sharing of good practice between schools with regard to equal opportunities. The advent of specialist schools is a potential cause for concern. Encouraging 11-year-old students to opt for a school specializing in sciences or languages, for example, is fraught with dangers of choice associated with sex stereotyping, especially as schools are not legally allowed to use sex (even to ensure a balanced entry) as a selection criterion (see Anne Madden's Chapter 3). This will need careful monitoring of this initiative.

The local management of schools alongside the arrival of the grant-maintained sector has meant less money being held centrally and more devolved to schools. Money that previously was used by LEAs to promote equal opportunities initiatives, such as those described in this book, is now held by the schools. Consequently LEAs have less power (and financial inducements) to encourage schools to address these issues. Some of them, though, retain considerable influence. It is still possible for LEAs to offer support in this area, though probably on a buy-back basis. This raises the usual concern that schools that are aware of the issues and want to address them are the ones that will be prepared to pay for support to do so. What can and should be done (if anything) about the schools that are not concerned at all about equality of opportunity or have other more urgent priorities?

Current concerns

During the period this book was written it seemed like concern about the 'gender gap' featured in one way or another, virtually every week in the *TES*. As has been mentioned earlier in this book, the concern has been much more public since the gender gap has been interpreted as boys not doing as well as girls. It is interesting to ponder why this is the case. Why was it so difficult in the late 1970s and early 1980s to get the issues about girls' achievement taken seriously and why is it so easy to do the same about boys? The paradox about the difference of concern shown towards achievement of boys and achievement of girls is developed in an article about Key Stage 2 results published in early 1999 under the headline 'Gender gap widens to a gulf' (Cassidy 1999: 6). Most of the column explains how boys are underachieving in literacy and how this will make it difficult for the Secretary of State, David Blunkett, to achieve his target of 80 per cent of 11-year-olds reaching level 4 by 2002. The last paragraph says: 'However, boys are keeping pace with girls in maths tests taken by all 11-year-olds. Girls are ahead in only one third of local authorities and then only by up to 5 percentage points' (Cassidy 1999: 6). Well, that's all right then. But is it? What is happening to girls in two-thirds of LEAs? Should this information alert us to a possible concern about girls' achievement in mathematics? It may well do but because the current discourse within education focuses so much on boys, there seems to be no room to consider where girls need help and support too.

In fact the Blair government has expressed concern about the plight of some young women. The Women's Unit in the Cabinet Office has raised some of the issues discussed above as areas of concern and will be undertaking a study to examine them. It is planning to build 'on the work already being undertaken by the Social Exclusion Unit and Department of Health

Table 14.1 Entry rates of GCE A level candidates aged 16–18, in 1997/98

Subject	Males	Females
English	24,155	55,970
Mathematics	35,895	20,635
Physics	23,119	6553
Biology	19,822	29,070
French	5899	13,730

Source: DfEE 1998a

on teenage parenthood and complementing that on teenage boys being led by the Home Office' (Cabinet Office 1999: 2). The unit is intending to work in conjunction with the Department of Health, the DfEE and the DTI (but no mention in the information about working with the EOC). It is to be hoped that this work infiltrates into the education discourse.

One area that warrants attention in this discourse, where there are still startling differences, is subject choice as illustrated in Table 14.1.

> In 'female-dominated' subjects, [A levels] such as English and Modern Foreign Languages, there is still a large entry gap in favour of girls. However, it has been decreasing over the last decade . . . , more male students have been taking these subjects. In contrast, in 'male-dominated' subjects such as Physics, Mathematics, Computer Studies, Economics and Technology, there has still been a large gap in entries. There has been no narrowing of the entry gap in Mathematics and Computer Studies over the last decade whilst in Physics, Technology and Economics, male dominance in terms of entry has actually increased over time.
> (Arnot *et al.* 1998a: 15)

And just as worrying, 'Gender differences in the mid-1990s among the 16–19 age-group in terms of the subjects studied for vocational qualifications is just as strong as at A-level' (Arnot *et al.* 1998a: 18).

> Students continue to choose vocational courses (e.g. BTEC) according to conventional sex-stereotypes, with young women opting, for example, for courses in Business and Commerce, Hairdressing and Beauty, Caring Services (e.g. Nursery Nursing) and Science (e.g. dental assisting). Young men continue to opt for courses in Engineering and Construction and mainstream Science subjects (e.g. Physics, Chemistry).
> (Arnot *et al.* 1996: xiv)

The sex segregation with regard to the take-up of modern apprenticeships confirms this trend (see Table 14.2) which becomes even more worrying when vocation is linked to salary (see Table 14.3).

Table 14.2   Gender segregation in modern apprenticeships

Sector	Proportion of total starters (%)	Sex of participant	
		Male (%)	Female (%)
Business administration	15	20	80
Engineering manufacture	13	96	4
Retailing	10	43	57
Motor industry	8	97	3
Construction	7	99	1
Hairdressing	7	8	92
Hotel and catering	7	52	48
Electrical installation engineering	4	99	1
Health and social care	4	11	89
Childcare	3	3	97
Accounting	3	42	58
Information technology	2	67	33
Travel service	2	14	86
Plumbing	1	99	1
Healthcare	1	13	87

Source: DfEe 1998b

Table 14.3   Modern apprenticeships salary record: April–December 1997

Sector	Average weekly salary (£)
Information technology	140.00
Retail	127.45
Accountancy	120.22
Insurance	118.59
Chemical industry	117.55
Sport and recreation	116.77
Engineering	114.75
Printing	108.21
Business administration	107.06
Care	98.33
Floristry	90.00
Travel services	88.14
Media	85.00
Construction	81.01
Electrical installation	72.68
Childcare	67.25
Hairdressing	62.50

Source: Data supplied by Manchester TEC, Modern Apprenticeships Vacancy Unit

The old, the new and the unanticipated

Some, but by no means all, of the issues that the initiatives and projects described in this book have been successfully tackled. It must be remembered that while girls' achievements at GCSE and A level should indeed be acknowledged and celebrated, there is still a long way to go in particular with regard to their career prospects, feelings of self-worth, earnings and carer obligations as discussed in Chapter 1.

Linked with this is subject choice; girls' and boys' differing aspirations as well as their differing perceptions of their abilities and aptitudes; particular groups of boys' underachievement; and how race and class interrelate with all of these issues are just some of the 'old' areas still to be addressed. As the world changes, new areas arise. Some we can anticipate but others are not yet apparent. For example, one area becoming increasingly important for work and leisure that we can anticipate as a cause for concern is equal access to information technology.

'The distribution of home PCs [personal computers] is becoming increasingly skewed towards middle-class homes, however, putting children from poorer backgrounds at a major disadvantage when it comes to information technology' (Scales 1999: 30). Unfortunately these data are not disaggregated by race and gender so we can only hypothesize that there may be further differences to investigate. What we do know is that those who have early and easy access to this technology are going to have considerable advantage when it comes to their school work, skills needed for employment and being able to operate in a society increasingly dependent on this type of technology.

As more and more information is made available electronically, and teachers are no longer seen as the font of all knowledge, schooling will have to change. There are many exciting possibilities being discussed, including the arrival of the 24 hour school where young people and adults share the same resources (learning centre equipped with latest technology, fitness centre, cafeteria, and so on, with different groups having priority access at different times).

New issues like these and ones we cannot yet even imagine could result in the increase of inequalities in the brave new world – but this is not inevitable. If we are to address areas we already know about and prepare for new ones as they emerge, it is vital that equality issues are seen as a central part of the planning agenda.

The main problem though is that there is now no obvious mechanism for taking them on board. While central control has been increased, local authorities have seen a reduction in their powers and centrally held budgets. Their future is not assured. One consequence of this is that local authorities are much less likely to take a lead in the way that many did in the 1980s, including those whose contributions are described in this book – ILEA, Brent and Ealing.

The role of the LEAs in this climate was significantly lessened and in 1995, most LEAs surveyed were relatively uninvolved in policy issues such as gender equality and reported playing little strategic role in promoting gender equality in schools.

(Arnot *et al.* 1998b: 9)

LEAs' time is now taken up with following and supporting government initiatives such as the literacy hour, rather than initiating their own. The EOC has neither the structure nor the budget to oversee projects such as GIST (see Barbara Smail's Chapter 9) or the Equal Opportunities in Education Project (jointly sponsored with the SCDC in 1986). The Qualifications and Curriculum Authority does not run projects in the same way that some of its predecessors did (such as the Schools Council and SCDC).

Recommendations abound (in this volume and for example Arnot *et al.* 1998a, 1998b) but although Ofsted has highlighted some of the issues by commissioning a research overview (Arnot *et al.* 1998a) no one seems to have the authority or resources to coordinate a concerted and consistent move to address them. One obvious solution would be to resurrect a strong education section in the EOC with a remit to coordinate gender equality work in education in association with a similar section in the CRE (so that the interrelationship between race and gender informs all work). The brief would include:

- facilitating networking (for example by establishing an interactive web site where those working on these issues could learn from each other)
- advising on initial teacher training
- advising on professional development for those working in LEAs, EAZs, DfEE, Ofsted and quangos
- advising on professional development for teachers, aspiring teachers and heads
- commissioning relevant research and learning from successful practice in the UK and overseas
- anticipating the equality consequences of all other initiatives
- coordinating the work of other government departments.

Perhaps the most important role of this body would be to keep equality issues in the public arena.

We are on the threshold of a new millennium and perhaps a new world. Educationalists have a major contribution to make about the future relative roles of women and men in our society. The young people who will be the decision makers in the near future are in our schools now. They will also be the parents of the next generation of decision makers. How we equip them for this task is up to us.

References

Arnot, M., David, M. and Weiner, G. (1996) *Educational Reforms and Gender Equality in Schools*, Research Discussion Series no. 17. Manchester: Equal Opportunities Commission.

Arnot, M., Gray, J., James, M., Ruddock, J. with Duveen, G. (1998a) *Recent Research on Gender and Educational Performance*, Ofsted Reviews of Research. London: The Stationery Office.

Arnot, M., Millen, D. and Maton, K. (1998b) *Current Innovative Practice in Schools in the United Kingdom: Network Strategy Research Study on Education as a Policy Issue of Gender Equality*, Final Report, November, University of Cambridge.

Cabinet Office (1999) Teenage girls, Factsheet. London: Cabinet Office.

Cassidy, S. (1999) Gender gap widens to a gulf, *Times Educational Supplement*, 29 January: 6.

DfEE (1998a) *Statistical First Release*, 557/98. London: DfEE.

DfEE (1998b) *Modern Apprenticeships Research Project 1998*, QPID. London: DfEE.

Elwood, J. (1995) Undermining gender stereotypes: examination and coursework performance in the UK at 16, *Assessment in Education*, 2(3): 283–303.

Fullan, M. (1987a) Managing curriculum change, in *Curriculum at the Crossroads*. Report of the SCDC Conference on Aspects of Curriculum Change, Leeds University, mimeo.

Fullan, M. (1987b) Implementing educational change: what we know. Paper presented for the World Bank, Washington DC.

Gillborn, D. and Gipps, C. (1996) *Recent Research on the Achievements of Ethnic Minority Pupils*. Institute of Education, University of London for Ofsted, London: HMSO.

Hargreaves, D.H. (chairman) (1984) *Improving Secondary Schools: Report of the Committee on the Curriculum and Organisation of Secondary Schools*. London: ILEA.

Mac An Ghaill, M. (1994) *The Making of Men: Masculinities, Sexualities and Schooling*. Buckingham: Open University Press.

MacGilchrist, B., Myers, K. and Reed, J. (1997) *The Intelligent School*. London: Paul Chapman.

Myers, K. (1998) The LEA's role in managing school improvement projects, *Improving Schools*, 1(2): 63–7.

Scales, J. (1999) Home PCs delete hope for the poorest, *Times Educational Supplement*, 22 January: 30.

Index

and the Schools Council Sex Role
Differentiation Project, 134
and the Women's Education Group,
168
see also anti-racist work; ethnicity
Race Relations Act (1976), 15, 79
and the ILEA, 88
*Recent Research on Gender and
Educational Performance*, 50–1
Redbridge, and the Equal
Opportunities Consortium, 111
Richardson, Jo, 138
rights, and entitlement, 197
Ross, Carol, 160, 163, 164
Rumbold, Angela, 115

Sarland, Charles, 206–7
SATIS (Science and Technology in
Society) project, 153
SATs (Standard Assessment Tasks), 21,
44, 45, 49, 224
SCAA (Schools Curriculum and
Assessment Authority), 47, 48,
191
SCDC (School Curriculum
Development Committee), 37,
138
EOC/SCDC project, 110, 111, 112,
138, 143, 223
The School Curriculum (DES), 17
School Curriculum Development
Committee, *see* SCDC
school improvement, 123
school uniform, 34
Schools Council, 131
and Brent Council, 95
closure of the, 130
commitment to sex equality in
schools, 131–2
and Ealing Council, 120
and the EOC, 37, 41, 203
Equal Opportunities in Education
Information Centre, 136–7
Equal Opportunities in Education
Project, 131
GIST (Girls Into Science and
Technology Project), 36, 131–2,
143–54, 221, 229

project report (1985), 141
Sex Role Differentiation Project,
129, 131–41, 217, 220–1,
223
and Hackney Downs school,
158–9, 165
and teacher group work, 132–5
and the Women's Education Group,
167
Schools' Organizations Committees
and Adjudicators, 46
science
children's attitudes to, 145, 149
and employment opportunities, 18
and girls, 25, 153
in the 1970s, 30
in the 1990s, 48, 52
at A level, 151
attitudes to, 145, 149, 150
curriculum access arguments,
161
and the EOC, 33
and the National Curriculum, 46
performance in, 192
and teachers' attitudes, 148, 221
and the National Curriculum, 18
race, class and gender, and access to
science education, 150
and sex differences in the
curriculum, in the 1970s, 15
staged model for curriculum change
in, 152–3
teachers, male-female ratios, 146
see also GIST; technology
Scotland, male/female ratios in science
subjects, 151–2
Scruton, Roger, 81
secondary schools
allocation systems, banding, 81–2
curriculum
in the 1970s, 3, 14, 15
and the EOC, 30, 33
equal opportunities policies, 49
male hierarchies in, 191
pupils' attitudes to science, 145
Seeing is Believing, 97
Self-Government for Schools, 46
Selsdon Group, 80